Community Art

The Politics of Trespassing

Paul De Bruyne &
Pascal Gielen (eds.)

Antennae
Valiz, Amsterdam

With contributions by
Tilde Björfors
Bertus Borgers
Paul De Bruyne
Luigi Coppola
An De bisschop
Miguel Escobar Varela
Jan Fabre
Alison M. Friedman
Pascal Gielen
Sonja Lavaert
Carol Martin
Antonio Negri
Alida Neslo
Tessa Overbeek
Lionel Popkin
Richard Schechner
Hein Schoer
Ricky Seabra
Jonas Staal
Klaas Tindemans
Luk Van den Dries
Quirijn Lennert van den Hoogen
Hans van Maanen
Bart Van Nuffelen
Karel Vanhaesebrouck
Zhang Changcheng

One of the unintended consequences
of modern capitalism is that it has
strengthened the value of place,
aroused a longing for community.

Richard Sennett, The Corrosion of
Character, 1998

Community Art: The Politics of Trespassing

Paul De Bruyne & Pascal Gielen (eds.)

Introduction **1**
Between the Individual
and the Common
Paul De Bruyne &
Pascal Gielen

Part I
Definitions

Mapping Community Art **15**
Pascal Gielen

Community Art as a **35**
Contested Artistic Practice
The Case of MET-X, Brussels
Paul De Bruyne

Community Art is What **51**
We Say and Write It is
An De bisschop

Through Zina's Eyes **75**
Community Artists as
Artistic Professionals
Quirijn Lennert van den
Hoogen &
Hans van Maanen

Part II
The Artist's Voice

The Vernissage by **91**
the MartHa!tentatief
A Play about Untameable Life at the
Beginning of the Twenty-first Century
Bart Van Nuffelen

Alakondre **109**
A Journey to the Invisible
Alida Neslo

The Advantage of Elephants **123**
Building a Community of
Artists One Trunk at a Time
Lionel Popkin

Portrait of the Activist-Artist **135**
as an Ageing Artist-Activist
Ricky Seabra

The Kids of Mitrovica **149**
Bertus Borgers

Part III
Rethinking Basic Concepts

Art and Common **165**
A Conversation with
Antonio Negri
Pascal Gielen &
Sonja Lavaert

Revolution from Within: **195**
A Grandson of Government
Changes Chinese Art Policy
An Interview with Zhang Changcheng
Alison M. Friedman

'We're in a Cage, ... **211**
but it's a Very Big Cage'
An Interview with Richard Schechner
and Carol Martin
Klaas Tindemans &
Karel Vanhaesebrouck

Part IV
Public Sphere and Activism

From Community Art to **239**
Communal Art
Paul De Bruyne

Chief Robert Duncan's **251**
Transformation Mask
The Native Carvers of Alert Bay
Hein Schoer

Michelangelo Pistoletto **265**
and the People of Corniglia
'We've Come a Long Way Together'
Luigi Coppola

About the Political Potential **275**
of Contemporary Art
Jonas Staal

Ruangrupa **287**
Experimental Video Workshops
and Activism in Indonesia
Miguel Escobar Varela

Out of Order: Cirkus Cirkör **299**
An Interview with Tilde Björfors
Tessa Overbeek

Epilogue **325**
Jan Fabre
The Revolution in My Own Flesh
Luk Van den Dries

Afterword & Arts in Society Series ... **341**
Rien van der Vleuten

Biographies **345**

Index of Names **353**

Geographical Index **363**

Colophon **371**

Introduction Between the Individual and the Common

Paul De Bruyne
& Pascal Gielen

Community Art is part of a series of books made by the research group Arts *in* Society (at the Netherlands-based Fontys College for the Arts), which examines the relation between societal transformations and artistic creation. In our previous publications, *The Murmuring of the Artistic Multitude* (Gielen 2009) and *Being an Artist in Post-Fordist Times* (Gielen and De Bruyne eds. 2009), we explored the contemporary art scene in relation to the parallel development of the new capitalist economy and neoliberal politics. During the course of a number of book launches, we noticed that, perhaps surprisingly, many artists and art mediators (especially younger ones), largely accepted the description of our modern society and art world as 'post-Fordist'. By this, we mean a working environment ruled by economic flexibility, mental and physical mobility, project work, informality and 'adaptivity', such as that whipped up by the creative and cultural industries. Some of the people we spoke to felt quite oppressed by this situation; others even spoke of a 'totalitarian regime' and, in that context, we were asked about possible ways out of this impasse. Is there still a place for subversion, or are there other art practices that can elude the *dispositif* of post-Fordism? This book is a response to these frequently asked questions. We wondered whether the recent worldwide boom in community art might be part of the answer. By offering theoretical viewpoints, historical and geographical contextualization and artists' testimonies, this book provides an overview of, and insight into, contemporary community art practice and context. In attempting this, however, we are explicitly disinterested in mounting a defence of, or offensive against, community art. In the first place, we wanted to make resources accessible which allow community art (and thus art in general) to be understood in its societal context.

The social artistic 'genre' — with its roots in the 1920s and 1930s (Proletarian Art and New Deal Art) and the 1960s and 1970s (countercultural art) — became dormant in the 1980s and 1990s only to be revived strongly over the past decade. Even artists who enjoy a lot of recognition in official art circles have begun to demonstrate considerably more interest in the community around them. This results in a colourful artistic palette, encompassing relational aesthetics, new social commitment and radical political art.

  Community Art attempts to explain this third upsurge in artistic concern for society. The various essays and interviews included here are not restricted to attempts to explain this revival;

they also offer critical reflection, posing such questions as: does the new generation of committed artists really possess the same sincerity and naivety as the previous ones or are we now dealing with a smarter, more strategic, but perhaps also more opportunistic, specimen? Is the revival of community art merely a perverted side effect of ongoing neoliberalization and the dismantling of the welfare state, or does the community now offer a powerful alternative to hyper-individualization and endless flexibility? Will art always remain a fiction, or can it, in fact, generate societal change?

In keeping with the logic of the series of books, *Arts in Society*, this publication assembles a variety of artists, sociologists, cultural critics and philosophers. Following on from *Being an Artist in Post-Fordist Times*, we confront dominant concepts by offering the insights of a number of thinkers who, in our eyes, have shifted or broadened discourse in relation to the subject at hand. While Paolo Virno and Michael Hardt fulfilled this function in *Being an Artist...*, it is Carol Martin, Antonio Negri, Richard Schechner and Zhang Changcheng who assume the role in this book.

Common

In 2009, the Italian philosopher, Antonio Negri, published the book *Commonwealth* which he co-authored with the American literary scientist Michael Hardt. This book concludes a trilogy, begun with *Empire* and *Multitude*, of radical political philosophy that attempts to reinvigorate communism. Ideology aside, both supporters and detractors of Negri and Hardt acknowledge the importance of their critical analyses of global capitalism and neoliberalism. Whether or not the solutions and strategies they propose make sense remains open for debate. What is important here, however, is the way in which Negri and Hardt breathed life into forgotten, supplanted and sometimes denounced concepts to offer different ways of looking at the world. Obsolete notions such as 'multitude', 'general intellect', 'bio-power' and also 'love' are re-actualized and refined for up-to-date societal analysis.

For our book, the concept of 'common' is of essential relevance; in *Being an Artist in Post-Fordist Times*, Michael Hardt explains that this notion is already centuries old. When, in the sixteenth and seventeenth century, first in England and then all over Europe, the meadows, where animals grazed, and the forests, where everyone could gather wood, were privatized, the conflict about common ground was born. From the Christian side came the argument that

God had given the earth and its beauty to all of humankind and that it should, therefore, be used in common.

Since the 1980s, the battle over the common has re-emerged, in a new guise and without transcendental allure, in a bid to oppose the advancing neoliberalization of government, which seeks to contract out national resources — such as water, soil and oil — to private enterprise. Some say that the state has conducted a full-scale clearance sale over the past thirty years, thus forfeiting its political grip on society. In cyber culture, a similar debate over 'information commons', 'creative' and 'cultural commons' has been going on for almost a decade. With these examples in mind, Hardt and Negri argue that the common is not limited to natural resources, but that man continually contributes to the production of language, knowledge, codes, information, emotion, affect, etc., which exist solely by virtue of social interactions and are easily shared. Forms of expression, creativity and art would lose their potency and dynamics if they could no longer draw on that common. Therefore, Hardt and Negri fervently resist the privatization of cultural products such as information, ideas and species of animals and plants. For them, open access to the natural and cultural common, the life source of community, is a prerequisite for a free and egalitarian society. By contrast, our times increasingly seem to deny that open access to the common.

As an antidote to the general trend, initiatives like community art — which, defined very broadly, thrives on the creation of affection and the nurturing of a practice of community between sponsor, artist, artwork and public — has an affiliation with the common. This approach stands diametrically opposed to the equally strong desire for the individualization of artistry in modern times, especially in the arts influenced by the avant-garde movement. Any community art project is catapulted back and forth between the poles of the common and the individual, and any theory about community art that doesn't take this observation as its starting point is doomed not to understand the complexity of the dynamics involved.

The Individual as Protagonist

Since the modernist era, the professional art world has thrived on such myths as individual creative genius, which deny or supplant the importance of a common. In their classic study, *Canvasses and Careers* (1965), Harrison and Cynthia White implicitly demonstrate the source of this individualization. Their study predictably begins with the rupture of the academic visual arts system and proceeds to outline some important shifts in the conception of the artist. When, due to morphological pressure, the Académie des Peinture et Sculpture in Paris and the annual Salon began to fall apart, it signified the birth of what the Whites refer to as the 'dealer-critic' system. In this system, not only does the immaterial principle of language play an important role — with the emergence of art criticism — but the role of the artist also undergoes a profound change, with personal style becoming more important than conforming to a uniform system of rules. While the long-awaited masterpiece no longer mattered, what was needed was a coherent oeuvre that guaranteed the lasting reputation of the artist. In other words, when the *Académie* lost its monopoly, one no longer bet on masterpieces, but the pedigree of the artist became prominent. Or, as the title of White and White's study clearly underscores, in a post-academic art system, the focus is less on the canvas and more on the career of the artist. Behind this shift, however, lurks simple market logic as the potential buyer needs to be convinced of the quality of the work of art; the most important arguments dealers use nowadays are, on the one hand, the aforementioned critiques of the work and, on the other, the positive perception of previous works. In other words, within an artist's oeuvre, already-delivered quality functions as a promise of future quality. This kind of mechanism may be read as the 'retro-prospective' character of an artistic career. Our contemporary understanding of the individual artist, their authorship and oeuvre, is as much a product of democratization as of the marketing of the art world, which got off to a flying start in the nineteenth century.

Indeed, when craftsmanship and academic rules disappeared as the hallmark of art, only the maker remained as binding agent and reliable point of reference. In other words, only the signature, which connects a work to an individual artist, determines the market value of a work of art. It is, perhaps, no coincidence that liberalism, with its strong belief in the beneficence of the market, embraces the individual as protagonist. Moreover, from an historical perspective, the development of liberal ideology and the invention of the artist as individual run remarkably parallel to one another. In short, the myth of the individual artist is a product of the mental space of free market capitalism, with works and signature often functioning as a brand.

While White and White illustrate their argument with examples from the visual arts, we can observe the same phenomenon in other artistic disciplines, where individualization is often even more evident as group processes and creations are traced back and attributed to individual authors. So, although dance companies, theatre groups and orchestras are collectives, attention is drawn to a single creator, who then ranks most highly in the symbolic hierarchy. This 'authorizing' of collective creative processes reduces them to the (genius) work of an individual, despite a more generalized acceptance that new creations imply shared responsibility and thus a common achievement.

From the tendency towards individualization outlined here, it follows that, within the modern (and Western) concept of art and the artist, the notion of community art constitutes a contradiction in terms. The demand for singularity on the part of the artist is hard to reconcile with social consciousness and the commitment to a community. This is perhaps one of the reasons why part of the professional art world still struggles to accept community art as a positive development. In return, community workers in all forms and formats have trouble accepting the arts as a possible means for creating the common.

The Power of Trespassing

Returning to the questions posed by young artists at the launch events for *Being an Artist…*, our answers in relation to community art can only ever be tentative and partial. There is no prevailing way out of the contradictions that the post-Fordist context imposes on the art world. Neither is there a way out of the tension between the will and desire to strive for an (artistic) common and the deeply rooted exigencies of the autonomy of contemporary art. Every community art project needs to be evaluated in relation to its concrete environment and its potentially therapeutic, subversive, critical, aesthetic or political impact. However, the readers of *Being an Artist…* ensured that questions regarding the activist and revelatory potential of the arts in general and community art in particular, are continuously present in this book.

The paradoxical position of community art is a leitmotif within this book. On the one hand, various articles and testimonies point towards the potency of art in influencing a community or, at least, allowing it to view itself in a different way. For example, different forms of community art reclaim the streets, in the broadest sense of the term, salvaging a public and democratic space, sometimes even literally laying claim to a 'common'. Other artistic projects direct our attention to the loss of common space and make the effects of this loss felt, sometimes personally. Whenever art leaves its own individualistic boundaries and trespasses into the forbidden terrain of community bonding, it becomes de facto politics.

On the other hand, some contributions, from the artistic as well as from the societal perspective, testify to considerable distrust. That there are governmental authorities willing to support a dose of subversion (albeit in a controllable way) casts suspicion over any kind of subsidized artistic activism. That 'community art for sale' is particularly pre-eminent in neoliberal regimes raises further questions about whose politics community art is serving. Living in post-Fordist times might imply that the correct political thing to do for the arts is to celebrate its autonomy and retreat into an artistic exile, which (just like its counterpart) is increasingly becoming forbidden terrain because it is anti-social in tendency.

By bringing both ways of trespassing together in this book (and, of course, the shades of grey in between), we attempt to create a nuanced image of the phenomenon. This image can never be objective, but it will take shape precisely because of the many subjective positions and interpretations that constitute it.

Four Parts and an Epilogue

Community Art is divided into four sections. In the first part, 'Definitions', we undertake a number of attempts to define the concept of community art beyond the rather unrevealing supposition that community art has something to do with searching in and through the arts for the creation of a community based on place, interest or curiosity.

In 'Mapping Community Art', Pascal Gielen develops, amongst other things, a cartography of community art through which concrete projects can be mapped, in terms of their subversive or digestive nature or in terms of the orientation of participating artists towards individualism or towards other people. The result is a compass rose which enables the full diversity of possible community art projects to be visualized in a single image. This serves as a prelude to Gielen's extensive consideration of the subversive possibilities of various practices.

In 'Community Art as a Contested Artistic Practice', Paul

De Bruyne analyzes one of the longest-running community art projects in Europe, the Brussels–based multicultural music production organization, MET-X, in an attempt to define community art as a constellation of positions on a scale of diverse dynamics in the process of producing, distributing and consuming artworks. He concludes that community art cannot be regarded as an artistic genre nor can it be understood from the perspective of only one actor involved in the construction of a network. Rather, the concepts of 'community' and 'art' can only be understood in the context of specific projects.

In 'Community Art is What We Say and Write it is', An De bisschop defines community art as a discourse that is being developed by, amongst others, the government and the press. She compares the policy and press discourses in the community art contexts of the Western Cape (South Africa) and Flanders (Belgium), outlining disparate interpretative frameworks and discovering similarities and differences between the situation in the West and that in South Africa.

Concluding this section, Quirijn Lennert van den Hoogen and Hans van Maanen define community art from the starting point of the specific values that can make art (in general) effective in society. To this theoretical analysis, they add a description of an intriguing community art project in Groningen (The Netherlands).

In the second part of the book, 'The Artist's Voice', several artists join the debate by drawing on their own projects and experiences. In their own words, they prove that 'believers' in community art are not naive puppets who think that their work will save the world. As it turns out, artists are capable of critically evaluating their own practice, both defending it and acknowledging its limitations. The Belgian director, Bart Van Nuffelen, describes how his group leaves the safety of the rehearsal room and takes the step towards a specific public square with its defeated and addicted residents. It is there that their work affects the social fabric, making people become more articulate and leading to new insights on the part of the artists, which publicly exposes the reality of the square. Alida Neslo, from Surinam, describes her artistic and educational development, which has led her to a youth prison in Paramaribo where she is developing a project with imprisoned children.

A completely different point of view is offered by the American choreographer, Lionel Popkin, who regards artists themselves as a community that has to be created, which is partly a response to the new distribution circumstances in the US, where the free market is more dominant than ever. The Brazilian visual artist, Ricky Seabra, situates his activist projects within the framework of developments in visual art to ask the core question: under which circumstances can art and activism be combined? Bertus Borgers, artistic director of the Dutch Fontys Rockacademy, describes how his rock institute contributes to restoring peace in the war-torn Serbian/Albanian city of Mitrovica.

The third part of the book, 'Rethinking Basic Concepts', provides room for a more conceptual discussion on the basic terms that frame community art: what is art? In which political-economic-cultural constellation do we live and how do art and the social relate to each other? In an interview by Pascal Gielen and Sonja Lavaert, Antonio Negri addresses the nature of art, of capitalist society since the 1970s and of the relationship between labour and art, the art market and the common in an attempt to elaborate the potency of art as a tool of resistance. This conversation with the critical (but marginalized) communist is followed by an interview with the Chinese Communist Party member, Zhang Changcheng, grandson of one of the leaders of Mao's Long March and one of the most influential forces behind the renewal of art policy in China. In conversation with Alison Friedman, Zhang describes the ways in which arts policy and thinking around art have evolved from Mao until now. Expressing ideas infused with the spirit of Confucius, the concepts of critical art, communism and politics are interpreted from a Chinese perspective.
      A final interview, with Richard Schechner and Carol Martin, completes this section. This conversation, conducted by Karel Vanhaesebrouck and Klaas Tindemans, once again plunges us deep into the history of the Western avant-garde and the relationship between art, economics and politics over the past half-century.

In the fourth part of this book, 'Public Sphere and Activism', a number of community art projects are analyzed in relation to their subversive power in public space. In 'From Community Art to Communal Art', Paul De Bruyne analyzes various forms of art that consolidate or contest the prevalent definitions and practices of public space. Between a conformist and a revolutionary attitude towards the public space, a 'third way' is introduced. From the contribution of Hein Schoer, about art in societies that have preserved a part of their pre-modern roots, it becomes clear that community art could only arise once the idea of community had largely been lost in modernity. From this moment on, art becomes not only an agent for social integration and cultural stabilization, but also a factor within disorientation. Only then could it be charged with the artistic (and ethical) duty for change, renewal and being different. As the 'natural' tie to community was lost, it had to be reconstructed.

As an example of this process at work, Luigi Coppola takes the artist, Michelangelo Pistoletto, whose practice has attempted to create a communal situation over several decades. Meanwhile, the Dutch visual artist, Jonas Staal, points in his work and his essay to the everyday certainties that we take for granted, such as freedom and democracy, especially in public space. In considering that freedom takes shape within strict conditions and that democracy is not a natural state but merely an ideology that is maintained by force, Staal discusses the idea of 'democratism' as a prelude to pointing towards an ever-changing possible reality. In considering how video-makers in Indonesia can only work in relation to the dominant characteristics of their televisual landscape, Miguel Escobar Varela argues that artistic and activist expressions of the margin are always determined by the dominant forms in relation to which they are marginalized. In the final contribution to this section, Tessa Overbeek introduces and interviews Tilde Björfors, the founding mother of the contemporary Swedish circus movement. This encounter describes the practice of circus as a critique of the dominant values of the Swedish political and cultural mentality (moderation, modesty and the avoidance of risk).

Community Art concludes with an epilogue that goes against the grain, taken from the diaries of the visual artist, Jan Fabre, which demonstrates that artistic self-creation can be understood as a political act. 'The Revolution in My Own Flesh' might be considered to be diametrically opposed to community art, but, in our view, it isn't. Every specific artistic and socio-economic situation demands from the artist an attitude of truth towards himself, his art and the relevant community. Sometimes, as is the case for Fabre, self-revolution is on the agenda; at other times, bonding and commonality are at stake. Each situation asks for an answer to the question of how community and art should relate to each other, there and then.

There are no universal answers.

We trust that the four parts of this book combine to stimulate discussion on the role of the arts *in* a globalizing society beyond easy glorification or revulsion. Anyone who wishes to comment on the book and the issues raised in it are welcome to do so through the different channels that are listed at the end. The research group will take up the thoughts and critique of the readers in its next projects. Let's inspire each other.

Part I
Definitions

Mapping Community Art

Pascal Gielen

The Impotence of Art

An illegal immigrant hesitantly expresses his criticism of an artist in front of a television camera. The man had promised to co-operate in a public intervention by the Belgian artist, Benjamin Verdonck. The project focused attention on the problems of refugees, illegal immigrants and other stateless people. The socially engaged artist had put up a cardboard house in the middle of the street on which he had written familiar advertising slogans, such as 'Nokia, connecting people' and 'My home is where my Stella is' (Stella Artois is a Belgian brand of beer). In the framework of Verdonck's artistic action, these slogans suddenly acquired a rather ambivalent, even bitter, undertone. Nobody missed the point. Apart from this fragile abode, the artist had also drawn up a pamphlet, in which he solicited understanding of the precarious condition in which these people who have turned nomads — often not of their own choosing — find themselves. During the artistic manifestation, illegal immigrants distributed this pamphlet. However, the man in front of the camera was slightly displeased with the form in which the artist had formulated his message. The childish handwriting, in which the leaflet was written, was not very convincing, according to him. This immigrant thought that his cause, and that of his companions, was not being taken seriously. Verdonck defended himself, in front of the same camera, with the argument that this childlike writing was simply part of his own particular artistic style ...

The short circuit which occurred between the illegal immigrant and the artist could well be considered symptomatic of all art venturing beyond the boundaries of its own world. Whenever art leaves the familiar surroundings of the museum or theatre, it falls prey to different opinions, perspectives and comments. It does not even have to flirt with social engagement or political activism for that matter. Even an aesthetically sound and 'nice' image in public space can provoke a storm of protest, if only because of the simple fact that it stands in the way of pedestrians and others. In the afore-mentioned account, however, something more is going on. With his artistic intervention, Verdonck chooses not only to break free from his pre-ordained place, but he also ventures to make a statement about society which is addressed to a specific part of that society.

All art — exhibited or performed inside or outside the confines of a museum, a concert hall or a theatre — makes a statement about society to a particular part of society. In other words, all art is *relational*. Even the artistic work of the most idiosyncratic hermit needs to be seen or heard — or there is always a relationship with a public necessary — in order to pass for art as such. Even the most abstract art, shown in a highly exclusive environment to which only a select group of insiders has access, makes a statement *about* society, *in* society and *to* society. French curator and art theoretician, Nicolas Bourriaud, made a rather poor choice when he used the word 'relational' to shed light on a specific segment and tendency in the art world, for art is *de facto* relational or it is not art.[1] Nevertheless, Bourriaud uses the concept *esthétique relationnelle* for a particular form of art, though his examples seem only to indicate a specific attitude held by certain artists. In Bourriaud's terms, the attitude of the relational artist may be described as consciously seeking communication with their public. Moreover, he actively includes this aspect in his work. The kind of art he applies to this purpose does not stand entirely apart from this endeavour, but may be considered as secondary to it. In fact, it does not matter so much what his art has to say about society and in which context it takes place. As long as the artist actively seeks a relationship with the public and attempts to engage it in a dialogue, a relational aesthetic is at work, according to the French curator. This does not imply that the relational artist makes critical, let alone subversive, work. The only criticism one might detect in his artistic work is rather indirect, with his explicit hunger for communication and dialogue perhaps expressing a lack of sociability in contemporary society.

The example of Verdonck and the illegal immigrant, given in the opening paragraph, goes beyond that, however, for Verdonck explicitly denounces a social problem. With his action, the artist not only seeks a relationship with a public, but he also serves this public a critical message. The playful packaging of the artistic statement barely covers its clear, political, perhaps slightly subversive, character. It goes without saying that this particular artist clearly chooses the side of illegal immigrants. His action is explicitly aimed at denouncing their situation. Yet, why was one particular illegal immigrant not completely satisfied? The answer has already been given: He takes offence at a particular aesthetic form. So, Verdonck's authentic artistic signature does not really seem to serve the good cause. The credibility of his action, with its real political claims, gets lost in an impotent world of fiction because, in the first place, the artist aims to realize an artistic project rather than a political statement with serious societal consequences. No matter how well-intentioned his engagement may be, his civil action always comes second. While what matters for the

---

1 Nicolas Bourriaud, Relational Aesthetics (Dijon: Les presses du réel, 1998).

illegal immigrant is that his social appeal might not be taken seriously, for the artist, the possible loss of his artistic prerogative seems scary. First and foremost, his childish touch keeps him rooted within the art world, and it is this which distinguishes the artist from the activist and distinguishes the artistic world from the political and artistic work from social work. The question as to whether the illegal immigrant is better served or becomes happier is an entirely different matter.

Meanwhile, it is quite certain that Verdonck counts himself lucky because, a year after his intervention, the material traces of his action can be admired in a museum for contemporary art. The work on display stimulated the imagination; it was poetic and, at times, even critical of society. It will come as no surprise that the unanimous public nodded approvingly when it ascertained that the political message it had deciphered was the correct one. The very same project which, in the street, enjoyed a certain degree of subversion, dissolved into common sense in the museum. Indeed, the significance and especially the effect of art depend very much on its context. Inside the museum, Verdonck's work met the strict criteria of contemporary art. One thing seems certain: with or without Stella, the artist has come home. Meanwhile, the question as to whether the illegal immigrant is able to enjoy a home rather than drowning himself in Stella, is somewhat more difficult to answer. From an artistic point of view, it is also completely irrelevant; aesthetics and ethics are two different things.

Aesthetics without Art

The lesson of Verdonck teaches us that an engaged artist, who sincerely wishes to make a political statement, forces himself into a particularly complex role. This is especially the case when he tries to substantiate this social claim from an artistic position. Building on the insights of Bourriaud, Verdonck's position — or at least the artistic project described here — could be described as *auto-relational*. In the long run, the relational bond with a public, including the political evocation of the fight for the rights of illegal immigrants, serves the identity of the artist. In this case, illegal immigrants involved are made complicit in a project which, in the end, will disembark safely in the art world.

The notion of auto-relational aesthetics, however, presupposes the existence of something called *allo-relational* art. Is it possible to detect projects or manifestations in the history of modern art which do not serve the identity of the artist or the artistic collective, but rather that of another person or the Other? Do forms of expression exist which ultimately emphasize the relational more than the artistic? A modest quest in modern art history leads us to the case of the Situationists. At the end of the 1960s, their artistic happenings and social provocations completely dissolved into society. Their art simply became politics. In the words of the Italian philosopher, Paolo Virno,

> The Situationists were very important when they became a political movement, but from that moment on they were no longer avant-garde art: it's about two modes of existence. They clearly illustrate this double take. Before 1960 they were an artistic movement rooted in Dadaism and Surrealism, afterwards they participated in social resistance, making the same mistakes or gaining the same merits as other political activists'.[2]

Allo-relational art can, then, lead to artistic suicide. However, it does not preclude the fact that the happenings of the Situationists inspired many activists following in their footsteps. In the feminist movement and the gay movement, among environmental activists and anti-globalizationists, one can find Situationist-inspired costume plays, theatrical expressions and other aesthetic forms which seek to highlight (at times literally) a certain social subversion. Especially within so-called identity politics, artistic forms of expression seem to be a favoured way of reinforcing one's social claims. People literarily colour their own cultural subjectivity. Moreover, in the artistic act of a costume play, for example, new subjectivities are generated. In other words, the pleasure of the play and the aesthetics are a substantial, constituent part of subversive movements. In an analysis of Baruch Spinoza, philosophers, Antonio Negri and Michael Hardt, claim that:

> The path of joy is constantly to open new possibilities, to expand our field of imagination, our abilities to feel and be affected, our capacities for action and passion. In Spinoza's thought, in fact, there is a correspondence between our

2   Sonja Lavaert and Pascal Gielen, 'The Dismeasure of Art: An Interview with Paolo Virno,' Being an Artist in Post-Fordist Times, eds. Pascal Gielen and Paul De Bruyne (Rotterdam: NAi Publishers, 2009).

power to affect and our power to be affected. The greater our mind's ability to think, the greater its capacity to be affected by the ideas of others; the greater our body's ability to act, the greater its capacity to be affected by other bodies.[3]

Contrary to Negri and Hardt's allusion, however, the relational power of aesthetic expression need not necessarily have subversive intention. In her article on community art, Jan Cohen-Cruz points out that not all strains within the community art movement have a progressive, political character.[4] She reinforces her argument by suggesting that the Nuremberg party rallies of Adolf Hitler were an aesthetic, communal ritual. During those rallies, not only blond, athletic workers paraded, but there were also women in traditional Teutonic attire performing folk dances. Cohen-Cruz's example leads us to a next point. Without necessarily subscribing to Nazi ideology, folk art is often intended to bring people together. This target beyond art binds the late Situationists to clog dancers and farce. Both make allo-relational art — in both cases, the artistic aspect is subsumed by other goals — the political (in the case of the Situationists) or the communal (in the case of folk art). Making a public complicit, therefore, may serve goals beyond merely artistic ones. It is this which distinguishes the political faction of the Situationists from those of Benjamin Verdonck. The latter is auto-relational because, in the end, his political act is instrumentalized for his own individual artistic career, whereas some of the Situationists allowed their art to become political.

Mapping Community Art

Gradually, gropingly, the vectors of community art start to emerge in the account above. Yet, before going into greater detail, it seems sensible to attempt a possible definition of these artistic acts. The relationship with people is at the centre of this type of cultural practice. All community art is, therefore, at the very least relational art. In order for a work to be considered community art, the bottom line is that it actively involves people in an artistic process or in the production of a work of art. With this in mind, is a director who engages professional actors for a theatre production also making community art? The earlier-quoted Cohen-Cruz would probably answer that the process of involving people in a work of art should at least be as important as any artistic process or project. In short, the community is at least as crucial as the art. The fact that the people participating are often not professionals, not even art connoisseurs per se, only serves to further delineate the territory concerned. Certainly, a community art project has only 'succeeded' when it realizes an interaction between participants and the artist and wider community at which it was aimed. The purpose of such interactions may be political or subversive, social, identity-forming or therapeutic, but the aesthetic aspect will only ever serve as a formal tool. Only when symmetry has been achieved between the community and the art does the expressive form have a claim within the professional art world. In other words, a relational work may well be aesthetic, but it is not necessarily a successful work of art. By the same token, an artistic project involving a community is not necessarily a successful community project.

The story of Verdonck teaches us that serving both the community and the art presupposes a very precarious balancing act. In the terms outlined earlier, it calls for the right balance between auto- and allo-relational aesthetics. This distinction immediately suggests two directions that community art may navigate. The first is that community art mostly abides by the rules of professional art; the second is that it merely serves social interaction. The possible purpose of this social interaction adds two more directions to the map, as a distinction needs to be made between Situationists and farce. Whereas the first possible direction aims at radical subversion, the second group is only interested in the socially integrating effect. The latter dimension may be called the *digestive* effect of community art. In much the same way as a digestive remedy helps to enhance one's metabolism, this form of art helps to integrate social groups into society. This is done without questioning the dominant values, norms or habits. Digestive community art is, if you wish, a form of 'naturalizing art'. It conforms to rules that are already in place within society. In some cases, community artists are deliberately put in place and subsidized — by companies, governments, or other official agencies — to bring about integration. Conformity and non-obstruction are at the centre of this way of working, which makes digestive art the opposite of the subversive artistic act. However, the division between both poles is not insurmountable, as integration may lead to emancipation — for example becoming conscious of one's own rights and of the possible injustice one is suffering — which subsequently elicits (more) effective subversive strategies.

3 Michael Hardt and Antonio Negri, Commonwealth (Cambridge, MA: Harvard University Press, 2009).

4 Jan Cohen-Cruz, 'An Introduction to Community Art and Activism' (2002), www.communityarts.net/readingroom/archivefiles/2002/02/an_introduction.php

When the poles of auto- and allo-relational, digestive and subversive art cross one another, a wind-flower with four directions comes into being, as should be the case in any cartography worthy of the name. In this configuration, the North stands for what is reasoned and slightly hypothermic, as opposed to the warm and sanguineous South. The clichés the wind directions evoke serve as ideal metaphors to contrast digestion with subversion. In the West, the cult of the individual dominates, with his own identity at its centre, whereas Oriental philosophy — in particular Buddhism — regards the self or the ego (*atman*) as an illusion. The West and the East, therefore, form ideal regions to which auto- and allo-relational art can come home.

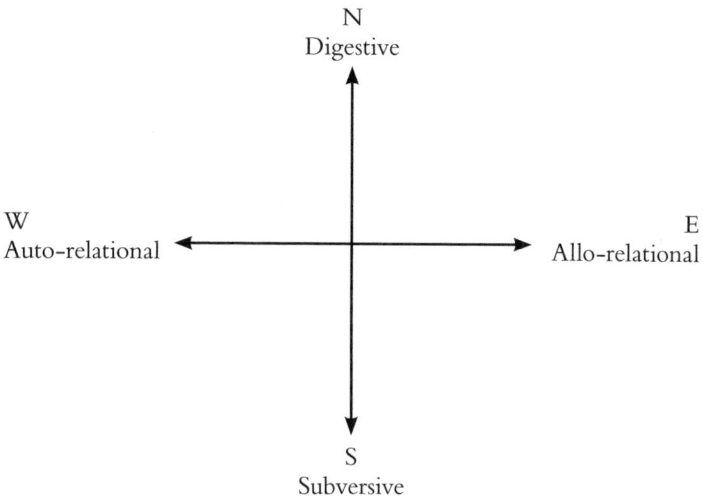

However, in the same way that only a few inhabitants of this globe actually live in the far North or South, community art will mostly be located in 'impure' places. The distinction between auto- and allo-relational art should, therefore, also be understood as the distinction between digestive and subversive, in other words as a gradation rather than an end point. Moreover, there is also a North-West or a South-East, at which interesting hybrids thrive. In this cartography, it is only possible to locate oneself in relation to another point of reference. Inter-relations are always relative; x lies more to the South of y and more to the West but more to the South of x, and so on. Over time, artistic trajectories may also transmute or change directions. This means that the development of an artistic idea may at first be merely an auto-relational matter, which opens up into a digestive allo-relational (repetitive) process, after which the final product is again summarized auto-relationally (though it may be highly offensive for the artistic in-crowd confronted with it). The afore-mentioned shift undergone by Verdonck, from a public intervention with illegal immigrants on the street to an exhibition with the remaining artefacts in a museum, illustrates that, on the map of community art, different itineraries are possible. Whereas an intervention on the street fluctuates between slightly subversive auto- and allo-relational art, the museum exhibition has a far more digestive auto-relational character, which has nothing to do with the artistic quality and persuasive power of that particular exhibition. The context and an amenable public together decide on the place at which an artistic project may be located on the community map. To illustrate this, we will use our compass to navigate a number of concrete examples.

Digestive Auto-Relational Art

Art in public space which has to mark a district or the history of a region and confirm its identity is often a form of digestive art. The artistic work at least has the goal of 'livening up' public space, without questioning it and certainly without sabotaging it. When the artist who took on the assignment (for it is often commissioned art) actively involves the community of the place where the work will be realized in the development and possibly the execution of his project, as we have seen this qualifies as community art. When the artist is able to channel all the involved social powers — often including the government commissioning agency, companies or businesses and local inhabitants — so he can seal them with his own particular artistic signature, we are dealing with auto-relational work. Organizations such as Les Nouveaux Commanditaires (the New Sponsors) in France and Belgium or de Stichting Kunst in de Openbare Ruimte (the Foundation for Art in Public Space) in the Netherlands often act as intermediaries in realizing such digestive auto-relational art. On the one hand, they explore the wishes of the sponsors and look for a 'matching artist', whereas, on the other hand, they also guard the singular identity of the latter. Through consultation, any frictions between artist and community are smoothed out beforehand.

Art-scientist, Simone Kleinhout, for example, describes a project by Les Nouveaux Commanditaires in the small French village of Blessey.[5] In this village with only twenty-three inhabitants, a laundry was being restored and the mayor and inhabitants wanted a work of art to be included in this project. The artist, Rémy Zaugg, was willing to take on the job. He was confronted with a population of mainly farmers who barely knew anything about contemporary art but who knew very well which requirements the work of art had to meet. It had to be in harmony with the sensitivity of the location and have favourable economic consequences. They even had an idea as to which material should be used to realize the work, which should include the characteristics of the environment such as water, stone and plants. And, as the sponsors thought his work also had to have favourable social consequences, in the end Zaugg was reluctantly forced to realize his work in the framework of a social integration project. The realization of Zaugg's work would take almost ten years, a period during which he had to go through the trial of many negotiations. For example, he chose to work with concrete, a material that did not immediately fit with the rustic image the inhabitants had in mind. The artist did finally manage to carry his decision through in this matter and, in doing so, to leave his mark on the work of art. Anyone who goes to look at the work in the French Bourgogne region has to admit that this is a real 'Zaugg'. Meanwhile, *Le Lavoir de Blessey* (2007), as the work is retrospectively called, blends in almost perfectly with the natural slopes and the heritage of the area, confirming the history and identity of the village. In other words, through the intervention of himself and Les Nouveaux Commanditaires, Zaugg succeeded in making a perfectly digestive auto-relational work of art, to which the inhabitants even relinquished part of their private premises. Let us be clear once and for all, then, that the word 'digestive' is certainly not synonymous with 'bad' art.

Digestive Allo-Relational Art

In the United States, the Law Enforcement Assistance Administration and the National Endowment for the Arts joined forces in 1977 to inaugurate a programme in which artists realized projects in prisons. With this in mind, the Federal Bureau of Prisons kindly organized 'arts-in-corrections' training. The purpose of artistic interventions was to facilitate the transformation of criminals into economically productive citizens.[6] Although this federal initiative eventually disappeared, several state governments (including those of California and Mississippi) continued to develop similar projects. In the case of

California, several millions of dollars were invested in such projects, which demonstrates that belief in the healing effects of the arts is remarkably strong in certain regions. Grady Hillman defends the project by saying that

> The evolving arts-in-corrections model is more than the intervention model of an arts residency in a penitentiary or juvenile detention center. It is a prevention, intervention and after-care model. [...] The benefit of this criminal-justice community is that it brings coherency to a system that is largely incoherent... .[7]

It goes without saying that this kind of community art programme primarily aims at social integration, with the artistic signature of the artist coming second. On the map, such programmes clearly orientate themselves in a North-Easterly direction, where digestion and allo-relatedness meet each other.

Subversive Auto-Relational Art

Let us remain awhile in the United States where, in 1989, the republican senator, Jesse Helms, was appalled by the 'distasteful' catalogue for *The Perfect Moment*, which showed the explicitly homoerotic and sadomasochistic work of photographer, Robert Mapplethorpe. In the meantime, the affair has become world famous, so it does not make much sense to further elaborate on it. Even twenty years after the incident, few people doubt that Mapplethorpe's act may be interpreted as subversive. Yet, whether the exuberant artist's work can be simply categorized as community art may well be contested. Certainly, his art is relational, for, as was mentioned earlier, all art seeks a relationship with a public. Few people would contradict the fact that the artist managed to capitalize on his own artistic signature — though perhaps quite a few people, including Helms, would venture to question the work's status as 'art'. But whether the artist was actively seeking

5   Simone Kleinhout, Kunst projecten in de openbare ruimte: Waarde(n)volle ondernemingen, **Masters Thesis, Art Culture and Media (Groningen: Rijksuniversiteit Groningen, 2010).**
6   **Grady Hillman, 'A Journey of Discouragement and Hope: An Introduction to Arts and Corrections' (2001),**
      www.communityarts.net/readingroom/archivefiles/corrections_all2/index.php.
7   **Ibid.**

communication with a public, in the sense that Bourriaud intends, is very much in question. Apart from the group of homosexual friends who posed for the photographs, it is difficult to find any traces pointing at a community. Yet, one could defend the position that Mapplethorpe makes auto-relational art. His *esthétique relationnelle* is not so much to be found in the social attitude of the artist, but in his photographs. Whether consciously intended or not, his work fits perfectly with the kind of identity politics in which a community finds expression. In any case, the work of Mapplethorpe may not only be read as a manifestation for the right to artistic freedom, but also as an expression of the right to make the (often socially suppressed) culture of a specific community visible. Mapplethorpe proceeds as an anthropologist in his own country, confronting American society with its own fantasies, self-indulgence or 'alterity'. By launching evidence of an extravagant lifestyle into public space, the photographer makes a case for its legitimacy, which may well be understood to be a political act. In this respect, the work of this individual is perhaps far more community-forming and community-affirming than much deliberately community-orientated artistic fieldwork. The hypothesis is defended that it is perfectly possible for an artist to make community art without addressing his work to a particular community. However, Mapplethorpe does explicitly embed the gay community in order to shape it in his oeuvre. Exactly this aspect makes him an extremely *auto*-relational artist.

Subversive Allo-Relational Art

Let us linger a bit longer in homosexual circles. Gay Pride is a relevant example of exuberant aesthetics shaping a community. The parades which are organized in an increasing number of cities often remind one of the 'carnivalesque', as the Russian philosopher and literary critic, Mikhail Bakhtin, understood it. Bakhtin attributes a specific social function to the carnival — a temporary reversal of the existing hierarchy of power relations.[8] It is by now well known that he called that mechanism 'symbolic inversion'. This inversion is, indeed, only symbolic; after the temporary costume play, one returns to the social order of the day. And, although a carnival may well offer space to 'vent' one's criticism, it is the very existence of a *ventil* (air valve) which prevents a certain kind of atmosphere from turning into an actual revolution. Only when Gay Pride transcends the temporality of the feast to point to the political rights of homosexuals does the manifestation find itself in the field of subversion. The aesthetics are invested, however, in serving the rights of the community rather than an individual artistic identity. Therefore, on the map, this type of practice navigates a South-Easterly direction as subversive allo-relational art.

Nowadays, many (municipal) governments vie with each other for their own Gay Pride. Politicians hope that the colourful parade will highlight the openness of their city and, at the same time, attract a new type of tourism. According to the work of the American social geographer Richard Florida, in the rush to form creative cities, a solid population of homosexuals is synonymous with a proportionately high creative potential.[9] By this rationale, Gay Pride simply serves to tap into a new economy, as 'alter-sexuals' constitute a substantial part of the creative class. Given the generally established belief in the potency of this class and its industry, each homophobic policy demonstrates economic irresponsibility. Conversely, the tolerance of the administration, whether feigned or not, raises questions as to whether Gay Pride and other alternative manifestations have lost their subversive feathers. In a wider context, it opens up a discussion on the social position of any form of community art.

Repressive Tolerance and Pastoral Art

In 2007, the Belgian independent research group, BAVO, made an important contribution to this discussion. In their analysis, concerning the recent revival of politically engaged art, they denounce problematic forms of art such as so-called NGO[10]-art, putting forth the following proposition concerning this new type of political engagement:

> It is noble and necessary that artists proceed to take direct action against the often harrowing abuses typical of these times. However, when it comes to judging the effectiveness of these politically engaged practices in tackling the current problems in a more fundamental way, they often leave much to be desired. [...] They tend to reason and operate in the same manner

8   Mikhail Bakhtin, Rabelais and his World (Cambridge, MA: MIT Press, 1968).
9   Richard Florida, The Rise of the Creative Class: And How It's Transforming Work, Leisure, Community and Everyday Life (New York: Basic Books, 2002).
10 i.e. non-governmental organization.

as humanitarian organizations or NGOs: rather than tackling large-scale, political problems, they focus on what they can do immediately, here and now, within the confines of what is obtainable [...]. In the same way as is the case with humanitarian organizations one may detect self-censorship in this so-called NGO-art. Humanitarian organizations consciously do not make statements about political questions, because this could interfere with their relief operations, [...]. NGO-art is in fact characterized by a denial of politics: above all it has to do with the practicability of a given action. These artists deliberately avoid confrontation with governments or sponsors, because the concessions or funding which they need to execute their actions, may be compromised by such politics. The question as to what can be done, here and now, and how this can be realized in the most efficient manner, is more important than exposing and fighting deeper lying structures – which is in fact the quintessence of politics.[11]

In the Netherlands — where quite a few community art projects are currently being financed by municipal administrations — one often feels the limits of this form of artistic engagement. For example, artists are often approached by policy makers to liven up the social life of one or other disadvantaged neighbourhood. When the politically engaged artist discovers, half way through the execution of such a project, that the problem of structural disadvantage does not rest on the individual shoulders of a few 'anti-social' residents, but that the negligent policy of a housing organization is to blame, the civil servants who commissioned the project suddenly become slightly nervous. The artist might well publicly expose the fact that the putative 'win–win situation' of private-public co-operation between the housing organization and the administration leads to little gain for the inhabitants. With such a threat hanging over them, the bureaucrats would rather halt this once much-welcomed community project.

When social engagement turns into political engagement, administrations prefer to withdraw their financial engagement. Considered in terms of the cartography outlined above, be it auto-relational or allo-relational, once the border between digestion and subversion is crossed, politicians and civil servants would rather rid themselves of such art. Therefore, it is very much a question of what a municipal administration would do with Gay Pride which would expose the embedded homophobia that lurks behind the façade of verbal tolerance.

The peculiar relationship between potentially subversive art and established power also emerges in the story of Verdonck. His public action, described earlier, formed part of a series of interventions by the artist in the Belgian city of Antwerp which took place over an entire year. These were included in a controversial documentary, in which the story of the critical illegal immigrant was also represented. At the beginning of the documentary, we see how Verdonck enthusiastically introduces his not-always-uncritical actions during a meeting with the cultural and political actors of Antwerp, including the mayor. At the end of the meeting, the mayor gives Verdonck a verbal pat on the shoulder and wishes him success, after which the mayor leaves the meeting with a benign smile on his face. In other words, the artist receives the green light from the incumbent power to demonstrate some subversive behaviour. This conforms to Herbert Marcuse's understanding of repressive tolerance,[12] a hegemonic strategy which neutralizes undesirable ideas by granting them a place. The possibility of such a mechanism inevitably raises questions about whether subsidized community art can acquire any sort of subversive power.

Moreover, it is striking that (often digestive) community art frequently surfaces in countries with pronounced neoliberal regimes, such as in Great Britain, Australia, the United States and nowadays also the Netherlands. An attempt seems to be made to compensate for the absence or imminent breakdown of a strong social infrastructure, typical of the welfare state, through artistic operations. Perhaps that is the very reason why community art is currently experiencing a comeback. It is generally accepted that, with the fall of the Berlin Wall, neoliberalism spread rapidly to become a hegemonic

11 BAVO, Cultural Activism Today: The Art of Over-Identification (Rotterdam: Episode Publishers, 2007).

12 Herbert Marcuse, 'Repressive Tolerance,' A Critique of Pure Tolerance, Robert Paul Wolff, Barrington Moore Jr. and Herbert Marcuse (Boston: Beacon Press, 1965).

ideology. What is striking, in the Netherlands for example, is that the government stimulates community art in precisely those areas from which it withdrew crucial social services ten years ago. Community art becomes a cheaper form of social work, especially as it is usually offered on a project basis, whereas social services, including local schools and hospitals, call for a more serious, structural investment. It is very doubtful whether one can effectively tackle serious issues, such as social deprivation and disintegration, with temporary projects and similarly temporary responsibilities. Who will take responsibility when the artist — who lives in the neighbourhood for anything from a couple of months to a year to set up a nice piece of art — leaves the neighbourhood?

Now that a connection has been made between government, social work and community art, one final point of discussion remains. This trinity suggests a specific ongoing form of power and disciplinary practice, which is further affirmed by the afore-mentioned example of the 'arts-in-corrections' programmes in the United States, leading as it does to the work of Michel Foucault, the French philosopher who was particularly interested in prisons. In his world-famous work, *Discipline and Punish*, dating from 1975, Foucault describes the birth of the prison. He goes on to show how punishments gradually acquire an increasingly 'humane' character. Public torture and executions recede into the background, to be replaced by confinement and an expanding army of nurses, psychologists and social workers. The crux of Foucault's theorem is that this model of discipline is disseminated throughout society, through institutions such as hospitals and schools. This research into the execution of power was continued in Foucault's lectures at the Collège de France, delivered during the 1977-1978 academic year, in which he unravelled the notion of 'pastoral power'. This is based on an idea of the shepherd who 'manages' his herd in a particular manner, which allows him to pay attention to the needs of an individual animal without losing sight of the rest of his herd. Subsequently, the church has applied this method of herding to human beings and institutionalized it, according to Foucault. The central point of pastoral power is that human life is shepherded from the cradle to the grave. The art of the shepherd, or pastor, consists of addressing the members of one's parish as individually as possible, penetrating their private lives and taking note of their deepest secrets through confession. The pastor performs a sort of micro-politics, through which he is able to continuously evaluate and correct the members of his herd, in order to keep them on, or lead them onto, the right path.

Distinct from the sovereign power of the nation state, pastoral power does not deal with geographically delineated territory, but is aimed at people of flesh and blood. For this reason, pastoral power is also a form of 'bio-power' — administration directed at life itself. On the basis of in-depth interviews, French sociologist, Maurizio Lazzarato, demonstrates how this pastoral power is part of an official 'system of correction'.[13] In doing so, the inspecting civil servant constantly oversteps the dividing line between public and private territory, in order to get through to the deepest intimacy of the 'client'. Wielding the threat of possible sanctions (the withdrawal of social benefits), he checks toothbrush usage and whether beds have been slept in. Conversely, the inspector of the unemployment office hopes to help the person who is eligible to receive social benefits on the right — productive — path. Via elaborate registration and records in individual dossiers, the life of the person eligible for social benefits 'doubles' in a paper or digital register in which each personal step is carefully followed. Though the client is constantly reminded of his own freedom and individual responsibility, he is, in fact, placed in an asymmetrical power game in which he is constantly shown 'the right path'. Within the welfare state, not only the inspection services, but also a large group of psychologists and social workers form an extension of 'police power' of which pastoral power is just one strategy. In a subtle way, they infiltrate the daily private sphere to register, correct and make economically productive (again) the most intimate parts of life. The point has now been reached whereby quite a few community art projects — especially when orchestrated by the government — are at the service of this police power. In the afore-mentioned 'arts-in-corrections' programme in the United States, this was all too obvious, where a community art project was explicitly launched to turn detained people into 'productive citizens'. Yet, even artists who enter into disadvantaged neighbourhoods with the best of intentions are often unaware of the fact that they are stepping into this 'correctional' logic. So, for example, quite a few artists would consider themselves exceedingly original to distribute photo or video cameras to socially disadvantaged families, asking them to record their lives and those of their neighbours. While the social worker on a house visit records their intimate details on paper and in files, the community artist goes a step further, as the confidential document is traded in

13 Maurizio Lazzarato, 'Pastoral Power: Beyond Public and Private,' Open No. 19: Cahier on Art and the Public Domain, 2010, pp. 18-33.

31

for a registration which may become public at any given moment. In other words, the artist enthusiastically encourages residents to participate in a 'public confession' of their own misery. Like religious confession, this is one of the pastoral power techniques for keeping the herd under control. In the case of the priest, the psychologist and the social worker, such confession still takes place in relative confidentiality; for the artist, however, precarious social misery has an expressive character. While the socially engaged artist, with all his good intentions, thought he was fighting against injustice in the world, he finds himself at the service of the power which maintains the injustice.

Beyond Community Art

Many a community artist might grow weary when reading the above discussion. Others might treat the arguments with disbelief and attempt to neutralize them with as many counterexamples as possible. A mapping of community art shows us that this world is full of good intentions, sometimes even revolutionary thoughts, but also that great naivety, and even incompetence, exists. This discussion is not, therefore, intended to discourage community art, but to permit some self-reflection. Hopefully, this will help to better clarify the position of the socially engaged artist, allowing her or him to develop effective strategies in the future. Whoever thinks that the above analysis demonstrates that community art is best carried to its grave has missed the point. Firstly, let it be clear that the digestive, integrating power of some artistic projects is particularly useful when counting the growing number of diaspora and homeless people in a globalized world. Apart from that, it should also be noted that the notion of community art nowadays carries with it a remarkably subversive potency, which is hidden in the very word 'community'. Within a neoliberal world, in which individuality, personal gain, competition and speculation have become the prevailing strategies of the day, exerting their influence over the social fabric, the community gives rise to associations which may sound naive but which are no less revolutionary within the current hegemony. When the community does not retreat into itself, but consequently uses its principles to the defence of an unknown other and the other, it might well offer an unexpected ideological counterforce to neoliberal hyper-individualism. In short, nowadays the community still stands for an alternative way of life. According to the American philosopher, Richard Sennett, it even provides the most important architecture against the current, hostile economic order.[14]

In contemporary network society, the community can no

longer be understood as a closed social form with mere face-to-face relations, as the romantic *Gemeinschaft*, Ferdinand Tönnies, once described it.[15] The new or alter-community does, however, evoke associations with 'the common', and the possibility of property to which everybody has an unalienable right. It also points in the direction of lasting solidarity across generations, inside and between neighbourhoods or (world) regions. Finally, it indicates a form of love which reaches beyond the walls of private family life. These new communities operate as neo-tribal groups in an alter-modern network world. The latter group implies, amongst other things, that it does not stick to its own identity, but is continuously transforming and having it transformed through new meetings. These worlds of stateless communities develop their own economies of leisure, pleasure, love and knowledge, as islands within neoliberal hegemony.

'Keep on dreaming, baby', sounds like a sober yet ironic voice, very near. Dreams probably do contain a sense of reality; perhaps it is the role of art to transform them into concrete forms — it will certainly take a lot of imaginative power to shape new communities. To move beyond community art presupposes, first of all, an art of communities, in which artistic reflection is not at the service of the evident questions posed by the mass media and neoliberalism, in which the aesthetic does not serve to slavishly patch up the holes a blind capitalism leaves behind. The art of communities knows how to occupy these holes in a meaningful way and to tactically manage them by constantly generating ways of escape. In short, community art only makes sense when it refuses to be used as an instrument of a uniform, homogenizing, calculating logic, and when it produces the most divergent communities through the confrontation of many singular and dissonant forms of imaginative power.

14 Richard Sennett, The Corrosion of Character: The Personal Consequences of Work in the New Capitalism **(London: W.W. Norton & Company, 1998)**.
15 Ferdinand Tönnies, Gemeinschaft und Gesellschaft **(Fues's Verlag: Leipzig, 1887)**.

Community Art as a Contested Artistic Practice

The Case of MET-X, Brussels

Paul De Bruyne

In the social and political field, community art is usually understood as an art form dedicated to forming a community in which politically correct values, such as solidarity, fellowship and community spirit, are encouraged or confirmed. It is, first and foremost, a social concept, not an artistic one. In the legitimacy debate of the subsidizer (which, in Continental Europe, is often the government but, in other contexts, may be a semi-private or private entity), community art is assigned great potency for forming or maintaining social cohesion and for creating individual and/or group identities. Indeed, community art is valued extremely highly in that discourse.

Since its social goals aim (too) high, are ethically (too) pure, not artistic in nature and, on top of that, the actual effects of projects are extremely hard to measure, community art is heavily criticized from several sides. In particular, this criticism comes from those political and social forces which urge that it is not the duty of the state to support cultural projects (neoliberals), from political forces which think the community arts are, by definition, in league with the prevailing hegemony (ultra left), from forces which feel that, under the guise of politically correct values, an unjust policy of positive discrimination is pursued with regard to socially damaging forces ('Islam', 'loitering teens', 'criminals') (ultra right) or from the artistic sector which urges that the autonomy of the arts is under pressure by art that is used in an instrumental way, since it is serving goals other than aesthetic ones ('this isn't art, this is social work'). Seen from a social and political point of view, community art is an expression of social democracy and related political movements, a typical welfare state product.

But if you take the trouble to research the history of the community art organizations in detail, you will soon discover that the concept contains very complex practices that cannot be understood, defended or attacked quite so easily according to their social goals, let alone their (alleged) social effects. And if you want to put in a word about the *artistic* identity of community arts, you stumble upon an even bigger complexity.

With this essay, I intend, by analysing the work of one of the longest running community art organizations in Europe, to contribute to defining artistic projects that have a clear social or political accent, be it subtle or more obvious. This defines community art as a constellation of positions between several artistic and social dynamics. The advantage of this approach is that the voice of the artist is heard more clearly within the debate on community art. Artists tend to think in terms of production and distribution processes, rather than according to the logic of social intentions and effect, typical of politicians, producers and social workers.

MET-X

MET-X is a Brussels-based organization, which, since 1982, has mainly set up music projects that we would call community art in the current parlance. Set up by a pool of musicians and visual artists, the core figure of the organization was and is the saxophonist, composer and curator, Luc Mishalle (b. 1953). Since the mid-1970s, he has been an important force in Belgium, organizing and artistically animating music and theatre projects into which musicians from the new wave of immigrants (initially mostly Moroccans and Turks and, later, also musicians from the sub-Saharan countries) were welcomed. Mishalle quickly became known as the country's leading multicultural, or intercultural, musician, who consciously tried to give shape to the new sociological diversity of Europe in a musical way. The music he makes is usually based on a combination of Western (reed) players, on the one hand (sax, trombone, trumpet, tuba), and non-Western percussion on the other hand (goblet drum *darbouka*, frame drum *bendir*, and the castanet-like *krakeb*). The structures in which he shapes his music have their roots in jazz, the new Western classical music and the non-Western (often Maghreb) folk music. Since Mishalle has defined his work, in interviews, as not only artistic but also social and political, he quickly came to be regarded as the founder of critical community art in the Belgian music world. Twenty-five years after the foundation of MET-X, the Flemish government funding it considers the organization to be the most important (best subsidized) music institute with a multicultural, educational and socio-artistic effect. Within the production house MET-X, multiple music bands and educational projects have been and continue to be developed which are put on the international market, sometimes with great success, sometimes with less success but always within the self-declared mission that is defined as follows on its website: 'MET-X is a house for and from musicians. We transform sounds from the belly of the city into a unique musical universe. In close collaboration with enthusiastic artists coming from the most different horizons we manufacture the creative elements in order to form bands, events and educational processes. Our acoustic universe is closely linked to that of the steaming capital, sometimes loud, sometimes soft, sometimes beautiful sometimes ugly. Never smooth. Always exciting. Moving music. Music that moves.'

There is no mention of community art in this description; rather, it refers to Urban Art, in which the concept of 'moving' has several meanings. It is about both the 'emotion', the literal 'movements in the street' and the more metaphorical 'putting things in motion'.

In subsidy applications to the government, though, MET-X emphasizes the idea of cooperation with people 'from the most different horizons' and 'educational processes', that is the idea of community art. MET-X involves 'through musical activities migrants of predominantly Moroccan origin in the cultural life, it improves the transfer to regular education through teaching programmes, and brings about a cross-pollination between Moroccan and Flemish musical culture'. These two different discourses (one on the website, for the general audience, with an emotional and artistic profile, and one for the subsidizing government, with an educational and social point of view) already hint at the complexity one is faced with when shaping the concept of community art in actual practice. It is a prime example of how an artist-driven organization in its communication with government has to/wants to adapt the discourse of that government.

In order to understand the concept of community art from the standpoint of the artist and to observe how an organization like MET-X operates within that concept, we have to introduce the various dynamics that might be important in describing the uniqueness of specific artistic projects. Those dynamics occur at three phases in the artistic process: production, distribution and reception or effect. Within this schema, seven different dynamics may be distinguished. They form a scale that makes the constellation of a specific project visible and, therefore, comparable to other projects. I call that scale, not without irony, the Brown Scale (my name means Brown in English).

In the production process, four dynamics are distinguished: the virtuosity in the process (whereby low virtuosity is usually the hallmark of the amateur and high virtuosity that of the professional artist), the autonomy of the process (whereby autonomy is inversely proportional to the extent to which a project is instrumentalized), the collective nature of the process (whereby collectivity stands in opposition to individual work) and, lastly, the diversity of cultures involved (whereby high diversity opposes a monoculture). In the distribution process, we witness the dynamic of the number of potential spectators ranging from limited (elitist) to general (popular). In the reception process, the disruption of expectations on the part of the audience is a significant factor, both at an artistic and social level, whereby low aesthetic disruption is the hallmark of entertainment,

38

high disruption is the hallmark of (modernist) art. A low social disruption is the hallmark of a conforming artistic product, a high one the hallmark of subversive or activist art. The Brown Scale looks as follows:

(versus)

Low Virtuosity	*High Virtuosity*
Instrumental	*Autonomous*
Individual	*Collective*
Monocultural	*Multicultural*
General Audience	*Limited Audience*
Entertainment	*Art*
Conformism	*Subversiveness*

This scale enables us to draw up a constellation of a hypothetical ideal community art performance as it would appear within social and political discourse. The 'ideal' community art performance is characterized by the use of non-virtuoso artistry because it is developed in cooperation with amateurs. The production has a high instrumental nature because the creation of a community through any means necessary is the motivation and goal of the event. For much the same reason, the development of the performance is a collective event for a general audience, which, therefore, has an entertaining and conformist nature. Whether the performance is monocultural or multicultural in nature depends on the kind of community that needs to be created. Thus, the constellation of the 'ideal' community art performance, from the viewpoint of the social workers and politicians, looks as follows. The sign 'CA' (Community Art) identifies the ideal community art performance on each rung of the scale. The combined signs constitute the constellation. CA visualizes the spot on the various rungs of the scale.

(versus)

Low Virtuosity CA		*High Virtuosity*
Instrumental CA		*Autonomous*
Individual	CA	*Collective*
Monocultural		*Multicultural*
General Audience CA		*Limited Audience*
Entertainment CA		*Art*
Conformism CA		*Subversiveness*

39

If, however, one studies the concrete artistic reality of community art, we notice that the social and political discourse surrounding it is too simple. The example of MET-X will demonstrate that community art projects can vary enormously at the scale of underlying production and consumption dynamics.

A Multitude of Projects

Al Harmoniah (1995–2004) was a project in which Mishalle formulated an answer to the decline of the traditional fanfare and brass band culture that had been a part of popular city and village life long into the twentieth century but is now disappearing under the influence of (post-)modernity. *Al Harmoniah* was a typical community art project because it tried to shape the new reality of the big city through which autochthonous and migrant communities could meet each other in a shared musical project. *Al Harmoniah* was a fanfare that left the marches and polkas, performed in processions and parades by the previous generation, far behind. It was replaced by music that was pollinated by the many musical genres from all over the world, from Latin America to Africa.

Al Harmoniah brought together amateur musicians from various origins who practised newly composed music that was rhythmically rooted in Maghreb culture and which was melodiously governed by the heritage of jazz. One could hardly call *Al Harmoniah* a mere amateur fanfare since, besides Mishalle, a number of other professional musicians (like the Moroccan percussionist, Abdallah Marakchi) took the lead in the artistic and organizational development of the group. The high virtuosity of the professional musicians was embedded into the lower virtuosity of the amateurs.

Because of the musical contribution of professionals looking for a new form of authentic contemporary urban music, *Al Harmoniah* was a group that considered the 'autonomy' of playing music more important than the instrumental support of the 'multicultural cause', although the performance environment could often be called politically correct (multicultural venues, multicultural festivals and the like). The production process of *Al Harmoniah* was highly defined by the amateurs' limited artistic and social potential. The collective working process was more important than the personal ambitions of any of the professionals involved. It was immediately clear that *Al Harmoniah* was driven by the will to undertake an intercultural action. Although the group's ambition was to create music that would be appreciated by many, that ambition was restricted by the limited possibilities an amateur group has for widespread distribution; the number of concerts that amateurs can play is quite limited. On another rung of the scale, the music of *Al Harmoniah* can primarily be labelled as entertainment, although the non-Western rhythm, the use of instruments uncommon in the West and the jazzy melodic lines must have sounded strange and (therefore) 'different' to some spectators. When judging the subversive quality of the work of this group, the last rung of the scale, one can reasonably assume that it was not subversive at all because the group of spectators and organizers had a positive bias towards any intercultural encounter.

When one positions *Al Harmoniah* on the Brown Scale, the constellation appears as follows (*Al Harmoniah* appears as an X):

<pre>
                          (versus)

Low Virtuosity   X   High Virtuosity
Instrumental   X   Autonomous
Individual   X   Collective
Monocultural   X   Multicultural
General Audience   X   Limited Audience
Entertainment   X   Art
Conformism   X   Subversiveness
</pre>

Al Harmoniah deviates from the presupposed ideal standard constellation of community art projects at a number of points. It was considerably more virtuoso, autonomous and artistic and considerably less collective.

Marakbar (1992–1998) is a MET-X project that generates a distinct constellation on the Brown Scale compared to *Al Harmoniah*. It was conceived when Antwerp, a city with large Moroccan and Turkish communities, became Cultural Capital of Europe in 1993, and the preparations for that cultural event were thwarted by a major political event. During the council elections of 24 November 1991, the extreme right and nationalistic party, Vlaams Blok (Flemish Block), which had a rabid anti-Islam programme became Antwerp's largest political party. The organizers of Antwerp '93 searched desperately for an answer to this result, which they perceived as dangerous. They asked Luc Mishalle to make an artistic statement that would depict the cultural diversity of the city as a positive thing; a statement that would show the enriching possibility of an intercultural cooperation in an illustrative and exemplary manner. In short, *Marakbar* was a community art project that was commissioned by the subsidizing governments and their cultural representatives.

From the start, then, *Marakbar* should be understood as a very instrumental, hardly autonomous project. Whether this also makes it a conformist project in the minds of the spectators is not so easily determined. But one may safely assume that both the Vlaams Blok voters and the anti-racist members of the audience were confirmed in their socio-political opinions and emotions by the intercultural music and spectacle, rather than being induced to change them.

Marakbar was an almost professional event, in terms of virtuosity and from an industrial-sociological perspective, since the best musicians from the Moroccan wedding party circuit and Antwerp pop and jazz circles were recruited. Artistically speaking, the mixture of musical styles (Raï, Shaabi, rap, funk and pop) resulted in entertaining, popular concerts. To quote the newspapers, 'Marakbar is a top-class act. Inspired singing, accurate percussion, attractive synths, authoritative saxes, the scratchwork of Grazhoppa that was beautifully integrated in the total sound and the brilliantly rapping T.L.P. [...] very enthusiastic audience [...] modern, warm pop music with many references to rap and reggae [...] the concept "multicultural" is finally becoming tangible for the general audience.'

On the scale, *Marakbar* (O) appears as follows in relation to *Al Harmoniah* (X):

(versus)

```
Low Virtuosity            X                      O  High Virtuosity
Instrumental   O              X                        Autonomous
Individual                        X O                     Collective
Monocultural                                 O X  Multicultural
General Audience O                      X      Limited Audience
Entertainment            O X                              Art
Conformism           O X                        Subversiveness
```

On this scale, *Marakbar* appears as an almost ideal community art project, albeit with a higher degree of virtuosity than usual. The resemblances between the production/consumption constellation of *Al Harmoniah* and *Marakbar* are evident at some rungs of the scale (multiculturalism, entertainment, conformism), especially at the level of virtuosity (professionalism), instrumentality and manner of distribution.

42

If one takes the complete history of MET-X productions into consideration, one notices that community art in MET-X style seems able to go in any direction in its production, distribution and reception dynamics.

In many MET-X projects, the autonomous nature of the production process is dominant. *Saxafabra* (2005–), led by the Polish saxophonist, Cezariusz Gadzina, is one such example. *Saxafabra* is a project that can justifiably be called a community art project but one of a completely different kind than *Al Harmoniah* or *Marakbar*. It is financed by the European Union and brings saxophonists from various member countries together in a series of concerts throughout Europe, with the goal of shaping the concept of European cooperation. *Saxafabra* is a project wherein the production process is characterized by a high level of professionalism, virtuosity, autonomy and safeguarding of the individual artistic interest of the project's participants. On top of that, it is monocultural because it is rooted in the world of professional saxophonists. Concerts are held within the art circuit and the circuit of the advanced art schools. Socially speaking, it completely conforms to the laws of the art world. It is community art because it intends to create a 'European' artistic identity. And, as for production and consumption practice, it creates a momentum of fellowship and joint exploration in the world of saxophonists or at least aims to do so.

On the Brown Scale, this project holds a radically different position from previous projects. *Saxafabra* is represented in the following scheme by ★:

(versus)

```
Low Virtuosity            X                        O ★High  Virtuosity
Instrumental  O                    X                   ★      Autonomous
Individual  ★                             X O                  Collective
Monocultural   ★                               O X  Multicultural
General Audience O                          X   ★ Limited  Audience
Entertainment            O X                             ★ Art
Conformism      ★    O X                           Subversiveness
```

If you drew the constellation of the dozens of projects initiated by MET-X, it would become obvious that some projects are set at a low level of virtuosity, others at a very high level, with everything in between. Some projects are completely instrumental, others are autonomous, with everything in between. Some production processes are highly individually driven, others are collective, with everything in between. Some processes are monocultural, others extremely multicultural, with everything in between. In terms of distribution, projects span the entire range from popular to very elitist. In terms of artistic reception, both entertainment and high art and everything in between is present in the history of MET-X. In terms of social reception, both conforming and subversive activism is present. This last dynamic deserves a closer study.

Conformism and Subversiveness

Community art projects are, almost by definition, both in artistic and social terms, projects with a conforming effect. Their goal is identity *formation*, not identity destruction; it is to defend values and norms (solidarity, fellowship, community spirit) that very few people want to undermine. Yet, there are a few community art projects that intend to exercise a certain subversive influence. MET-X also gave rise to an interesting example of this in the *Marockinettes* project (1996-1998).

The *Marockinettes* was a training programme for young women of Moroccan origin who would learn to sing and make music, supervised by Mishalle and long time member of MET-X, Mohammed El Ouazghari. To many institutions involved with integration problems, this project was a godsend since it targeted one of the most difficult segments of their field, literally and figuratively providing young Moroccan women with a public stage. The rehearsals went well — although secrecy and lies were necessary on the part of some of the women before they could attend — but the first performance was a disaster. The girls made a fabulous start but, during the third song, a woman from the audience walked on stage. She started pulling the arm of one of the singers, screaming and swearing in fury. It turned out to be a mother who was thoroughly upset because her daughter was on stage. The concert was spoiled, the atmosphere ruined and the *Marockinettes* project slowly petered out. Obviously, something had been attempted that broke taboos but, in the end, it had no chance of succeeding.

Transposed onto the Brown Scale, this project appears to be subversive, if not activist. MET-X and a number of Moroccan musicians developed a performance that operated at, and eventually crossed, the boundaries of (Moroccan) decency. Yet, we have to formulate a few remarks to clarify the complexity of the phenomenon of subversiveness in relation to community art. It is true that the project had a subversive relationship with the rising re-fundamentalization of the Moroccan-Flemish community that became obvious in the late 1990s. But it is also true that the project was very conformist in relation to the progressive, multiculturally-minded Western artistic and intellectual community. The project was, therefore, *simultaneously* conformist and subversive, and the *Marockinettes* were caught in the crossfire. Community art appears to have no chance if the community cannot be, or does not want to be, formed, because the values and norms of the participants exclude each other. At this point, the art of meeting each other seems to fail, but perhaps not completely.

The *Stitou & Mishalle* project (2006–) demonstrates how cooperation between (representatives of) communities, with little or nothing in common, can still engage in a (musical) conversation.

Stitou rules, like an African chieftain, over a number of suburban Brussels-based Gnawa musicians who are usually illegal and hidden deep in society. He is, in every way, the boss of the Gnawa musician in Brussels. As in Morocco, the Gnawa are a very closed and self-orientated community, steeped in Sub-Saharan influences and blood ties; the Gnawas are usually the Moroccans with the darkest skin. Mishalle found their music attractive, saying 'I like the rawness of these musicians. Concepts like beautiful, swinging or cosy are truly far away'. But cooperation was not a walk in the park.

Stitou wanted to perform *Aïsha*, a traditional Moroccan song, with MET-X musicians. Mishalle recorded a version of the song and composed an arrangement for, amongst other things, an electric guitar and four members of the wind section, an arrangement with a considerable number of clever variations. When the MET-X musicians and the Gnawas came together, Stitou played the piece at about twice the speed of the original recording. Naturally, the arrangements didn't fit any more. Despite repeated and very clear instructions (at least on the part of the MET-X musicians) about the right tempo, the Western musicians had to guess at the speed during performances. They were unable to come up with a satisfactory way to reach consensus. One by one, the Western-schooled musicians quit. Mishalle felt inhibited as well; the arrangements did not come across as the Gnawa did not keep their end of the musical bargain. For instance, the agreed-upon structure (2x solo singing, 2x refrain, 2x instrumental, improvisation trumpet on A, back to instrumental) was mangled to, for example, 3x singing, 1x refrain, the percussion joined in too late, solo on B and suddenly singing again. Chaos abounded.

Community art seemed impossible here, but there has been a way out in *Stitou & Mishalle*. Both lead musicians have accepted the free, improvising method of playing together. For Mishalle, this means falling back on his musical sources — the free jazz in which ensemble is created virtually without any shared material or agreements. In *Stitou & Mishalle*, a musical community arises that doesn't lead to mutual adaptation but to mutual drifting apart, without letting go of each other. Each party retains its own roots, going flat out, which leads to an uncompromising dialogue between traditional and improvisational music. This practice provides an interesting piste for thinking about the dynamic 'conformism versus subversiveness' in community art (and beyond). The practice of *Stitou & Mishalle* is subversive towards all the musical cultures involved and, in that sense, it is activist art. At the same time, each musical culture stays true to its own tradition and logic. Improvisation is the key word with regard to a possible encounter of cultures far apart.

When we add the practices of the *Marockinettes* and of *Stitou & Mishalle* to the scale, it appears that the concept of community art is not a distinguishing concept, seen from the logic of the dynamics of production and consumption processes of artworks. The Scale slowly fills up. (The *Marockinettes* project is shown as M; *Stitou & Mishalle* is shown as &):

(versus)

```
Low Virtuosity M            X                    O & ★ High Virtuosity
Instrumental  O M               X                    & ★ Autonomous
Individual  ★ &                     X O                    M Collective
Monocultural  ★                                O X & M Multicultural
General Audience O M &                      X   ★ Limited Audience
Entertainment         M O X                          & ★    Art
Conformism     ★   O X M                      & M Subversiveness
```

If we assume that the projects of Mishalle and MET-X are representative of the world of community art, then it is evident that the concept is not clearly distinguished as a type of artistic production or consumption. It is not an artistic genre. It shows a much more complex identity than what might be expected from the social and political definition. But, at this point, some differentiation is necessary. There are many community art projects in all branches of the art and culture field that do not exhibit such a host of choices in constellations as MET-X does. The majority may well be projects where a low virtuosity, a highly instrumental nature, a collective production and a monocultural

46

production group actually go hand in hand with a focus on a wide general audience through entertaining and conformist productions. The example of MET-X proves that this is not necessarily so. Above all, it shows that, within the same organizational concept, the tension between modernist individualist art and the attraction of the creation of a community and the communal can still go hand in hand. The MET-X concept is an example of how the autonomy of the artist and instrumentality can work together in an interesting fashion.

A Contested Cultural Practice

The way of Mishalle and MET-X shows not only a colourful artistic practice, it also provides a differentiated answer to some criticisms formulated on community art.

MET-X has a special relationship with the experimental, autonomous music scene in Belgium. Nobody from the highbrow art sector can deny the occasionally avant-garde nature of MET-X music. MET-X concerts are therefore performed in the most prestigious music temples in cities across the world. The most remarkable characteristic of the organization is that, next to these prestigious arenas, they also sought out the arenas of the street and run-down locations. It is a custom that rebukes the criticism of the autonomous artist by reformulating the age-old question: who do you want to play for? Merely for an informed elite? And must you give up autonomy and artistic experimentation if you want to play for a large general audience? The community art projects of MET-X answer these questions in a differentiated way.

The criticism of neo-conservatives and the ultra right, that community art projects are pernicious examples of positive discrimination being shown towards socially undermining forces, cuts no ice in the case of MET-X because every participant is always selected for his or her artistic abilities, never his or her origin, level of persecution and so on. This is not positive discrimination; it is a positive attitude tout court. The projects offer a place to all cultures, dominant and marginal. The entire process is aimed at using the differences between cultures positively, in a productive manner. Nobody and nothing is discriminated against, including (and that is the fear behind the criticism) the ruling culture.

MET-X has to plead guilty, nevertheless, to two forms of criticism. If you support the neoliberal point of view, that the state should not support cultural projects because the free market should play its role, then MET-X is an obvious target. The entire project couldn't exist without subsidies from the welfare state. This is true not only of the direct subsidies received by the MET-X organization but also of the concerts set up by similarly subsidized organizers. Community art, as shaped by MET-X, functions entirely within the state-financed economic-cultural circuit.

Met-X, and with them the entire community art movement, also has no real answer to the ultra left criticism. Community art never rebels against the foundations of our current culture and society. It is, to use the terms of the most outspoken critics, the Belgian theoretical activists, BAVO, in the influential essay, 'Cultural Activism Today', typical NGO (non-governmental organization) art; art that does, indeed, articulate very strongly the dominant concepts of solidarity, fellowship and community spirit but always operates, partly due to subsidies, within the logic and organizational structures of current ideology.

Community art projects that develop mainly from a social goal, and receive their subsidies on that basis, are vulnerable from an artistic avant-garde point of view. Community art projects that present themselves mainly as artistic (e.g. *Saxafabra*) usually function within already privileged surroundings. It is the strength of MET-X that the group fully accepts the tension between both of the central concepts within which community art exists, namely the artistic idiosyncratic and the communal. The relationship of MET-X projects to the subsidizing government is always a relationship that emphasizes both the artistic and the social nature. MET-X can negotiate with the government in terms of social and artistic terms. It is both its strength and its weakness. But the artistic production does justice to the complexity of the position of the arts in our time, including and in particular that of community art.

Community Art is What We Say and Write It is

An De bisschop

Things in themselves rarely, if ever, have any one, single, fixed and unchanging meaning. Even something as obvious as a stone can be a stone, a boundary marker or a piece of sculpture, depending on what it means — that is, within a certain *context* of use [...] It is by our use of things, and what we say, think and feel about them — how we represent them — that we give them a meaning.[1]

'What does community art mean?' — that is the question. Like the stone in Stuart Hall's quotation above, the term 'community art' has no meaning in itself, but we give it meaning. Just as a Sunday painter and the curator of a prestigious artistic happening define the concept of 'art' in different ways or the CEO of a multinational and a single mother with four children relate to the concept of poverty entirely differently, so too the meaning of community art is created from various contexts.

To address the issue of the meaning of community art, we have to consider the question of how humankind gives meaning to 'things' as essential and, as Wittgenstein emphasized, 'The meaning of a word is its use in the *language*'.[2] Community art should, therefore, be examined from the perspective of discourse, whereby it is viewed as a collection of coherent linguistic statements that give meaning to the term, even though this language often has the tendency to erase the traces of its own construction. As Foucault said, 'Discourses are practices that systematically form the objects of which they speak. Discourses are not about objects, they do not identify objects, they constitute them and in the practice of doing so conceal their own invention'.[3]

A rigorous focus on language and on the language patterns that are used to speak and write about community art is, therefore, necessary. But — and here we return to Stuart Hall — no less important is that such an approach of discourse also focuses attention on the context of this language, in particular the social context. Discourse analysis is, after all, more than language analysis without obligation; it is critical of the social structure in the sense that it links language study to a broader social picture — who says what and from which position? What purpose do the arguments serve? Which argumentation survives over time and which doesn't and why? Terry Threadgold summarizes this critical discourse view as follows: 'We should not "burrow" into discourse looking for meanings. We should look for the external conditions of its existence, appearance and regularity. We should explore the conditions of its possibility. Just how it is possible to think that, to say that — these are the questions we should be asking.'[4]

In light of the above, discourse analysis into community art has the ambition of questioning the obvious meanings around community art, based on the idea that discourse is always connected to power, and therefore the obvious meanings should be viewed with suspicion.[5] 'Deconstruction, if such a thing exists, should open-up', Derrida wrote. This means that the analysis of discourse should bring new or subordinate meanings to the forefront in an attempt to withdraw the construction of meaning from dominant power structures. Or, as Shapiro formulates, 'Deconstruction has the power to show how every social order rests on a forgetting of the exclusion practices through which one set of meanings has been institutionalized and various other possibilities have been marginalized.'[6]

In the following essay, I describe the results of discourse-analytical research into the assigning of meaning in community art which I have based on these principles.

Leading Metaphors for the Research Scheme: the Travel and Theatre Metaphor

The starting point for my analysis is the manner in which various players in Flanders give meaning to socio-artistic projects. But, since the manner of speaking and writing always takes place in a context, it is necessary to confront various contexts with each other. After all, it is only through difference that the familiar becomes apparent.

The Travel Metaphor: Community Art in Flanders and South Africa

The simplest way to put this methodology into operation is to conduct parallel research in two radically different geographical contexts. This is how we achieve a 'comparative consciousness';[7] the confrontation

1   Stuart Hall, Representation: Cultural Representation and Signifying Practices (London: Sage/The Open University, 1997), p. 3.
2   Ludwig Wittgenstein, Philosophical Investigations, (Oxford: Blackwell, 1953), §43, p. 20.
3   Michel Foucault, The Archaeology of Knowledge (New York: Harper & Row, 1972), p. 49. Trans. of L'archéologie du savoir (Paris: Gallimard, 1969).
4   Terry Threadgold, 'Poststructuralism and Discourse Analysis,' Culture and Text: Discourse and Methodology in Social Research and Cultural Studies, eds. Alison Lee and Cate Poynton (Lanham, MD: Rowman & Litllefield, 2000), p. 49.
5   Maggie MacLure, Discourse in Educational and Social Research (Buckingham/Philadelphia: Open University Press, 2003), pp. 9-12.
6   Michael Shapiro, 'Textualizing Global Politics,' Discourse Theory and Practice: A Reader, eds. Margaret Wetherell, Stephanie Taylor, and Simeon J. Yates (London: Sage, 2001), pp. 318-324, p. 231.
7   Laura Nader, 'Comparative Consciousness,' Assessing Cultural Anthropology, ed. Robert Borofsky (New York: McGraw Hill, 1993), pp. 84-96, p. 89.

with a strange context teaches us to look at the familiar context in a whole new manner. The metaphor of 'travel' can be regarded as central to grasping this 'context consciousness' in a geographical sense. As Margaret Meade put it, 'the traveller who has once been from home is wiser than the one who has never left his doorstep' (1928).

For this research, two radically different geographical contexts were selected: the Flemish context, which is illustrative of many Western meanings attributed to community art, and the Western Cape province of South Africa, which differs from the Flemish context in various respects.

In Flanders, community art projects have a relatively short history; they have only been officially and structurally supported as 'socio-artistic projects' since 2000, in a way that is very well delineated in cultural policy. The Flemish context is also notable by its affluence in the socio-economic sphere and in the long tradition of democracy in the political sphere.

The South African context is entirely different. Firstly, the history of the community arts in South Africa is much older and, above all, far more complex. This dates back to the 1950s and 1960s, when the South African government and some missionary services saw it as their duty to keep the culture of the 'blacks' alive in the 'homelands' by offering them recreational possibilities (read: stripping art and culture of its political dimension and preventing rebellions against the apartheid regime).

A completely different form of community art arose in the seventies, associated with independent artists who made art education accessible to black people (who were not allowed in art schools supported by the regime). This tradition, linked with emancipation, was also a great carrier of political resistance against the apartheid regime, which immediately makes the community art history in South Africa politically loaded. Next to that, of course, are the general social, economic and political qualities that determine the uniqueness of the South African context, together with, amongst others things, inequalities in income and recently introduced democracy.

The Theatre Metaphor: Community Art in Policy and Press Discourse

Discourses, however, are not merely defined by geography but also by institutions; the worlds of science, the media, policy-making and practice all have their own traditions of speaking and writing, based on a number of formal and procedural rules that govern public speech. Paralleling comparative awareness being related to the travel metaphor, the theatre metaphor steers towards role-awareness. In the opening lines of Shakespeare's *As You Like It*, the notion that 'all the world is a stage, and men and women are merely players' pre-empted the thought which summarizes the *theatrum-mundi* metaphor.[8] Based on Goffman[9] and theatrical studies,[10] we can state that every speaker in the discourse plays his or her specific role (the journalist, the scientist, the policy-maker).

This research concretely aimed at two discourse domains: those of policy and of the print media. In the policy domain, meaning is first created around community art by including or excluding community art in funding categories. In the press domain, meaning is constructed in the way the press packages the news, the specific language in which it is written, the position an article is given in a newspaper, the choice of a certain headline, the people quoted in the article, etc.

Methodological Framework and Mode of Operation: Interpretative Repertoires

Within the range of discourse-analytical methods available, I selected the methodological framework of 'interpretative repertoires'. This frame originates in discursive psychology and is defined as 'systematically related sets of terms, often used with stylistic and grammatical coherence, and often organized around one or more metaphors. They are historically developed and are a major part of the 'common sense' of a culture, although some repertoires can be specific for certain institutional domains'.[11] The choice for this research framework was made because of a number of consistencies with the vision above on the construction of meaning around community. Firstly, I searched the data for the concrete repertoires that people use when they speak

8   Howard D. Pearce, 'A Phenomenological Approach to the Theatrum Mundi Metaphor,' PMLA, 95 (1980) 1: pp. 42-57, p. 42.
9   Erving Goffman, Strategic Interaction (Philadelphia: University of Pennsylvania Press, 1969); Erving Goffman, Relations in Public: Microstudies of the Public Order (New York: Basic Books, 1971).
10 Richard Schechner, Theater Anthropologie: Spiel und Ritual im Kulturvergleich (Reinbeck bei Hamburg: Rowolt Taschenbuch Verlag, 1990); Erika Fischer Lichte, 'Theatralität und Inszenierung,' Inszenierung und Authentizität, Erika Fischer-Lichte and Isabel Pflung (Tübingen: Francke Verlag, 1995), pp. 11-27.
11 Jonathan Potter, 'Discourse Analysis and Constructionist Approaches: Theoretical Background,' Handbook of Qualitative Research Methods for Psychology and the Social Sciences, ed. John T. Richardson (Leicester: BPS Books, 1996), pp. 125-141, p. 131.

or write about community art. These interpretative repertoires are putting discourse thought into operation on a smaller scale, which offers us the possibility of looking for discourse in texts and interviews 'as they happen'. Secondly, the framework of interpretative repertoires pays special attention to the relationship between the language people use, the position from which someone speaks and, by extension, the function that using a specific repertoire has to a certain individual.[12] Interpretative repertoires allow us to study 'the utterances of persons in social context, thereby giving our attention to the relation between language and action'.[13] Thirdly, the theme of the relationship between language and position or between language and action also implies that attention is paid to the *subject* (the one who speaks/writes) and, more specifically, to the degrees of freedom the subjects have and may or may not use to construct meaning within a specific discourse domain. The subject here is not an 'authentic person'; he or she is not an unambiguous and indivisible person but is a role player. We are talking about 'a subject in the plural'.[14] Fourthly, the foregoing means that we pay attention not only to structural or systematic patterns in language use, but also to variations in the way people talk about community art. Other than, for example, the Foucauldian discourse movement, the framework of interpretative repertoires starts from the idea that subjects actually have margins of freedom and are not completely determined by discourse that, as Foucault saw it, is merely playing a game with so-called subjects.[15] Finally, Jonathan Potter's description also suggests an historical perspective. Compared to the historicizing tendency of the discourse analysis of Foucault, our interest in history in this research is limited to the 'traces' of history that can still be found in current speaking and writing. So, we make a cross section of the way people talk about community art today. Compared to the historical sensitivity that Foucault demonstrated in his research, this method has a greater sensitivity for the rhetorical dimension of discourse.[16] It is beyond the scope of this article to go into any more detail about how I came to interpretative repertoires and to discuss them integrally; I refer to my doctoral thesis for this reason.[17] In this essay, I will limit myself to a concise discussion of the repertoires of each context- and domain-specific part of research in so far as they are useful for the debate.

Reconstruction of Discourse in Interpretative Repertoires

Flanders Policy Discourse

It is worth mentioning a few structural characteristics as structural attention to socio-artistic work is a rather recent phenomenon within Flemish policy discourse. And this attention is also very rigidly delineated within a single policy domain, namely the cultural policy and its 'Kunstendecreet' (Decree on the Arts). Throughout this section, it is worth bearing in mind that policy tightly regulates each project, using assessment criteria and a specific committee, which results in a conveniently arranged discourse that is accessible without too much investigation.

In Flemish policy discourse, we firstly distinguish the repertoire of the *Mirror of the arts*, in which meaning is attributed to socio-artistic work as if it were identical to the regular arts. This interpretation mirrors arts logic in the sense that, with regard to content, both discourses use the same anchoring points to substantiate whether something is good or bad. Moreover, strategic resistance against socio-artistic work as the 'little brother' of the arts exists.

Diametrically opposed, in a way, is the repertoire of the *Other arts*, which assigns meaning to socio-artistic work through a fundamental difference between art and socio-artistic work. Socio-artistic work is art but different art, in the sense that it brings different symbols to the fore, uses different artistic codes and replaces the technical quality of the regular arts with a different form of quality which is

12 I am referring to the pragmatic or functional movement in language analysis, Wittgenstein, op cit.; Chris Barker, Making Sense of Cultural Studies: Central Problems and Critical Debates (London: Sage Publications, 2002); Jonathan Potter et al., 'Discourse: Noun, Verb or Social Practice?,' Philosophical Psychology, 3 (1990) 2-3, pp. 205-218.
13 Barker, op cit., 15.
14 Ian Parker, Critical Discursive Psychology (Hampshire, NY: Palgrave/ MacMillan, 2002), p. 126.
15 Foucault, op cit., p. 183.
16 'We might argue that, with regard to "the grand discourse" (as performative speaking, as power-bound organizations, as a monolithic block that wants to mask the constructedness of objects), rhetoric is a devil that can be compared to history: just as we would like to forget how differently things were viewed in the past, we also want to forget how both speaking and writing has the dual goal of persuasing and convincing. Both accents are thus equivalent "strategies of alienation"'. (Jan Goldstein, 'Foucault Among the Sociologists: the "Disciplines" and the History of the Professions,' History and Theory, 23 (1984) 2: pp. 70-192, pp. 170-172.
17 An De bisschop, Community art als discursieve constructie, PhD (Ghent: Ugent, 2009).

described in terms of 'expression', believability', 'chemistry'.

A third repertoire lets go of the possible contradistinctions be-tween social and artistic, and is held together by the logic of *Cultural rights*. With frequent references to the basic right to culture for every human being, this repertoire problematizes the limited access to the regular arts and sets the latter against active cultural production in socio-artistic work. One speaks metaphorically about 'giving a voice' to people and about the artistic transformation of the 'individual story' of these people, which is supposed to have an emancipatory value. The meaning of socio-artistic projects is, thus, partly situated on a different platform; the artistic meaning of projects is a derivative of their social meaning and dissidence is not encouraged.

In the repertoire of *Inclusion and positive diversity*, one expands upon the social aspect of this reasoning to emphasize the equality and equivalence which is the foundation of the rights approach. From this starting point, easy accessibility is the ultimate criterion of quality and inclusive projects are viewed more favourably than those which exclusively target a specific group. After all, there is nothing wrong with diversity in society. This diversity is an opportunity and not a problem. This idea is not only valid for a substance-based discussion about quality in socio-artistic work, but it is also strategic in the sense that one opposes the separated position of socio-artistic work in the arts — an integrated position of socio-artistic work within the regular art disciplines ought to be a *conditio sine qua non*.

In a sense, the repertoire of the *(Other) social work* builds on this strategic substantiation and views the current framework within the Flemish Kunstendecreet as a handicap, which, sadly enough, limits the policy argumentation. With this, we find ourselves once again in the logic of contradistinction between the social and the artistic. There have been long and productive debates about whether or not using the artistic as a means instead of as a goal is legitimate. After all, socio-artistic work has historical connections with social work meth-odologies and should, therefore, be evaluated partly on the basis of its process. Sometimes the reasoning is added that this kind of practice is different from 'regular social work' in the sense that an approach based on the competencies of target groups is the central point and that, precisely by using the artistic as a means, they appeal to a type of educational freedom that is ignored by regular social work with its solution-orientated focus on people's problems. Seen in this context, using the artistic as a means is potentially transformative; it has the potency to change people.

Finally, in the repertoire of the *Socially engineered society*, this transformative potency is extended to the social sphere; socio-artistic work has a de-acidifying effect, a community-forming effect, and it is a lever for a better society. This repertoire is mostly dominant in the rhetoric of general policy documents and affects subsidy decisions by emphasizing that socio-artistic work should be socially committed or socially conscious. It is not value-free, it is not reality television but it genuinely wants to change something about society by using art. Long-term processes and growth opportunities for participants are, therefore, the quality criteria that this repertoire aims for on a project level. At a policy level, a transversal approach is intended; multiple policy domains would have to support socio-artistic projects if the leverage function is to succeed.

Flanders – Media Discourse

Press discourse about socio-artistic work takes as a starting point the introduction of the terminology into policy discourse, which makes socio-artistic work a recent newspaper topic. When it comes to the structural characteristics of this discourse, the considerable number of articles about socio-artistic work, both in the broadsheet press and in the popular press, is noteworthy. It is also interesting that the reporting method is mostly comprised of reviews on culture pages. Additionally, it is usually art critics who write the articles, which almost automatically results in a language dominated by the vocabulary of art and culture. In the popular press, these projects are sometimes discussed from a different point of view, for instance from a societal perspective, and they are occasionally published in the regional pages.

In the repertoire of the *Lesser of the arts*, journalists use artistic criteria (although often without explicitly mentioning them) to indicate that they expect less from socio-artistic work. 'Lesser' refers mainly to the participants of projects, who are not real actors, dancers or sculptors, which, of course, means that the performances are 'not as good', or 'not perfect'. Often, performances are 'pleasant, intimate, charming' but these so-called qualities are frequently used as the opposite of that which is artistically valuable.

The repertoire of *Universal art* differs slightly; its leitmotiv in the construction of meaning is the quality demanded of art, which must create universal symbols. Sometimes, socio-artistic projects do not live up to this quality standard but, then again, sometimes they do. Socio-artistic projects should transcend the anecdotal and the therapeutic, and autobiographical elements have to be adapted in order to give them a universal character. Sometimes, they fail and critics speak of a 'zoo effect' or of 'throwing miserable stories for a scramble', but often they do succeed, lending a unique added value to socio-artistic work with respect to the regular arts. As one journalist said, 'even the best film maker couldn't have achieved this with a classic, professional crew'.

Relating policy and press discourse, these first two repertoires in press discourse can be seen as a de-duplication of the previously discussed repertoire, *Mirror of the arts,* in the sense that the construction of meaning in both repertoires starts from a set of quality criteria typical of the regular arts, but they each do this in their own way.

The repertoire of *Human art* emphasizes the relationship between humans and art in socio-artistic projects to convey three meanings: socio-artistic work is art coming *from within* people, made *by* people and meant *for* people. In this repertoire, socio-artistic work is the metaphorical 'mirror of life', as if art and life were always inherently connected. This 'people art' or 'reality theatre' — as one calls socio-artistic work — is emphatically counted among the arts, with which one also expresses critical comments on the so-called contours of what nowadays is generally acknowledged as artistic and on the so-called quality criteria of the arts.

The repertoire of *Socially committed art* differs from the previous repertoire through the finality attributed to art. Art is not a mirror of life but a lever for change. Art has to make itself necessary again, it is said, and, in order to succeed in this, it has to strengthen its ties with social reality. In this repertoire, socio-artistic work is offered as an example of how art can live up to this assignment. The noticeable commitment in many projects is much more credible than in the regular arts where social commitment, if present at all, is limited to pretty words. In this repertoire, socio-artistic projects create art out of necessity, sometimes as accusation, and they operate by catalysing in social problems. But, at the same time, this repertoire is critical with regard to policy, the type of policy that so loves to hear words like 'social consciousness' that it is almost a rhetorical pose, especially considering the fact that the projects receive relatively low subsidy amounts in comparison to the regular arts. In this respect, socio-artistic work cannot be a token gesture for a social conscience in the arts.

Relating policy and press discourse again, the repertoires of *Human art* and *Socially committed art* can be seen as a de-duplication of the previously discussed repertoire of the *Other art.*

The repertoire of the *Other social work* is built on the social foundations of socio-artistic work, and it largely discards attempts to oppose the regular arts. In socio-artistic work by this definition, it is all about empowerment, about helping to give meaning to people's lives, to give them the happy feeling of being accepted into a group, and so on. And yet this is not about social work in the traditional sense, since socio-artistic work doesn't focus on problems and their solutions. Socio-artistic work is different from social work in the sense that it starts from the strength of people and it is not paternalistic due to the unique means being used, namely art. Reporters indicate that they use a different codex when assessing a project of this type; among the elements being assessed for quality in these cases are the background of participants, the impact on participants and the attention that is devoted to the process of creating.

Finally, this discourse domain is characterized by the repertoire of the *Imaging*, in which socio-artistic projects are typified as instruments that try to change the image of target groups. It is not so much about measurable social effects or about artistic quality but about an audience-oriented logic; the stigma clinging to target groups persist through the perception of the audience and it is through moments of public display that these stigma become nuanced or removed. The core metaphor here is the perception or the view that one wants to change. Reporters also see a role for themselves in this process; they explicitly reflect on the way they write about the target groups.

Western Cape – Policy

Within the policy discourse of the Western Cape, a number of structural characteristics are key to a proper understanding of the repertoires. Firstly, the discourse about community art is a discourse coloured by anti-apartheid history; community art traditionally meant black art while 'the arts' signified Western, white art. The continuation of this history is even more complex because of the various traditions within community art, with a government-directed tradition going hand in hand with the apartheid regime as opposed to an independent tradition of committed artists and art schools for blacks that wanted the complete opposite, which sought to abolish apartheid. Currently in Western Cape policy, community art is present as a topic across several departments: Social Development, Economic Development and Tourism, Health and Arts and Culture. The main reason for this is that community art is largely used to achieve two transversal policy goals, namely combating poverty and creating jobs. Secondly, it is also more obviously part of these policy domains because, according to African tradition, art is connected to life in a far more natural way. This fragmentation of community art over various policy domains results in a more ambiguous discourse. An important structural characteristic in this respect is the absence of formal quality criteria with regard to content; projects are approved on the basis of administrative criteria, based on site visits, rather than on content.

In the repertoire of *Unequal access to art*, the meaning of community art is centred on three historic and mutually reinforcing exclusion mechanisms: community art is art of the (1) socially neglected population, (2) the economically neglected population, and (3) the population that had no access to art under the apartheid regime. Community art is, therefore, art by and for previously disadvantaged people, that is acknowledged by policy-makers as having just as much quality as regular art. So, what distinguishes community art from regular art is not quality but access — access to art education, to the financial means of creating art and to the socio-political stage. This repertoire builds upon the historical connotations of community art and also immediately makes a theme of these connotated exclusion mechanisms, even before pondering the possible core of what community art is.

The same thing happens in the repertoire of the *Indigenous art*, albeit that this repertoire does not so much cite unequal opportunities as a reason for differentiation, but rather the contradistinction between indigenous art forms and so-called professional art forms, which are no more than the metaphorical cultural bomb dropped by imperialism. Community art is habitual art here, art connected to traditions and to life itself, which can be found in public places such as villages, but not usually in a museum or in theatres — making this repertoire more a matter of arbitrary standards of quality than of an essential difference in quality. In this repertoire one problematizes the term 'craft', which is defined in terms of a tradition of (mostly) visual art that also has an economic function. Where Westerners thought up a term to separate this tradition from high art, the Western Cape makes no distinction between crafts and community art when it comes to quality assessments and the necessary social relevance.

In the repertoire of *Culture as part of development*, there is considerably less debate on the relative artistic status of projects, but the contribution of the projects to social development serves as a pivot for the construction of meaning. In this repertoire, culture is seen as a self-evident part of development and, in that sense, it has a political meaning. Just as art and culture were used for political purposes during apartheid, so too can art and culture be used for social goals. Art and culture can be used as tools and that is what the community art projects are trying to do: they use art as a means of healing, reconciliation, moral regeneration and poverty reduction. The meaning attributed to art and culture within projects is described as expression, as construction of meaning, as communication.

Next to this general interpretation of culture as development, we also find two repertoires that provide motivation for this type of development within the specific interpretation framework of South African policy discourse. The first of these is the repertoire of *Ubuntu*, which gives meaning to community art from the values of the Khoi San. Ubuntu means something like 'humankind' or 'humanity', and it signifies the idea that a person is only a person through other people. Under this unifying philosophy, community art projects are viewed as contributing to social inclusion. They take as their starting point the fundamental equality of all humans and contribute to the development of identity and self-awareness, to a feeling of brotherhood and to a positive attitude toward diversity. The frequently used rhetoric, that government aims to create 'a home for all', fits seamlessly into this picture and community art projects play an important part in this.

A second specific reference framework within the great denominator of 'culture as part of development' is the repertoire through which people assess community art projects for their *Economic potential*. The idea of art as a luxury is refuted, this time not from a right-to-culture ideal, but from a down-to-earth economic logic; art creates chances to make money and to sell. In this sense, community art projects are only sustainable when they create job opportunities for people and, in this sense, projects are motors for meaningful socio-economic transformation. This economic interpretation framework has significant consequences for the meaning community art projects acquire; not merely traditional target groups but also all support services (catering, media, transport) are seen as a target group, the education aspect is widened from art education to technical skills, even including management skills. Means have to be fairly divided among all the people involved. This repertoire produces a completely new terminology which is used to talk about projects and to discuss their quality, which is measured according to their management frameworks, human resource capacity, market-driven production, commodity work, self-sustainability, etc.

Finally, the repertoire of *Political and social transformation* differs from the previous repertoires because it does not ascribe a specific function to community art. This repertoire is related to the first repertoire of the policy discourse in the Western Cape in the sense that the apartheid system is frequently used as a reference point, but, as distinct from the repertoire of *Unequal access*, meaning is aimed at the future and far less based on the past. Community art is viewed as potentially important for the social and political transformation of South African society, precisely because it always puts the relationship between art and context at the centre; 'the desire for social transformation is what keeps community-based performance alive'.[18] This repertoire also produces a number of broadened meanings — not merely the black people but also the advanced communities are viewed as target groups for projects because, in the post-apartheid system, it is often these so-called developed populations which participate very little in meaningful art. People plead for more partnerships between government-linked art institutions and independent community art projects, to ensure that the democratic transformation of the current art and culture institutions succeeds. And one finally undermines the contradiction between community art and professional art in the sense that they are both placed on an educational ladder (where community art stands for the first step on the road to a career in art) and that both are evaluated in terms of their transformational power (where community art feeds professional art, helps it to develop and to reflect on the way they develop a symbol system).

Western Cape – Media

As far as the structural characteristics of this discourse domain are concerned, the first thing we notice is that, despite the long tradition of community art in South Africa, community art is relatively ignored by the print media. In the popular press, ninety-five percent of community art projects are discussed in the culture pages. In the regional press they are often discussed in the form of preliminary reviews, while the broadsheet press uses a greater diversity in formats (culture columns, extensive interviews with community artists, in-depth reviews, etc.). Noticeable in the style of reporting is the often very critical and sometimes humorous style that is used in the broadsheet press.

In the repertoire of *Mainstream art*, the meaning of community art is attributed according to the criteria of the mainstream arts. The underlying perception guiding this repertoire is that community art does not fundamentally differ from mainstream art products and it is not, therefore, to be assessed and described any differently. The ultimate quality criterion for community art is that it has found a market, that profits have been generated; therefore, the undertone is a market-orientated, popular interpretation of arts, rather than the quality framework that we associate with the (Western) high art tradition. Community art must, first and foremost, entertain, it must be light, fashionable, humorous, if it is to be met with approval in this press repertoire. This goes hand in hand with the business practices of the newspapers themselves, in which selling advertisements to companies and private investors is the top priority, and the contents are adapted accordingly. Viewed in this light, community art projects often have little appeal: 'no one would like to advertise on the same page as where you find a community art review'.[19]

In the repertoire of *Unequal access to art*, people are critical about mainstream art as a reference point because it implies unfair competition.[20] As a reaction to the fundamental difference in commercial power (caused by the unequal opportunities in art during apartheid), people focus on qualities like accessibility of art productions, on empowerment of the participants, on working with historically neglected people and on the undeserved negative quality connotations that cling to community art. Construction of meaning in this repertoire is, therefore, founded on a socio-historical criticism.

In the repertoire of *Indigenous art*, the same quality argument is followed, but one also reduces the perceived difference from other aesthetics which is typical of indigenous art. In that sense, 'community art aesthetics' are often compared to 'bourgeois aesthetics', but what makes this distinction valid is not so much a distinction in quality but a distinction in the functions of art. Community art connects with the functions of indigenous art, in which social embedding is of major importance. Community art is rooted in speaking to the conditions of a particular community. It is also about art for ordinary people, about ordinary subjects, about traditional language forms and about a great solidarity between art and life.

In the repertoire of *Culture as part of development*, community art is viewed not so much as a different form of art but as an artistic means that is subservient and useful to the function of development. Reviews in the newspaper often refer to community development programmes of which community art projects are a part. The art aspect of community art is an unproblematic tool here, whereby art is employed to achieve far more concrete goals — nation-building, anti-crime

18 Le Roux, interview 2006.
19 Van Graan, interview 2007.
20 Mane, interview 2007.

action, rehabilitation, job creation, healing perceived social diseases, etc. People sometimes differentiate between the intentions of projects and their actual effects, whereby community art ultimately offers no statistically demonstrable guarantees but does offer hope, creates awareness, promotes reflection and, in that sense, is empowering.

In the *Ubuntu* repertoire, community art is connected to the typically African ethics of the collective. In the press, we read countless names of community art projects that refer to this ethic — like 'Ubuntu Production House', 'Ubuntu Marimba Group' — but the typical accents of this value framework are also reflected in the substantive meaning given to community art: community art projects start from the equality of all human beings and their common bonds, they emphasize the importance of identity as individuality-in-solidarity. They stand for people who take up responsibility for the community and work with diversity as a positive aspect of living together.

Finally, the repertoire of *Imaging* assigns to community art the meaning of problematizing and challenging the images we have come to consider normal. Perception and representation are the leading terms around which meaning is constructed and the stereotypical images of certain groups of people are denounced.

Community art projects have an empowering effect in the sense that they aim at an increased feeling of self-worth in neglected target groups by changing the view of the spectator in the first place. 'Empowerment is of course twofold: for these people to be really empowered in our world, it takes as much influencing the world and its images as it takes working with those people, by whatever therapeutic means you can imagine'.[21]

Discussion: A Plea against Self-Referential Cultural Logic and in Favour of Relational Social Action

In the final stage of my research, I compared the above repertoires along the axes of context (Flanders and Western Cape) and domain (media and policy). For the purpose of this article I focus on just one of these comparison axes, namely the geographical one. It is, after all, my opinion that the confrontation with discourse about community art from a radically different context will teach us to look at our own context in a different way, and, therefore, also to the limitations of the discourse we use.

The discourse in both geographical contexts shows a number of undeniable similarities. It is, for example, remarkable that policy discourse in both contexts is interspersed with overblown rhetoric, with words that have so many meanings that they no longer mean anything, but are nevertheless present everywhere. Examples would be 'a home for all', 'partnership' and 'needs' in the Western Cape, and 'participation', 'diversity' and 'acidification' in Flanders. It is also noticeable that policy discourse about community art in both contexts is subservient to the policy framework of a higher order, which curtails freedom to give community art meaning. From this point of view, the Kunstendecreet in Flanders fulfils the same function as the Reconstruction and Development Programme and the Investment in Culture Programme of the Western Cape.

Such similarities are less noticeable in press discourse, although here, too, similarities in form exist, like the formats in which community art is discussed and the continuous 'battle' to get community art mentioned in the newspaper at all. So, although the words used are often the same, the differences in content are nevertheless remarkable. We could go deeper into each of these differences but the leitmotiv in the comparison of context is the dominance of art-orientated repertoires in Flanders versus the dominance of socially-orientated repertoires in the Western Cape. This conclusion is all the more remarkable because socio-artistic work in Flanders is historically aimed at combating poverty (Article 23 projects), whereas, in South Africa, it is far more rooted in the arts, specifically in the art education, since the projects at the time of apartheid were the only option for black people to educate themselves in the arts.

In the Flemish policy context, which is very obviously coloured by the position of socio-artistic projects in the Kunstendecreet, the predominance of the *Mirror of the arts* and the *Other art* repertoire is considerable, while the *Cultural rights* repertoire is, as it were, the social completion of this discourse domain. In Flemish press discourse, the first repertoire is split into the repertoires of the *Lesser of the arts* and *Universal art*, and the second repertoire in its turn into the repertoires *Human art* and *Socially-committed art*. This results in no less than four art-orientated repertoires. All things considered, Flemish discourse has much to say about the relative art status of socio-artistic work, with major stumbling blocks to be found in ideas like 'art that is socially committed is no longer art', 'art serves no purpose but itself', 'art that serves a social goal is instrumental art and therefore not artistic', etc. In short, the means–ends debate about art is currently

21 Ibid.

the debate *par excellence* in relation to socio-artistic projects. This is a debate which — with one exception, namely the repertoire of the *Other social work* — is locked in the cultural sector and rarely refers to other social sectors. Two quotations from the advice of the assessment committee are very illustrative of the main theme of this debate: 'The organization uses the artistic mainly as a binding agent to achieve a social process, thereby disturbing the balance between social and artistic processes.' 'Apart from that, it appears that the artistic story in the socio-artistic concept of the organization is put too much in the service of the social and political aspect [...] The committee hopes they will not distance themselves from the artistic thinking.'

If we compare Western Cape repertoires with this, we immediately notice that the major questions about the arts that dominate Flemish discourse are far less important here. There is, for example, no real art-orientated repertoire in policy discourse, although there is a repertoire of unequal opportunities in art, but, from the outset, the artistic argument is accompanied by a social argument. Remarkable in this context is the great diversity in repertoires through which art and development are almost inextricably linked — the repertoires *Culture as part of development, Ubuntu, Economic potential* and *Social and political transformation* in the policy discourse, and the repertoires *Culture as part of development* and *Ubuntu* in the press discourse.

In the Western Cape, for a long time it has generally been acknowledged that art can be used as a means; this is self-evident. In the past, this implied the means to political transformation, and today it is a means based upon the obvious experience that culture is a part of development. From this point of view, combating poverty and aiming for job creation are legitimate goals for community art projects as shown by the repertoires dedicated to these goals. Particularly in a socio-economic context with sky-high unemployment rates and forty-five percent of the population having to live on $4 per day, these goals are understandably important and these social finalities need not exclude artistic development. On the contrary, it is felt that community art allows both goals to interact. What the discourse is really about is not so much a contradistinction between art and social finalities, but about the *connection* between art and society, about the social relevance of art. This idea is expressed in the following citations:

In South Africa the relevance of such a frivolous activity as the arts is always questioned. Why

> should we care about the arts when people
> are starving, unemployed and homeless? It's
> a difficult question, one that I can't always
> answer convincingly. But by taking the angle
> of community art, I think that we at least try to
> negotiate this question.[22]
>
> In the South African context, the notion of 'art
> for art's sake' is very problematic, when there
> are more pressing issues regarding human living
> conditions. I don't know if we have to look at
> professional theatre that way. It is indeed in
> some ways easier not to. But certainly at the
> moment, we are talking about art as a social
> function and its effect, so as to talk about the
> question of the relevance of the arts. Community
> art is the best illustration of this philosophy that
> art can and should to some extent be related
> to societal reality, rather than being a totally
> different register.[23]

Western Cape discourse about community art is, therefore, an example of a transversal discourse; it crosses several sectors and it connects art and culture with social affairs, economics, tourism, etc. This is most obvious in the policy discourse itself, but the press repertoire of *Mainstream art*, for example, can also be seen as a domain-specific translation of the policy repertoire of *Economic potential*. In these repertoires the ultimate indicator of quality for community art production is, after all, the commercial power and marketability of productions; is the audience big enough? Is the sale of the tickets high enough? Do performers make enough to live on? So community art has an economic pillar, as proven also by the arts and crafts, which are seen as part of community art and which aim to produce and sell small handiworks to (mostly) tourists and through export channels.

In the Flemish context, such economic or explicit social argumentation would be considered extremely odd, and yet some socio-artistic projects hesitantly make connections to, for example, the

22 Mbangu, interview 2006.
23 Le Roux, op cit.

social-economy. Rocsa, a socio-artistic project in the Belgian city of Ghent, set up a textile studio for women in the working-class area of Rabot, where, alongside being creative with needle and thread, the sale of products is a goal. But these projects are certainly not rewarded by subsidizers for thinking outside the box.

Economy and culture also appear to be a taboo marriage when we look at the cautiousness shown by some socio-artistic projects when they start performing their shows in different places — are tickets being sold, just like in the regular arts? If so, what are the wages for the actors involved? Do they share in the copyrights or are these reserved for the directors? In short, socio-artistic work in Flanders is definitely not a market, any more than it is a political movement; all justifications that are external to the art and culture domain are taboo, with the exception of the criterion of social process, which is only just acceptable because it ended up in the assessment criteria almost by accident.

How can this confinement of meaning in the Flemish context be explained? I think the discourse about socio-artistic work in Flanders is typical of broader art and culture discourse in Europe, which has become deeply estranged from society. When, in 1966, E.P. Thompson spoke about culture as a necessary middle term to explain the 'real silences' of Marxism, he might have been right; in focusing on the socio-economic positions of people, Marx failed to offer an explanation for whether class awareness develops or does not. Thompson corrected the so-called universality of socio-economic analysis with a theory that enables the serious treatment of cultural factors as a motor of development. Eight years earlier, Raymond Williams published a vision of culture that called into question the tradition that high art is worth more than popular culture; culture is ordinary and is a way of life, he wrote, thereby acknowledging the culture of the working class as equivalent to that of elitist cultures. According to him, culture is nothing more or nothing less than meaning-constructions. In the combination of these two thoughts — that culture is a relevant factor in development, on the one hand, and that culture is much broader than just high culture, on the other hand — Williams substantiates culture as a universal human right and justifies the implementation of a broad cultural concept in policy and science.

The right to culture also acts as the symbolic basis *par excellence* for the justification of community art in the West (in this case Flanders). For the predecessors of the current socio-artistic projects in Flanders, the article from the Belgian constitution that refers to the right of culture was chosen as their call sign: Article 23 projects. But from the reconstructed repertoire of current socio-artistic work in Flanders, it appears that the recognition of this right to culture is not really legitimized in relation to other social factors or sectors. The reverse seems to be happening; it merely posits the independency of the right to culture, as if it were an isolated notion that has no connection to the social reality to which this right relates. This independency of the right to culture is connected to the modern spirit through which policy sectors, including the cultural sector, are professionalized arenas that develop in relation to themselves much more than in relation to the society surrounding them. And this development, which is typical of modernity, is, at the same time, a mirror of our relatively great prosperity. The art and culture sector has a self-referential logic and gets cold feet when it comes to clarifying its relations to other social sectors, exactly because such a positioning was permitted in the prosperous Flemish context. The arts could afford to close themselves off from society because they were no longer necessary to harness all policy sectors in order to offer the population more and better chances for survival. In this sense, the cultural correction of the dogmatic nature of socio-economic models has retreated into its own dogma: a different one-sidedness which is no more productive than the social-economic one-sidedness.

This self-referential way of thinking and acting in relation to culture and art is, in any case, pernicious when considering the potential social power of community art projects, because community art projects work with the most underprivileged groups in society, for whom modernity has meant no significant improvement in their daily lives as compared to the Middle Ages. Similarly, democracy in South Africa has only minimally translated itself into better living conditions for the majority of the township inhabitants. For these underprivileged groups, it is essential to find a job, to make an extra buck to supplement their benefit, to feel accepted in a social network, next to the fact that they like to act. And, while equal opportunities for artistic expression are important, the right to culture is part of a greater corpus of human rights that should be realized in their coherent totality. If community art projects could favour a transversal approach, then they could significantly strengthen their social clout. Would they still be artistic enough for the world of the arts? It all depends on how urgently the art sector itself feels the need to strengthen its ties to society. Thompson's supplement to Marx was justified, but this does not mean that Marx's socio-economic analysis doesn't

hold up. In times of social and economic crisis (increased unemployment, an endless stream of asylum seekers, growing individualism,
etc.), Marx is more relevant than ever. It wouldn't be inappropriate
for the culture and art sectors to incorporate a certain measure of
socio-economic awareness and social action. Community art projects
can be a useful guide in this.

References

Billig, M. (1987). Arguing and Thinking: A Rhetorical Approach to Social
Psychology. **Cambridge: Cambridge University Press.**
Blumer, H. (1969). Symbolic Interactionism: Perspective and method. **New
Jersey: Prentice Hall.**
Derrida, J. (2001 [1968]). Writing and Difference. **London/New York: Routledge**
(vertaling van L'écriture et la difference, Paris: Gallimard).
De Saussure, F. (2002 [1916]). Ecrits de Linguistique Générale. **Editions critique**
de Bouquet, S. and Engler, R. (eds.) Paris: Gallimard.
Edwards, R., Nicoll, K., Solomon, N., and Usher, R. (2004). Rhetoric and
Educational Discourse. **London/New York: RoutledgeFalmer, Taylor & Francis
Group.**
Goffman, E. (1959). The Presentation of Self in Everyday Life. **New York: Anchor
Books.**
Hawkes, T. (1972). Metaphor. **London: Methuen.**
Lakoff, G., and Johnson, M. (2003 [1980]). Metaphors We Live By. **Chicago:**
University of Chicago Press.
Mead, M. (2001 [1928]). Coming of Age in Samoa. A Psychological Study of
Primitive Youth for Western Civilisation. **New York: Harper Perennial Modern
Classics.**
Meuser, M., Nagel, U. (1991). ExpertInneninterviews - vielfach erprobt, wenig
bedacht. Ein Beitrag zur qualitativen Methodendiskussion. In: Garz, D. and
Kraimer, K. (Hg.): Qualitativ-empirische Sozialforschung, **pp. 441-468. Opladen:
Westdeutscher Verlag.**
Thompson, E.P. (1966). The Making of the English Working Class.
Harmondsworth: Penguin.
Williams, R. (1958). Culture is Ordinary. In McKenzie, N. (ed.) Convictions.
London: MacGibbon & Kee.

Through Zina's Eyes

Community Artists as Artistic Professionals

Quirijn Lennert van den Hoogen & Hans van Maanen

In a way, the term community art can be regarded as a tautology, at least in the domain of those *performing arts* which (as is the nature of the beast) aim at groups of 'users' and, according to many, (should) make communities out of groups taking part in the performances. This is very obvious during pop concerts and somewhat less obvious during cabaret shows — both art forms in which the collective experience plays an important part — but it hardly applies to the visual arts since modern artists are usually focused on the individual reception of their work or operate in and for a circle of their closest friends and connoisseurs. By comparison to the visual arts, although reading is also an individual activity, literary reception plays far more of a part in social interaction systems and communication through the media. On the other hand, the reception of many forms of theatre (stage, kinetic, dance) has become highly individualized since the 1980s, mostly because of the rapid development of new and often specific languages and idioms by artists working in this discipline. Due to their conceptual, often complex and/or abstract nature, such forms are only appreciated by viewers who are more or less informed. In this sense, and because of the simultaneous increase of interest in the design of theatrical space, the theatrical arts have moved towards the visual arts in the way in which they function in society.

However, this development is diametrically opposed to the nature of the arts and the responsibility that many artists, *being artists*, feel for society or for certain communities within society. With Niklas Luhmann, we can conclude that the arts offer a way of distinguishing between reality and imagination 'and, consequently, a position from which something else can be determined as reality'.[1] This distinction immediately requires some specification of the relationship between reality and art, both in a theoretical sense and from the perspective of artistic practice. Apart from the generally accepted idea that by manipulating their medium (wood, language, body, etc.) artist play with forms, specifically the forms of experienced reality (matters), Luhmann signals a number of directions this game can take:

> [...] whether to 'imitate' what reality does not show (its essential forms, its Ideas, its divine perfection), to 'criticize' reality for what it does not want to admit (its shortcomings, its 'class rule', its commercial orientation), or to affirm reality by showing that its representation succeeds, in

fact, succeeds so well that creating the work of art and looking at it is a delight. The concepts imitation/critique/affirmation do not exhaust the possibilities. Another intent might address the observer as an individual and contrive a situation in which he faces reality (and ultimately himself) and learns how to observe it in ways he could never learn in real life.[2]

Luhmann makes a somewhat unusual distinction between the last approach, aimed at the individual (in which he agrees with Martha Nussbaum's opinion that 'the aesthetic attitude shows us the way'[3]), and the first three possibilities he mentioned, that seem to be more aimed at collective use. But this approach as a whole enables us to deduce two things: a) art communicates, in a reflective sense, about the realities and asks users for, at the very least, a mental response; b) art enables one to experience something that cannot be experienced outside art and therefore, in the strictest sense of the word, it always has a subversive nature even if the work of art does nothing more than stretch the boundaries of pleasure.

This second conclusion is, however, open to debate; the notion 'art' has blurred over the past two decades and has blended into the compound concept of 'art and culture', which usually doesn't differentiate between the two components. Besides that, under the influence of neoliberalism — opening the way for the free flow of capital and ignoring distinctions that hamper this — the definition of art has been stretched so far that it includes anything which is drawn, danced, sung etc. In itself, this is defensible if one accepts the idea that a characteristic feature of art is that it shapes matter into material in order to influence the perception and the imagination of users. This description applies as much to forms of art which require the user to adjust his or her perceptions, as it does to more comfortable forms that do not demand this. Both kinds of art offer different forms of aesthetic experiences; additionally, the former one may be called artistic and perhaps also subversive. It is precisely these possible differences in experience — which can occur with different (groups of) users of

1 Niklas Luhmann, Art as a Social System (Stanford: Stanford University Press, 2000), p. 142, trans. E.M. Knodt from Die Kunst der Gesellschaft (Frankfurt am Main: Suhrkamp Verlag, 1995).
2 Luhmann, op cit., p. 143.
3 Luhmann, op cit., p. 207.

various forms of art — that make it necessary to reinstate the distinctions in terminology between culture and art and between art that is comfortable and art that challenges, not only for theoretical reasons but also mostly because of the social interest in knowing which forms of culture and art can have which effects.

Considering what is stated above, one might wonder whether community art can be both a comfortable and a challenging form of art (initially the answer is yes) and whether community art can aim at bringing about experiences with individuals (initially the answer is no). As far as the individual experience is concerned, we can state that every collective experience begins with individual experiences; people who already feel they belong to a community, or who get this feeling during an aesthetic event, will always have to be touched by a work of art before they share these experiences with others more or less consciously. There is, however, no point in speaking of community art if this second phase is not intended, or better, is not achieved. By the way, even when 'users' of art would be personally appealed to in a completely comfortable way, the experience of collectivity can sometimes challenge the participants to perceive themselves and their environment in a new way.

The first matter, whether community art can be both comfortable and challenging, is not much more complicated than that. Obviously, it is possible for an organized aesthetic event, aimed at a community and organized with this community, to generate experiences that are familiar and do not ask people to use their imagination and/or for them to review their existing perceptions, neither on an individual nor on a collective level. It is important to clearly distinguish this form of community art from the one in which participants acquire artistic experiences, meaning forms of community art that challenge, undermine and renew the way a community sees itself; this is community art in the strictest sense of the word, because, in this process, the specific value of art is active, *by activating the imagination of people so that they can perceive reality in a different manner.* Or, in the words of the people responsible for social-artistic projects in Flanders, as formulated by Marie van Looveren: 'The familiar world of the participants is artistically manipulated during the process (and that) means that people step into the world of the imagination and of the symbolic' and 'This is the moment when people start looking at their own world as an outsider and start seeing the familiar as strange.'[4]

Whether or not this value can also be realized socially is a different and much more difficult question. Flemish colleagues, Van Kerkhoven, Laermans and Van den Dries, do actually see theatre art as functioning socially but only for the informed audience who see *the* (represented) reality being de-constructed on stage: 'the visualization of the constructed and rhetorical (rather than fictional) nature of the theatrical representation.[5] And François Stienen states that even 'Michael Moore can film whatever he wants; he will simply have no influence in a TV culture. Not even when his film is shown in the movie theatre'.[6] In other words, how effective is art when its meaning is immediately lost in the overwhelming force of current perception? The point is to offer the users of art the opportunity to give the artistic experience a 'productive' place in their experience of the world, 'so that it sticks' as Van Erven says.[7] And that is exactly what is expected from community art — that it creates a situation of aesthetic communication that makes it possible for the individual and collective experiences gained in this way to seep through to adjacent domains, both in the *minds* of the participants and, in particular, in the collective activity of the community. Only then, when the challenging collective experience continues in a second life, is the possible value of the event not only offered and consumed but also realized socially. In this case, we could speak of subversive art although, in a strict interpretation of the notion of 'art', that, too, would be tautological. An important first step on this road is the gathering of people who know each other or who have to deal with the same issues: communities. This was done, for example, by the consciousness-raising theatre of the seventies, Dario Fo in Italy and Théâtre du Soleil in France and is also carried out today by a large proportion of the artists *active* in the domain of community art. A second step in *community art* is taken by asking people to make something together; it is the basis for an interest in something new. Neither steps are taken in the regular arts, which, as a consequence of this and other factors, run the risk of losing their significance because they contribute too little to giving meaning to the world.

4   Marie van Looveren, 'Balanceren op de breuklijn tussen sociaal en artistiek', Boekman **82** (Spring 2010), p. 44.
5   Rudi Laermans, 'Theater/Politie: Enkele observaties', Bewakers van betekenis, eds. Yolande Melsert and Dennis Meyer (Amsterdam: TIN, 1996), pp. 75-83, p. 76.
6   François Stienen, 'Beelden zonder overredingskracht', Boekman **64** (Autumn 2005), p. 34.
7   Eugène van Erven, 'Op zoek naar de kern: Een verkenningstocht door de wereld van community art', Boekman **82** (Spring 2010), p. 12.

Three Dimensions of Community Art

And so emerge three dimensions with which we can think about community art and its meaning in society. The first dimension concerns the relationship between the nature of the imagination (of the material) and the intended group of users. When the manner of representation is familiar to the group and doesn't, therefore, challenge reception in itself — as in Gay Pride, mentioned by Gielen in the article 'Mapping Community Art' — all that is left is the collectivity of the experience which maintains the possibility of confounding existing schemes of perceptions. This could be the case for homosexuals in a one-horse town who do not meet many other homosexuals or people kindly disposed to them in daily life, preferring to trip over them in the Amsterdam canals on a sunny Saturday afternoon in August. The average urbanite gay person will experience the massiveness of Gay Pride as less challenging because it also occurs on an average Amsterdam regular night out in the Reguliersdwarsstraat.[8]

The second dimension concerns the extent to which the relationship with fields other than the artistic are encompassed by the community art project; in other words, the contextualization of the aesthetic experience.[9] If this contextualization is explicitly organized, for example by entering into a pact with social parties — like a housing corporation or institutions for social care — the chance that community art acts subversively, in a social sense, is much greater, although Marcuse's concept of repressive tolerance could also take effect here. Gielen justifiably remarks that when such institutions act as financiers, they will try hard to take the sting out of projects because they are not interested in commissioning aesthetic experiences that expose their own failings (as happens, for example, when residents who have been asked to film their world for a cultural project only show the shoddy maintenance of the commissioning housing corporation). Here, the social context in which a project is presented and in which the experience of the project can get 'a second life', is fundamental. When projects are presented in more traditional art institutions, it is obvious that the contextualization of the experience in adjacent domains is harder, if not impossible.

We can now construct a model of four quadrants to categorize community art (see fig. 1). But there is a third dimension in which community art practices can distinguish themselves from other artistic activities. In this dimension, members of the community play a central part in the project. At one extreme of this dimension is the situation in which the community supplies the matters for the aesthetic communication to professional artists, who proceed to work them out in their images. It makes sense that, in this case, artists will be more inclined to, as Gielen calls it, move in an artistic discourse, with the possible result of impeding the contextualization into other discourses. At the other extreme, members of the community are themselves on stage or behind the camera, with the possible consequence that 'recognition' occurs instead of an artistic (read: challenging) view on their own situation.[10] So now we can construct a three-dimensional model of eight 'cells' in which the quadrants listed above are processed (see fig. 2).

Fig.1. Four forms of community art

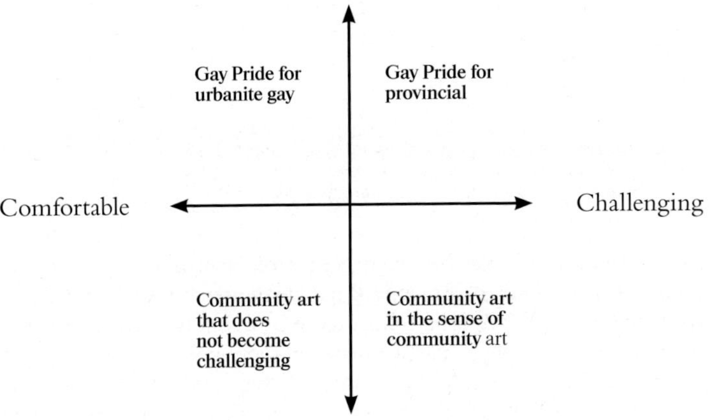

8   Although this street, the epicentre of the Amsterdam (and therefore Dutch) gay community, has less and less establishments specifically catering to gay people.

9   Hans van Maanen, How to Study Art Worlds: On the Societal Functioning of Aesthetic Values (Amsterdam: Amsterdam University Press, 2009).

10 This distinction is also valid for Gay Pride, in which homosexuals represent themselves as homosexuals not only to other homosexuals but also to the broader community.

Fig.2. Eight forms of community art

Orginization of effects in other fields

	No		Yes	
	Community supplies matters	Community also represents itself	Community supplies the matters	Community also represents itself
Comfortable*	A	B	E	F
Challenging	C	D	G	H

*N.B.: That the sign system in itself cannot lead to challenging experiences, strictly speaking excludes these forms of community art. However, since the subversiveness of these forms is experienced at the level of the collective, we can still consider them to be community art.

The extent of the likely subversiveness of community art projects increases as we move from upper left in the matrix to lower right, from cell A to cell H. In the cells A up to D, a contextualization of the experience is unlikely, and it is there, on the whole, that we find the projects that are generally not associated with community art. The previously mentioned Gay Pride is here (in cell B).[11] Also, the exhibition of Mapplethorpe, mentioned by Gielen, is in this part of the matrix, in cell A or C, depending on how provocative one perceives his aesthetic imagery to be. In general, we can assume that forms of community art that present themselves in traditional art institutions are located in the left part of the quadrant. In the right part of the matrix (cells E up to H), we find the more familiar forms of community art. The Rotterdams Wijktheater, a group that has been making theatre for over twenty-five years in the biggest port city of Europe, uses material that originates from its contacts with residents of the districts and these residents are found on stage as well. We find this group in cell F but, depending on how much experience the audience of these performances had in visiting the theatre or whether the players investigate their own situation more thoroughly artistically speaking, this form can also generate more challenging experiences, in which case it moves to cell H.

Zina neemt de wijk,[12]
Community Art in Groningen

The temporal nature of theatre can cause a production to move through multiple cells. We give the example of project *Zina neemt de wijk*, which was organized in the city of Groningen in May 2010. This project is a typical attempt to give social significance to cultural activity. This is hardly surprising given that the project was mostly financed through subsidies from the city of Groningen and from the Nederlandse Fonds Cultuurparticipatie, the fund that was set up in 2009 in order to strengthen cultural participation thereby increasing the importance of the arts in society. Community art figures prominently in the plans Dutch municipalities and provinces put together with this fund.

Zina Platform is a cooperation of female artists centred on the well-known Dutch actress, Adelheid Roosen. With her regular theatre group, Female Economy, Roosen has received a multiple-year subsidy from the national Fonds voor de Podiumkunsten and is therefore part of the established performing arts circuit.

In the policy plan of Female Economy the initiative for Zina Platform is mentioned. Zina is a platform for 'gentle' confrontation with the daily, sometimes tough but wondrous life.[13] The members of the platform derive from various ethnic backgrounds and have their own specific artistic practices: text writing, acting, story telling and cooking. The platform searches for the boundaries of traditional artistic practices, particularly with the link to food. Meeting the other is the focal point. After a number of successful projects in the working-class districts of Amsterdam and northern Holland — in which, for example, local residents were invited to hold a parade in a park they thought was only accessible to 'rich people' or migrants were

11 Although one can pose the question here as to whether or not by the emphatic ties between political and economic sectors (establishments that may or may not cater exclusively to gays), there could be some experience seeping through in these fields, although perhaps not of effects specific for the aesthetic characteristics of the experience.
12 This translates literally as 'Zina takes refuge' but it also means 'Zina takes the neighbourhood'.
13 See www.zinaplatform.nl.

asked to tell their stories in order to examine who they were — the company was invited to undertake a project in Groningen, the biggest city in the north of the Netherlands (187,000 inhabitants). This invitation came from four institutions: the local centre for creativity, which wanted to find out if community art was an art form they could use; the Noord Nederlandse Toneel (NNT), the largest theatre company in the north of the country which, being the city's company, wanted to connect more emphatically with the city; the foundation for Maatschappelijk Juridische Dienstverlening (Social legal services), which wanted to learn, as they put it, 'to look at the people in the neighbourhoods through their eyes' and Het Toevluchtsoord, an institution for women suffering from domestic violence, which wanted to make domestic violence more visible for those surrounding the victims. One decided to work in three old working-class districts in the city of Groningen. With this broad coalition of organizations, we can already say something about the first dimension mentioned above — the organization of the effect on other fields. The range of the coalition makes it clear that there was co-ordination of the relationship with other fields: the project was supposed to have an effect on both the local residents and the victims of domestic violence (the community) and on the social workers dealing with these groups on a professional basis. On the one hand, the involvement of welfare institutions guaranteed access to this community, while, on the other hand, it offered the *potential for* effect outside the community.

However, the decision to perform the show that would close the project in the NNT's own theatre moves in the other direction. Through this gesture it is obvious that they sought to place themselves within an artistic discourse. The Zinas emphatically see themselves as artists, rather than community artists. But the decision of the NNT to open itself up to the project had also everything to do with the wish to connect emphatically with life in the city. The city was almost literally drawn into the theatre.

The Zinas also devised strategies to organize the ties with the neighbourhoods in the artistic process itself. So, for the premiere and also later during the series of performances, residents were invited to come to the show, at the expense of the guests who ordinarily do not have to pay for their own ticket, but now had to. And an important part of the performance was the organization of a silent procession with local residents who walked from a point in the neighbourhood to the theatre, literally right through the performance. This way, these people were stimulated to come and see the performance itself as well.

As mentioned above, the community in which the project was organized consisted of two groups — the residents of three old working-class districts in the city and women suffering from domestic violence. Since Zina aims to collect the stories of people and to return them 'artistically processed' to the community from whence they came, a strategy was devised to make contact with the inhabitants of the working-class districts. Through the Maatschappelijk Juridisch Dienstverlening, host families were found in which members of the platform went 'into adoption' for two weeks. After the adoption period, the Zinas moved into a few houses in the neighbourhoods so that they would have a place of their own and could become part of life in the neighbourhood. Each member of the platform opted for a specific situation. One went into adoption with a single and socially isolated older man, another with a refugee family, a third with a handicapped man living together with a Moroccan woman. The Turkish-born Zina-member Nazmye Oral wanted to go into adoption with someone who would vote for the right-extreme Partij voor de Vrijheid. Adelheid Roosen herself went into adoption with Het Toevluchtsoord and lived with the women according to the occasionally strict rules of the organization. Apart from the adoptions, the Zinas gathered their material through a large number of activities. Dressed in pink wigs and coats, they organized movie screenings in the neighbourhoods, they participated in the annual cleaning action organized by the city and organized *Beauty Stories Salon*, an installation in which people wore headphones and listened to someone else's story while getting a hand massage. In this way, the Zinas were visible in the neighbourhood and they recorded the stories of the migrant and autochthonous citizens they met. So, the relationship to, and involvement with, the community was organized on a very personal level. Finally, Ola Mafaalani devised the structure of the stories the Zinas had collected and directed the show. It resulted in a performance of over two hours in which the Zinas, supplemented by a few other actors, alternately (re)presented themselves and people from the neighbourhoods. Films, projected on the walls of the hall, introduced the adoption families to the visitors, and actor, George Groot, standing amidst countless written notes fluttering down, read the stories of the neighbourhood residents aloud. One of these stories made it clear that a particular family didn't recognize itself at all in the way it was perceived by the professional welfare workers, namely as a 'multi-problem' family. The story showed the family's strength rather than its weaknesses. Some of the adopting families were present in the performance. Adelheid Roosen, for example, introduced two women from Het Toevluchtsoord who told what had happened to them and what it meant to them. Next to that, George Groot played the part of a man who beats up his ex-wife out of rage, thus creating empathy for both sides of the story. Groot also recounted, in the first person, the story of Gerrit, the socially isolated old man whose wife had grown demented, to whom he had slowly had to say goodbye. The man himself was present in his wheelchair and kept confirming his own story with little nods and a mumbled 'yes'. Adelheid Roosen acted out the frustration of a migrant woman who was ordered by her autochtonous husband to adjust while she feels he is so deadened and has so few contacts that he himself no longer fits into his own culture. Roosen and Groot also played a woman and man who knew each other in the past and meet again; for the woman, this represents an experience she has trouble opening up to but eventually surrenders to; for the man, it is closure and he ends the contact, which deeply grieves the woman.

At the end, the procession of local residents has moved once through the hall (the audience is not sitting in a tribune but on stacks of mattresses spread across the stage), then they enter the hall once more and introduce themselves to three members of the audience who they invite to eat from a very long table that suddenly has come down from the ridge of the hall. The table is set with a variety of snacks from various cultures. The show ends with a conversation between audience members, actors and residents from the procession. There is no applause and the audience either stays in the theatre for a long time or they leave the room in dribs and drabs. In this way, an alternation occurs between presenting, representing and being represented and visitors are challenged to connect to the sometimes familiar, some-times new stories of the residents. The implicit but obvious question the show asks of the audience is whether they are willing, and able, to open themselves up to meetings with 'the other', with whoever devi-ates from their own form of civilization, and to prove it immediately.

In doing so, the performance moves freely across all four fields E up to H in the matrix, but this community art project also leaves one question about the effect of the project unanswered: to what extent does the embedding of the project into the activities of two art institutes (the NNT and the Kunstencentrum) and two welfare institutes (Het Toevluchtsoord and the Maatschappelijk-Juridische Dienstverlening) guarantee or impede the social effect of the percep-tions that were realized in the project?

86

Community Art and Subversiveness

The question posed above is very similar to the one Gielen asks in his article 'Mapping Community Art' in this collection, namely whether community art has, by now, been so thoroughly encased that it no longer has any social effect, subversive or otherwise. We feel it is better not to talk about community art if it is not — in the artistic sense — subversive, in other words, if the experiences the community art invokes do not challenge people to look at reality in a different manner. The professionalism of the artists distinguishes them from street workers or from ombudsmen of housing corporations. Added to that, the relationship between artists and the *community* in question can play an important role since it is the artists who give the matter form in such a way that it is perceived in new ways. Here, we make a distinction between the authenticity of the matter (experienced reality), performed by its 'owner' and the artistic, imaginative representation of it by the artist. Also, in the first case, there *may* be some social (as opposed to aesthetic) subversiveness when a dominated or marginalized community (the 'other') reveals itself to itself and to others and wants to be seen. But one step further is when both forms of subversiveness are combined and the use of the produced perceptions have been organized within the project as well. After all, just as a railway is no longer a railway if no train travels over it and a dress is no longer a dress if it isn't worn, perceptions are not perceptions if they aren't used and disappear into nothingness.

Part II
The Artist's Voice

The Vernissage **by the MartHa!-tentatief**
A Play about Untameable Life at the Beginning of the Twenty-first Century

Bart Van Nuffelen

Preface

This story is set in the land of Belgium, which can be found somewhere between Germany, the Netherlands and France. The interesting thing about Belgium is that it diminishes year by year, or vaporizes more and more, if you prefer, and slowly morphs into two countries: the Walloon provinces and Flanders. This story is increasingly set in the country of Flanders, where more and more people become convinced that they work harder, are more enterprising and smarter than the people in the Walloon provinces. Most Flemish people speak Dutch and live in allotments that used to be part of nature. This story, however, takes place in a city in which most people do not speak Dutch and some children have never seen a real cow. This city is called Antwerp and it is one of the most beautiful cities in the world (in fact, only the lack of hills prevents us from calling it the most beautiful city in the world). There is a beautiful historic centre, there is a mighty stream that laps against the city, there is a world harbour, there are gorgeous decrepit neighbourhoods with paupers from all over the world and there are us, the united artists of the MartHa!tentatief.

In April 2010, the theatre cycle *The Revue of Untameable Life* began in Antwerp, a series of plays by the theatre company, the MartHa!tentatief, about the multicoloured city in the beginning of the twenty-first century. The first show, *The Vernissage*, was, by itself, remarkable for more than one reason. After years of trial and mostly error, the company finally found a way to represent the contemporary city in an authentic way.

Months of intense research on the Coninckplein (Coninck Square), which serves as a halfway house for people with serious drug problems, resulted in a remarkable show in which high artistic quality went hand in hand with active participation in the show by those square residents. In this article, and as writer and director of the performance, I try to explain why *The Vernissage* succeeded where many attempts to combine active participation with high artistic quality (including my own) had failed. And also why this performance might be a blueprint for further exploration of the stories of a modern city.

1. *Make a Humongous Failure*

One day, I read the following quotation by Anil Ramdas, a Dutch writer from Surinam, and it hit me like a bolt of lightning: 'Surely it is a humongous failure of the Dutch [Flemish] storytellers to fail to notice that their society has changed drastically in colour and nature over the past twenty years. While a million citizens swallow their daily humiliations, the Dutch [Flemish] writers look the other way.'[1]

We, too (I now speak on behalf of myself, the whole of MartHa!tentatief and virtually all other Flemish and, therefore white, playwriting, bourgeois boys), have not avoided this failure. As critic, Wouter Hillaert, notes in his article, 'Dover zien en sterven',[2] current Flemish theatre mainly demonstrates that the influx of migrants is not part of experienced or imagined reality. And I know why. It is hard enough to write about what you know, let alone about what and who you don't know.

For years, I have lived near the Coninckplein, a small run-down square near the train station of Antwerp. Even the building of a new central public library on this square (which began in 2003) and the matching efforts of the city council to make the square 're-spectable' — through urban renewal projects, by using frequent and repressive actions against annoyance, and the deployment of a battery of community workers and social organizations — were to no avail. Today, a group of people exists that calls the square 'home', with all its accompanying inconveniences such as nightly noise, street litter and drug-related criminality. For years, I have been fascinated by this group of the square's residents, by the mechanism of the square, by its impact on my own surroundings; over the course of time, I became a part of the square myself. And, while the square's residents (before this project I would have called them 'those addicts') seemed as threatening as they were incomprehensible, this slowly changed. I got to know them as neighbours. I learned that there are sociable square residents and surly ones, very cheerful ones and infinitely sad ones. But it wasn't until 2008, when I was invited to participate as a volunteer in a 'social artistic project', that I really got to know the square's residents.

Three years ago, 't Vlot and Free Clinic — two very different social organizations that care about the deplorable fate of these street residents — started cooperating on an arts project. It consisted of a se-ries of workshops in graphic art, drawing and theatre for the square's residents under the supervision of professional artists. And there, in the humble reception room of 't Vlot, the simple truth seeped in, week after week, that the addicted people are simply people like you

1 NRC Handelsblad, 14 March 1997.
2 Wouter Hillaert, 'Dover zien en sterven,' Rekto: Verso, No. 35, May-June 2009.

and me. It may seem to be a trite aphorism, but you wouldn't say that if you knew these people and how they sometimes hang out on the square with their spirit completely shattered. I had long and often laborious conversations with them and I slowly began to understand that these square residents had the same dreams as I did, despite their deplorable living conditions — that they want nothing more than to be understood and respected, as we all do. And, slowly, their addiction changed from being the main issue to becoming a side issue. And when the workshops were finished, when it turned out that the arts project would no longer be organized due to lack of funding and we searched for a way to try and continue this work, something started smouldering inside me. And, after reading two key books during the summer holidays, it burst into a holy fire.

2. *Go and Lie by a Tuscan Swimming Pool*
(and Read the Right Books)

I read those key books, I have to admit, by a sunlit swimming pool in Tuscany, which, as everyone knows, is the typical holiday destination for more or less affluent theatre directors such as me. But, after reading these books, I couldn't care less about that pool and I was hungry to return to my drab square because, at long last, I knew how to tell the story of that square.

In the ambitiously conceived and documented *Het land van aankomst (The Country of Arrival)*, the Dutch publicist and professor of urban policy, Paul Scheffer, painted a sombre picture of multicultural society. He described how the migrant wave of the past twenty-five years has remained invisible in our history and how it confronts our society with near-impossible challenges. Intriguing, for instance, is his statement that the evolution towards a 'global village' (cheap travel, lightning-fast internet connections, satellite TV) makes de facto integration impossible. Migrants retain family ties in their land of origin and look for brides there. Satellite dishes bring the daily news into their living room from a distant land. By contrast, they don't know the news of their land of arrival any more than they know her represented reality: the children's series, the soaps, the actors; none of it means anything to them. Not now. Not ever. The result is that the contemporary city will continue to evolve into a cluster of more or less isolated islands of migrants with their own background and represented reality. And so, more and more (until recently), the obvious bridges between those islands will be demolished. Paul Scheffer teaches us that we can no longer hide behind the old notion that, if we just wait long enough, the intercultural society will come about naturally, and that we will have to make an effort to make it happen — that we will have to get to know each other better than ever before, in all our diversity; that we have to get out there, to talk and to listen.

In *Bright Shiny Morning*, the US writer, James Frey, writes a biography of Los Angeles. In a staggering 400 pages, he describes many hundreds of lives connected by the siren call of LA and the shared belief in the Californian dream. Sometimes these lives are told in five sentences; sometimes in half a page; sometimes in a single sentence. And the sum of all those lives is a touching tribute to the modern metropolis as a collection of shared dreams. And so, suddenly, by that pool in Tuscany, I knew what I had to do — to really search for the stories of all those new people on the isolated islands of my old city, islands I would recognize when I returned to the city.

The night café, Capitole, where I like to write my texts in the evening, is a home from home for three very distinctive groups of people living right next to each other but not having (or wanting to have) anything whatsoever to do with each other. The back of the café is the territory of some form of drug dealing middle management that directs street dealers from there. At the front of the café stands a Pakistani billiard table (a smooth table designed for a game with black and white discs that have to be shoved into the cut-aways) around which dozens of Pakistanis and Indians jostle one another night after night. And everything tallies, except the café Capitole, which should have been located in a Pakistani valley and not near the train station of a medium-sized European city. Between the billiards table and the dealers are a number of small tables where homeless elders come to spend a part of the night and, on that island, my computer and I belong. And there, during summer nights, the plan was born that all those yet-to-be-conducted conversations with all those islanders would lead to a series of plays called *The Revue of Untameable Life*.

3. *Create an Ambitious Umbrella Project*
The Revue of Untameable Life is a series of ten plays about people who washed up here, yesterday or forty years ago, about people who have lived here their whole life to become a castaway in their own city, a year and a half of plays about a shadowy square, about Poles on a bench in the park, about a waiting room full of dead people, a school filled with children, a BMW full of Moroccans, about ourselves in our safe homes. It is, by the way, an odd theatrical paradox that real recognition only occurs when the lens zooms in maximally, as if the

spectator only recognizes his own life in another person when that other life is described and documented as intimately, as accurately and as authentically as possible. That is why we decided to zoom in on a very small spot in the city for each performance of the revue. While this may seem trite, it couldn't be further from the truth; every European city has a train station where lonely souls wash up (revue #1: *The Vernissage*); every metropolis is transected, by bus or subway lines (revue #2: *The Bus*), by the special schools for migrants (revue #3: *The old primary school De Groenstraat*), etc., etc.

According to the Dutch dictionary standard, Van Dale, a re-vue is 'a theatre play consisting of a series of separate tableaux [...] interspersed with song and dance in usually large-scale settings'. The large-scale settings, in our case, are the streets, squares and fallow ground of this city. The separate tableaux are seemingly daily occur-rences: people waiting for the tram at dusk, a small group of Poles in the park on a Sunday afternoon or a woman standing still for hours in the middle of the square. Song and dance take the shape of a cin-ematic soundtrack that tells the stories of the passers-by, the waiting people and the loitering people.

The glorious goal of it all is to show life in the multicoloured city at the beginning of the twenty-first century and to tap into the endless reservoir of modern stories and enable them to interact. And so, all these lives that are lived side by side on any other day — this, at least, is the theory — will start interacting over one night and make the many-sided universe of the modern city tangible. The first show, *The Vernissage,* made that ambition real in a wondrous way. '*The ver-nissage* offers something that reaches beyond the walls of the hall. The reality of 'out there' steals in here. The stories of the square remain with you; they move us without aiming for sentimentality, but mostly they make us consider all those who live beside us in the city and who we usually just pass by. That little piece of city will, once and for all, become a little bit different.'[3]

4. Remember – before you start – Your Glorious Defeats
It is an irrefutable law that a single failure will teach you infinitely more than ten victories. The play, *Leuvendijk* (2002), is one of these interesting failures, but, before I disclose the reasons behind that fail-ure, for your education and enjoyment, I must first tell you about the tradition that gave birth to this play.

Sometime in the late 1990s, the subsidy policy of the Flemish Government introduced a new subcategory: social artistic projects.

Suddenly, a not inconsiderable pot of money became available for projects that, next to artistic goals, also claimed to have a socially emancipatory aim. In most cases, this policy boiled down to professional theatre-makers and companies starting to work with so-called underprivileged groups: migrants, prisoners, addicts. *Leuvendijk* was one such social artistic project. With a dozen or so underprivileged people from Leuven (a small city in Flanders with a major university, the first town to be wrecked during World War One by the advancing German troops, which caused uproar all over the world at the time), we made an adaptation of *Waaiendijk*, the then-successful location performance of the 'phenomenal' MartHa!tentatief. (That is just the weird name of our company, we decided on it one drunken evening and now we are stuck with it and so are you). The idea was this: at the moment *Waaiendijk* was to play in Leuven, we would perform its adaptation by the underprivileged prior to the show, in order to give the esteemed audience the opportunity to compare the reality of real life (*Leuvendijk*) with its theatrical translation *(Waaiendijk)*. No sooner said than done.

Three months before the performances of *Waaiendijk* in Leuven, I canvassed the Leuven community houses and assembled a team of actors after an exhausting round of introduction and selection that brought together a motley crew of people who had become stuck in a deplorable situation due to misfortune or through their own stupidity. In the weeks following selection, we read the original play *(Waaiendijk)* and reflected on how the fictional story could be translated to their reality. And this was the fictional story: a young woman, on the run from her past, is sold a roller shutter door by a clever salesman and quickly realizes that this shutter will do her no good and undertakes a quest through the alien city to attempt to cancel the order. By conquering various obstacles, she regains her self-esteem and comes to terms with her past, and, you may find this hard to believe after this summary, but it was actually a fun play and no, it wasn't pounding home a message and yes, it was moving.

The translation of this story to a new play was the interesting part of the process. The participants told their own, often poignant, stories, compared them with the fictional story and together we made a new scenario, which, at several moments, created an interesting tension with the original stage version, because it was moving in all

<hr>

3   Ines Minten, 'Bruggen naar een eiland. Revue #1: de vernissage uit Revue van het ontembare leven van MartHa!tentatief', theatermaggezien.net.

its clumsy humanity and because it revealed that reality is sometimes more poetic than fiction. But then duty called and we shared out the parts, rehearsed for a few more weeks in a cardboard set and eventually performed our play, and it flopped big time.

Leuvendijk suffered from the same flaws as ninety-nine percent of the other social artistic projects of the time. It could certainly boast a certain level of social success (the participants lived an intense and comradely time, shared a valuable experience that some cherish today, almost ten years later), but artistically, the level was, to put it bluntly, insufficient. And I have given a great deal of thought as to why this play, like virtually every other social artistic production I have seen (I have seen dozens, maybe hundreds) failed, almost by definition. And, by now, I think I know the answer: because acting is a profession, whether we like it or not. Simply addressing an audience of several hundred people and, at the same time, pretending that what you're saying is a coincidence is an art in itself, which can only be successfully achieved after several years of training. I believe that a *rara avis* can achieve such a feat within a few months and with intensive supervision, but an entire company of inexperienced players will never succeed. This automatically brings us to the most hateful aspect of social artistic performances; as a spectator, you have to see past the incompetence of the actors in order to appreciate the real value of the play; you have to force yourself to forgive the actors all their incompetence, the uneasy fumbling, the self-assured blah-blah, the emphatic delivery of the text, the flat acting, the cringe-worthy singing. And the fact that I was unable to avoid these flaws in *Leuvendijk* was my reason for radically and immediately ceasing to make social artistic projects. Since that day, the phenomenal MartHa!tentatief has not made a social artistic project. But, what is worse, since that day we have never worked with non-actors *on the scene*. Until now, that is. So why now? To begin with, two equally important reasons:

The belief that actual reality sometimes surpasses represented reality
This is motivated by the regained belief that real stories of the city are definitely worth telling these days and, even more than this, that a writer could not make up stories as rich and layered as those from real life; in other words, the cliché of reality surpassing fiction. And believing also — and now I am really on a slippery slope — that 'real' people are more interesting to watch than actors. To put this differently I often see people on the streets who I would dearly love to see on a stage, simply because their 'being there' appears to be telling a

grand and compelling story. In the way they look around themselves, full of distrust or, by contrast, very openly, in the way their ebony skin glistens in the sun or in the way they cling to their shopping cart. But is not all of this in contradiction to the objections listed above against non-professional actors?

The solution to the problem is obvious
Although all of this only became clear years afterwards, it boils down to making plays that avoid the trap of 'acting'. In other words, by looking for a way to tell the story of these people, using actual people but without requiring them to act, finding a way in which they can just 'be' on stage. And, by simply 'being' on stage, they share their whole grand and compelling story with a large and increasingly excited audience. This would be the challenge for *The Vernissage* and, by extension, for the whole *Revue of Untameable Life.*

Once all the solemn oaths have been sworn, all grandiloquent previews have been written, everything has been placed on file, all insights have been put into words, the real work begins. And how, in God's name, do you start with one of the most difficult and incomprehensible squares in town?

5. *Let the Experts Help You*
As I found out in the years before the play was conceived, the world of the square residents is very closed and ruled by laws and codes that are incomprehensible to outsiders. It was obvious that we would have to get help from the relief organizations that were already present on the square, and that there was no better route than 'adopting' the arts project that had already introduced the square residents, in a very modest fashion, to graphics, photography and theatre three years earlier. The MartHa!tentatief requested, and was granted, an additional subsidy to continue the project and re-appoint one of the regular counsellors (Eduardo Tardaguilla, a Uruguayan photographer). But, even more importantly, in this way we automatically had access to the expertise of both organizations that were organizing the project ('t Vlot and Free Clinic); as this report will show, their experience was undoubtedly necessary for the success of the project.

After thorough consultation, we decided to make the project last longer (to run over five months instead of the previous three), to use a second counsellor from our own company (graphic designer, Tom Clement) and to work increasingly towards the themes that would be tackled during the play. The relief organizations had their

own logical demands: a low artistic, technical threshold, personal interest of the square residents had to take precedence over the artistic end result and a guarantee of anonymity for participants. And, above all, it was decided to continually evaluate the process and correct it where necessary.

This play, ladies and gentlemen, was to have been called *The Vernissage of the Expo Street Art by the Collected Addicts of the Square*, but that was vetoed by the department of public relations who had had enough of titles that were too long to remember. It was also vetoed by the social workers; just as patients of the La Borde psychiatric clinic aren't called patients but residents and the technicians of the MartHa!tentatief aren't technicians but designers, the addicts of the square could not be called addicts but instead were called 'guests' or 'men' or 'street residents' or 'street users'.

6. *Experience an Intense Research Period*

In November 2009, the arts project began, the weekly workshop (Monday 14-17.00 hours) in the dreary drop-in centre from 't Vlot, near the Coninck square. Under the supervision of Tom Clement and Eduardo Tardaguilla, an increasing number of square users used paint and cameras in an informal coffee-and-cake kind of atmosphere.

Some people came in, drew one perfect eyebrow and left again; others worked for hours on a self portrait only to crumple it up in the end; some people refused to be photographed, others were immortalized in hundreds of pictures; some people worked in an abstract way; others made still lives, and all of these people together made the following scene on 12 December 2009.

Scene 2 — young women (fragment from the play *The Vernissage*)

Two young women. She entered less than a minute ago. She already got herself a cup of coffee and three sachets of sugar. She already took off her black coat. Already sat down and stood up again, and she has already fired off fifteen questions to the other young woman, let's call her Marein. Whether that is normal? But then, what is normal these days? Do you think his behaviour is normal? What do you think I should do? Marein has already opened her mouth three times to answer, in vain. Is the doctor in today? Until when? Do you think it is normal that I have to go to the doctor by myself? Do you think it is normal that I always have to do everything by myself? Marein no longer tries to answer. She waits, and tries to keep listening. She sees things are going well today, many visitors, people walking in and back out again. She hears the cowboy with his high voice explaining to a man that today is 'self portrait'. She sees the man listening attentively and then drawing a cat. She sees the young woman getting up and getting another cup of coffee with three sachets of sugar. She sees her previous cup of coffee, standing untouched on the corner of the table. She sees a very young woman she has never seen before come in hesitantly, sees the way she looks ill at ease at all these people drawing on wood, how she zips open her coat, how it reveals a heavily pregnant belly, how the woman with the four lives disentangles herself quickly from the drawing table and offers the newcomer a cup of coffee while the questions keep flowing over her.

The remarkable thing about these weekly meetings was how the counsellors, an assortment of professionals and temps, quickly lost themselves in the project. The business manager of the MartHa!tentatief created the most psychedelic works week after week; the homeless man worked in an orderly and structured way. Caroline, the research girl with the yellow shirt, would love to start a new life, as would Dave. As with so many others, the volunteer, Diane, often lay awake at night, contemplating her life. Trainee, Carly, serenely told us one night how she used to play house with a heavy drug user, and everyone was occasionally overwhelmed by the life seeping in from the square. When the young woman eventually fired her questions at her image in the mirror. When a man softly sobbed. When the very young woman came in a week later, softly told us a baby had been born, and disappeared forever. We were glad when P. finally made a picture on the last but one workshop. And everybody developed a special affection for Fons, who came regularly every week, developed an entirely new art movement all by himself and posed for each and every photo session, and, in a way, became the embodiment of the project, which had as the goal of making essential works about life on the square, in order to be better able to tell the true story of the square in ten scenes.

As we had hoped, this arts project was the perfect 'lubricant' for penetrating quickly and purposefully into our first target group. At the margin of the workshops, we could have informal conversations that soon became official, meaning we continued them in a neutral domain and recorded them. Even more importantly, the entire group of square residents (including the majority of residents who did not participate with the arts project) started thinking of us as 'safe' or 'to be trusted', which allowed us to dwell on the square and talk to residents relatively unhindered (in sharp contrast with the reporters and photographers who were invariably chased off the square). Even more than before, this enabled us to observe the mechanisms of the square at close hand, by both day and night.

The research period was an intensive experience. Over several months, we practically lived on the square, we had long and often intense conversations about living and surviving in the contemporary city. We witnessed fights, we saw a tram derail, we saw cars bump into disappearing bollards of the firm Vialis on a daily basis. We learned who was buying drugs, who was selling drugs and who was selling drugs in order to buy drugs. We saw people use, we saw people cry, we saw people laugh till their sides split over a very strange joke. We immersed ourselves in an unknown, enchanting and sometimes horrifying world. And, now and then, it became too much and one of us fainted or had to stay away from the square for a day.

Over a six week period from January to March, we were able to hold approximately thirty intense interviews with (in our eyes) the representative members of this group of square residents. Because of the relative safety the square residents lent us, we could also reach the people that social workers can barely reach (the homeless and drug-addicted illegal immigrants, for example, who often operate as street dealers and whose fate is even more wretched than that of the Belgian addicts). Next to that, we had conversations with the social workers of the square, about the square, about the square users, about their vision of these things, their hopes, their disillusionment. In order to get an outlook that was as broad as possible, we also spoke with local residents, involved or not, with passers-by and/or library visitors and with the head of the drugs squad of the city of Antwerp.

7. Constantly Adapt Your Plans to the Changing Circumstances
The circumstances changed continually, as was to be foreseen and

expected. See, for example, this fragment of text of the performance:

> The street residents have been conspicuously absent for some weeks now, not only in the square, but even more obviously in the rooms of 't Vlot, where we wait for them expectantly every Monday evening to no avail. Week after week, fewer people show up, and, after a while, the whole thing becomes a little ridiculous. Us, sitting around with ten people, watching a single man drawing an eyebrow, you can see him thinking 'what did I get myself into?' and leaving quickly, never to return again. Caroline has waited for weeks for the return of the Babylonian, Mohammed, a boy who speaks eight languages and, as she writes one evening, 'always smiled so heart-rendingly kindly'. A female participant mails her demand that we remove all her work from the future exhibition since she feels that modern city man is only interested in the dark aspects of her life. Day after day, it becomes clearer that it will be extremely difficult to actually involve the people from the square in the performance, and, if that wasn't enough, it appears that the group has fallen apart right under our noses and without us even noticing it. And we wonder whether the cold is to blame or the snow that will fall tonight. Or maybe it is our fault, with our perpetual questions, our data hassle, our rules, our agreements, our schedules. You may notice that the artists of the MartHa!tentatief are momentarily at a loss.

More than with any previous project, we had to adjust our plans; a great many of our presuppositions turned out to be untrue or impossible to realize. Reality turned out to be even harder to handle than we had expected or feared. We also had to question our own laws and rules more than we cared to; so, for example, we could demand that no drugs were to be used during rehearsals, but that demand simply couldn't be enforced. We could demand that everyone had to present at 16.00 hours but some came around dinner time (18.00 hours) or around the time of the performance (20.00 hours), and others simply didn't turn up; they remained absent for an evening or we never saw them again. In the re-evaluation of our rules and agreements, the expertise of the insiders at 't Vlot and Free Clinic turned out to be indispensable. They helped us to look at matters from a different angle, and carefully guarded the interests of the participants. On the other hand, there was a growing tension in those final weeks of rehearsals between the artistic (MartHa!tentatief) needs and the social concerns ('t Vlot and Free Clinic), a very logical and unsolvable tension, which, just as logically, disappeared a few days after opening night.

8. *Be Persistent, However, in Pursuing the Earlier Artistic Dream*
It was our intention to make a play that would make the strange, enchanting and sometimes horrifying world of the square come to life on stage. We did that by isolating the 'magic sentences' from all the stories we recorded (from the interminable interviews) — sentences that summarize someone's entire truth. These sentences were edited into a bigger and overarching story of the square.

It was our dream to make a play about the modern multicoloured city. We did that by recording stories from around the whole world, next to the tales of square residents — how homeless Antonio Gomez from Guinea-Bissau suffers from the cold here at night, how Shirley May Wong washed up here twenty-three years ago, how Sarah made a beeline from Kinshasa to here and how she now cleans offices at night, how a nameless Pakistani fell to his death one day while mounting a satellite dish on his roof.

It was our dream to let the square residents 'be' in the play and not get caught in the trap of 'acting'. We achieved this by letting professional actors tell the overarching story of the square (like a documentary), a story that was interspersed with the magic sentences of the interviewees and accompanied by a clever soundtrack, to enhance the emotions. We achieved our aim by giving the esteemed audience a head-set, so that the story would penetrate intensely. And, finally, we achieved it by asking square residents, whose trust we had managed to gain over the preceding months, to be present and very occasionally play small, almost symbolic, scenes.

It was our dream to stage the play in the place where all these stories are lived, day in, day out, next to each other, interacting for about an hour and twenty minutes and making visible the many-sided universe of the contemporary city. We achieved this by inviting the audience to the opening of an exhibition of all the graphic art and pictures made during the workshops. We achieved this by changing the vernissage area into an almost hyper-theatrical room, over the course of the exhibition, where the audience itself becomes part of represented reality. We made the square come to life by using sensory perceptions like 'live' drawings and by projecting a series of images of the square on the walls of the room.[4]

9. *Have an Extraordinary Amount of Luck at the Right Time*

Be so lucky as to ask the right question at the right time. Be so lucky as to read the right book at the right time. Be so lucky as to make the right choice at the right time during the rehearsal. And, above all, be so lucky as to be able to work with the right people. If anywhere in the past 5700 words it might appear that I single-handedly came up with the idea of *The Vernissage* and produced it single-handedly as well, then that is completely untrue. It was the combined forces of as many free-thinking people as possible, as it should be in oral theatre about untameable life at the beginning of the twenty-first century.

10. *Live in the Neighbourhood Forever...*

Live in the neighbourhood forever, keep track of your characters and their experiences in blog messages[5] and stay in touch to see whether the prediction with which *The Vernissage* ended comes true.

And so it goes, always on and on. New people will wash up, year after year. Riet will leave and lead a fifth life elsewhere. The bollards of the firm Vialis will continue to get the best of cars. Trams will continue to come and go, during the day and during the night. The trees will bud, the leaves will fall, there will be young families with delivery bicycles who will start saying: 'yes, but all this dirt on the left and the dirt on the right should be cleaned up', and they will mean the street litter and the slum on the corner and the toothless people in that slum. Slums will be demolished and replaced by six apartments and a 'ground floor shop on a unique location

---

4   And if all of this remains foggy and abstract, then please watch the five minute compilation video of the exhibition on our website www.marthatentatief.be, then it will hit you immediately!

5   www.marthablog.be; www.marthatentatief.be.

in the city'. Shirley May Wong will live to be a hundred years old. Three blonde children will grow up and leave their house on the square. The woman who is supposed to optimize the data flow of a company that will later be called Traxis will be grateful for the wonderful years she spent here. The new people will keep searching the sky with satellites and form incomprehensible islands here. The woman in the coat in the middle of the square will cautiously keep building bridges between all those islands, all those people, all those lives, thinking back with love upon the time when the square was still a square, still a square of small groups of people who now hope for a better life in new out-of-the-way places in the city.

The End. Applause.

Alakondre
A Journey to the Invisible

Alida Neslo

When you are born in Surinam — a country in which countless Euro-colonial machinations randomly threw together a great number of peoples from virtually all over the world, miraculously without causing war or apartheid, creating a unique language and a situation in which everybody knows the dos and don'ts of several cultures — you are perplexed by the problems people experience through living alongside the 'other' in the free, affluent societies of twenty-first century Europe.

This contemporary discomfort is expressed by two modern philosophers.

The first one is the Dutch professor, Ad Verbrugge, who pleads for community in his book, *Tijd van onbehagen*, attributing the crisis in his own country to a loss of culture, the loss of a social culture that gives direction to life. The Enlightenment put humankind at the centre of the universe but was not unambiguously benevolent (Which human being did they mean? The one from the North? From the South?…).

The second one is the Frankfurter Schule thinker, Jürgen Habermas, who, after spending half his life pleading the 'disenchantment' of society, now argues that it is foolish to maintain that religion will disappear on its own if you only suppress and fight it for long enough. Habermas also claims that the European inability to become a community of citizens is caused by miscommunication between Muslims, Christians, unbelievers and others.

In my opinion — coloured by growing up in the Caribbean, the most 'mixed' area in the world, and by my theatrical studies in Western Europe — both scientists miss a point that has been missed since the beginning of the extolled Enlightenment: if one recognizes and/or acknowledges the *authenticity* of a phenomenon, it is not difficult to put your own imagination to work in order to make the 'strange' familiar. Sranan, the lingua franca of Surinam, is comprised of twenty-two different languages and uses the expression 'alakondre' (literally alla = *all*, kondre = *country*), which is difficult to translate but means something like 'the search for the other, for whatever differs from your own opinions, your own looks, your own vision of reality'.

In my area of expertise, the theatre, I have noticed that, despite obvious changes in society such as the composition of the population, European art schools generally think of their own 'standard' as the right one. Acknowledgement of authenticity, of 'the alien', is nowhere to be found. They still only teach a single art history; they always refer to the 'Enlightened Human' without noticing the shadowy side of the Enlightenment, and the fear of the unknown, caused by ignorance, is always, none too subtly present in intellectuals who should know better.

As a young student 'from afar', I therefore consciously went looking for ways to 'enlighten' the ignorance between various peoples; the idea of becoming a bridge-builder, or ferryman, was born; the search for amazement, for the other —which would take years longer than I had anticipated — had begun.

In and Out of the Comfort Zone

In the Flanders of the 1970s, I met the theatre pioneer, Tone Brulin. He preferred not to work with actors or actresses but with 'players' who were willing to go 'beyond applause', who didn't merely want to play a part, desiring instead to become familiar with an image — of any culture — in a unique, personal way, as a matter of life and death. His method was aptly expressed during our first rehearsal day. Tone drove up in his mobile home (!) and ordered us, a group of very young professional players, to get in. Without any explanation, he drove to the Antwerp Rubbish Dump and said, 'Take a good look around because what you see is yourself; actors are disposable products'. To drive his point home, he recommended that we take a piece of rubbish home, which we did, somewhat embarrassed.

Rehearsals started and Tone never mentioned the event until a week before the opening night. He asked us to bring the piece of rubbish we had taken home with us to the next rehearsal. Eventually, he integrated the various objects into the performance because 'dirt has poetry too'.

It wasn't until much later that I realized that this was an un-precedented lesson in humility vis à vis one's own knowledge, and a warning against snap judgements, or distaste, when confronted with unfamiliar material. Tone's vision about travelling with a theatre group (called 'TIE 3' — a company I would stay with for years) as a way of training through observation and improvisation, change of space and rhythm, also seemed to be his way of giving form to the credo of his teacher, the Flemish thinker/writer, Herman Teirlinck, in a personal manner: 'I am for a stage that claims the whole person and does not scorn a single (!) one of the human ways of expression.' I think that, in the Europe of the 1950s, 1960s and early 1970s, Tone Brulin was the director who came closest to breathing life into this vision.

The continuous change of space and rhythm inherent in this

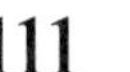

way of working started me thinking about words that are easily used in Europe in relation to immigrants and players from developing countries (the modern-day marginals) — words that many migrant artists have subconsciously adopted, by the way: origin, roots, (feeling at) home, trust, identity, authenticity and, last but not least, the hated word *quality*. These words set the tone in each interview, each review. That last word, in particular, makes me react in the same way as the South African poet, Breyten Breytenbach, who says that, as soon as he hears the quasi-innocently uttered words 'beauty' or 'culture' or 'quality' from the mouth of a Western European, he starts growling and barking like an angry dog. Breytenbach wants to express his displeasure about the way the 'Northerners' asked questions of the 'Southerners'. Echoing Breytenbach's questioning of these terms, Habermas notes that there is good reason to do so, as tolerance is often seen as synonymous with respect when, in fact, this is a misconception as, in European history, tolerance has usually been accompanied by lack of respect — minorities are despised, but tolerated.

I didn't exactly feel 'discriminated' against in light of the use of such words, but I thought about it in a more general, human sense, in terms of 'letting go and starting over again' (with the open-mindedness of a child). What effect would tolerance and respect have if structurally applied to the curriculum of an art school? When I was the artistic leader of the Dutch theatre group/preliminary training called 'DNA/Its DNA' — originally intended to prepare aspiring actors with a migrant background to attend regular theatre schools — these thoughts led me to establish 'DNA (lab)'. This was set up with the express purpose of seeing what effect a change in the curriculum could bring about for all of us, not merely for migrants. One of my guiding principles was a statement by the American critic, Neil Postman. In his book, *The End of Education*, he says that we will have to show the courage to take another critical look at the composition of the curriculum of our schools, which still conform to the distorted paradigm of Enlightenment thinking, based on a form of exclusion that is no longer tenable in a time that confronts us with an increasing number of people with multiple identities. The art that young people produce nowadays is becoming increasingly hybrid, multidisciplinary and intercultural; it is art that transcends the monoculture, art that throws off the slavery of unambiguous identity. Schools all too often ignore the fact that young people carry with them not only a national but also an international heritage and feel a pluralistic solidarity with events far beyond their native soil. An important source of inspiration for the coming generations is mobility, not merely in the physical sense (already noticeable in the rising choice of exotic destinations) but also in a more spiritual sense, perhaps suggesting a movement from identity to affinity.

Within the DNA (lab), I opted for a curriculum that contained the kinetic elements of several grand old cultures (India, Java, West Africa), elements within knowledge-transfer systems that were carelessly shoved aside by the early colonizers in favour of their own mechanisms. Such a curriculum became the point of entry for learning about multiple art histories, instead of a single one, and for forcing the students out of their comfort zone, sometimes gently, sometimes roughly.

Movement is a far more efficient way of getting in touch with an unknown aspect of the arts spectrum than discussion. Art is, first and foremost, a matter of taking action without wondering too much where you will end up, especially if, as in the theatre, there is a certain amount of transformation involved. I asked the (Dutch) students to record their inner reactions to the curriculum every few months and I let myself be partly guided by their remarks, over the months and years.

The following quotations give an impression of how the students evolved over their first year in the programme:

'After the first week I can say that the lessons in Java, Indian and African dance have made the deepest impression. The kinetic language of these kinds of dance is completely new to me, as opposed to the other lessons where I always recognize something, regardless of whether I can perform the movements or not'.

'I compare Indian dance with a jumping jack where the arms and legs are connected with strings to a long pull. If you pull the strings, the muscles of the arms and legs are pulled towards the spine. This is an absolutely new experience for my body. African dance is very open. You show your breast(s), your arm pits, your buttocks and spread your arms wide open. I conclude that my body language is much more closed (arms across each other, legs crossed). Java dance focuses strongly on the centre (the bellybutton). It feels as if a thread goes right through my bellybutton and that I can only walk backwards or forwards. Every swaying motion moving away from the centre eventually returns to the bellybutton very tightly. Next to that, we are really being trained to apply everything we learn in a lesson and to repeat it; to apply the information we absorb and recount it. In that sense DNA (lab) trains you from the start to adapt an attitude towards life that is both active and positive.'

'I notice that I feel very good under the physical training which is giving shape to my thoughts.'

'I have come to experience my body as a diary during the lessons with DNA (lab). I am still surprised by its strength. Before this, I mistrusted the physical and kept wanting to engage my head, as if my body didn't have a wisdom of its own [...].'

'Through the different forms of kinetic training I have discovered that, as an artist, the question 'What's next?' is far more useful than the question 'Why?' because the first one forces you to take action.'

'You can try to be as intercultural as you like but that doesn't mean that you are actually capable of it. You have to be prepared to set aside a few of your own feelings, to make room for new concepts, as if a new alphabet is created out of many alphabets.'

The female student that went through this inner development later went on tour to Surinam with the DNA theatre group, where she designed sets and costumes for a performance which dealt, amongst other things, with the issue of slavery. Her work touched the hearts of many, despite opting for a very austere design that seemed almost Japanese which was hardly common in the Caribbean, especially not in cases involving such a historically sensitive subject. Through her earlier learning experience, she had come to understand the intrinsic value of working in a different context, the discovery of the unknown and the non-conformity to the familiar so that the respectful integration of her own standard into the standard of another was possible without worrying about whether it would be understood by the supporters and/or the alien audience. And the audience — both alien and familiar — accepted and 'recognized' her style completely.

Over the years, it became clear to the DNA (lab) that it was possible to go beyond cultural diversity (and other terms) in search of a grammar, a new language of expression, created from multiform interpretations, identities and standards. Eventually, it would be possible to discover a 'confused' space; somewhere in an unknown location where everybody would discover a part of themselves, where everybody would feel like (s)he belonged. Analogous to the example of Sranan, this grammar would have to come about gradually, absolutely organically, without the tricks and manoeuvres used in Europe with the miserably failed experiment of Esperanto.

From Identity to Affinity

DasArts is the multi-disciplinary secondary level training and re-search centre for theatre and dance in Amsterdam's Hogeschool voor de Kunsten, a school with a flexible curriculum that is deeply influenced by the ideas of both native and foreign mentors. When I was put in charge, I was able to go a little further because I was dealing with an international group of students that had already worked professionally for several years and was looking forward to broadening and/or deepening their vision. It was customary to move DasArts into a different context (Belgium, Germany) every four years. I felt kinship with the training immediately although the contexts chosen were still too close to the comfort zone of the students, who were mostly 'Western' orientated.

In order to address this, I put together a programme with Germaine Acogny, the Senegalese choreographer/dancer/pioneer of modern African dance, for the school she founded, L'Ecole des Sables, which is based on the principles of pre-colonial and modern West Africa, located in Toubab Dialaw, Senegal, the land of one of the architects of the 'Négritude', the now-deceased president/poet Léopold Sédar Senghor.

Acogny calls her school 'Le Bois Sacré du 21e Siècle', referring to the mixture of transferral methods from the African past (for example, working in and with nature, supervised by a mentor) with the ideas of contemporary visiting lecturers from Africa, the African diaspora and the rest of the world.

Fragments from the report of a German student show how a profound change can occur, at an artistic and personal level, if one follows such an unfamiliar programme in completely alien surroundings.

First week

'In spring 2003, DasArts and L'Ecole des Sables, a centre for contemporary African dance […], ventured into a collaboration that, in a lot of ways, was the wet dream of any interculturally-minded arts official: twelve DasArts students, from eight different countries of the Northern Hemisphere, lived and worked with twelve students of L'Ecole des Sables; for two and a half months, they shared the same bedrooms, meals, dance spaces and media tools with young dancers/ choreographers from all over the African continent. The humanists' credo of the arts as the vehicle to bring humanity together was an ever present cliché, and I cringed slightly every time it would yet again be solemnly exclaimed by another visiting lecturer or visiting funding officer. My trouble with that cliché was in a strange way the same as my initial trouble with African rituals. I was concerned about the suggestive and 'fake' component in both the naïve multicultural dream-speak ('we are all the same') as well as in the joyful African ritual practice. Ritual, in my mind, needed a certain amount of sincerity and mysticism, not people making jokes all the way through, making me feel as if I am part of some birthday party… What could I take as authentic? What was simply fake? Does it amount to anything to exclaim that we are one big family of human beings or should we look into it much more critically before exclaiming anything? These things governed my thoughts […]

Just after the two and a half months' stay

What did Africa do to me?… This is such a difficult thing to say for me. I find it difficult, because it sounds so intimate when I write it down. […] I feel I should write something more analytic, or more artistic … whatever that's supposed to mean […]

I do not know when a change in my body and feelings made me understand something consciously and when conscious understanding caused a change in my body. It feels too mixed up, it feels as if trying to analyse it might not even be of any importance […]

The key moments, however, lay where my struggle between Western thinking and African being was the most prevalent; in the rituals, in the dancing, and in my working relationships with the other participants.

I discovered ambiguity, found out that something can be several things at the same time, that this actually is the way every living thing, every lived relationship functions. Dancing the Sabar (a West African dance style) is about showing off and about giving yourself away at the same time. Being part of a ritual is both socializing and worshipping, can be educating and joking at the very same moment. Working on contact and relationship is working on a piece of performance and vice versa […]

I do feel a lot less clever now than I felt before Africa. And although I feel that cleverness is not what is going to help me anymore if I want to keep growing, it feels rather uncomfortable […].'

About one year later

'More than a year later, I am preparing a performance project together with two fellow artists from DasArts, the postgraduate institute of the Theatre school in Amsterdam. They are a writer from the former

Yugoslavia and a visual artist from Brazil and I am a German with a theatrical background. Also in this context, the statement "we are all the same, everybody is different" is not helping us a lot. We come from different disciplines and more than once I felt that there was no way that we would ever be able to convey to each other directly what our respective disciplines are about. But we have been in Africa together and somehow, through the prism of that shared experience, we found each other and started working together.

Quite naturally, our work began to focus around crossing borders and building relationships between people, disciplines, countries and realities.

And if I want to talk about my theatre now, I have to start in Africa…'

The personal report of the second student clearly demonstrates that there has been almost a 'rebirth' as a person and as an artist. This becomes especially apparent if you know that this student asked me a week before we left for Senegal if 'we would meet people of our own level'. One can only have the deepest respect for the way he opened himself up, in all insecurity, enabling him to eventually take a different path, from identity to affinity.

In general, I could conclude, after quite a number of years, that working in different contexts triggers a variety of approaches and interpretations that keep the process unfinished, always *in transit* as it were, a handy method, especially in the case of young people, to stimulate them to life-long learning (including from and about 'others'). The remarkable thing, particularly with the internet-orientated 'zapper' generation, is that, in the end, the *in transit* room, or mental space, becomes more important than the 'conventional' room, even if the student's first response to this kind of pluralistic school programme is recalcitrant, especially if they have to step far outside their comfort zone. After a while, resistance disappears and (deep) personal changes gradually occur. Very often, a new work/life attitude surfaces, prejudices wither and people show themselves to be continually interested in crossing boundaries, remaining in transit and understanding this condition intrinsically. This attitude is best described by the Surinam term 'alakondre'.

North South

My recent return to Surinam was inspired by, amongst other things, the urge to give something back to the original source of inspiration.

It was also an attempt to escape *le théâtre du trop*, in the sense of 'trop loin de la source primordiale', the theatre of excess, which often confronted me in Europe and America. Habermas would perhaps use the term 'theatre of disenchantment'. After all these years, I once again felt the need for almost naive astonishment, open-mindedness, eagerness and surrender to the sacral (not in any ecclesiastical manner): man has always sought something beyond his pain, anxiety and sorrow. Something we might call sacred. Something that is nameless, beyond alleged quality and time — magic, perhaps.

From that desire, I became involved in something completely different — a cooperation project with the Ministry of Justice and Police in Surinam, which included setting up a teaching programme beyond the comfort zone of the students, and, for the first time, my own. The students in this case were minors between thirteen and eighteen years of age from underprivileged backgrounds who had ended up in prison through a faux pas and attended school in prison too. Rehabilitation through art? Most of them had never even heard of art and, at first, there were a lot of misunderstandings. Due to lack of proper schooling and abominable facilities, it was not possible to have a decent *basic* conversation with — highly suspicious, since abandoned — children who, besides being trapped behind bars, were also trapped in their inability to verbalize their teenage dreams. On top of that, some of them lived among adult criminals, which is completely against the International Rights of the Child. To find out what their dreams were, we had to start with what was present, in other words, with nothing at all. That took a little getting used to for someone who came from the world of the 'anything goes' DasArts school. In this place, everything — the necessary money, materials, location, staff — was *in transit*, in the most extreme sense of the term and, for the first time, all our actions were supervised. There was none of the freedom so characteristic of the arts. Added to this, the process started with literature, a heavy obstacle for semi-literates. The comfort zone concept took on a completely different dimension since the students were completely out of sorts in the place.

So, for the first time, it became necessary to reverse the process; we had to create an arts programme that had to *act* as comfort zone and lure the students (or pupils, as they are called in prison) into it, rather than chasing them out of it. Quite literally, the art of 'seduction'! The only advantage I had was that I didn't have to explain the concept of *Alakondre*. I dragged every foreign colleague that visited Surinam to the prison and made them give a workshop or performance.

This led to astonishing jam sessions, for example an improvisation on the music of Bach, between the wind section of the Amsterdam Conservatorium and the boys and girls, using instruments made from washing buckets connected with pieces of bicycle tyre. Despite, or perhaps because of, their harsh life experiences, the students demonstrated a remarkable capacity for improvisation which did not go unnoticed by several (elite) guests. This eventually resulted in a benefit action, which secured us a complete set of (electronic) instruments for the students. Four bands were formed that sometimes came to blows, so fierce was the competition and earnestness with which they gave themselves to the music.

This outcome was less than fun because the authorities forbade the students from making music, which had a counter-productive effect. They didn't really realize that the fighting wasn't about food or some object but, however clumsily worded by the pupils, about mental space. They knew of no other way to defend their artistic standpoints than to fight physically rather than verbally. In this case, essential elements of the Enlightenment were helpful instead of being a hindrance.

When the music-making was re-instated, slowly, they discovered a new space in the four disciplines of stage, music, dance and writing. On a smaller scale, it was the same space Nelson Mandela spoke about after his imprisonment. When, in the confines of a cell, all the rigmarole of a (hostile) world fell away and he focused exclusively on his own inner, creative thoughts, he noticed that, after a while, the inner space continued to grow, that there was even room for 'the enemy', that one changed his sometimes deeply rooted beliefs that involved mistrusting others; Mandela called it 'true' freedom. The psychologist who occasionally visited the youngsters told me that the children regarded those hours with the visiting lecturers as 'hours of freedom' in which they could express themselves in a way that wasn't possible anywhere else within the prison walls. Even the 'literary' field had created such a suitable outlet for some, meaning that the pile of notebooks containing stories with personal touches continued to grow. The personal talks between teachers and students went much better as well: the masks came off and some surprised us by revealing themselves as quadrilingual virtuosi during vocal improvisations. In contrast to the 'outside' world, audio media played a greater part than visual media. It became clear that the students increasingly wanted to go public — they had something to say to 'the enemy'. After a considerable effort I succeeded, to my own surprise, in finding them a stage.

Early one evening, forty-three prisoners, together with twenty-five guards, stood on the stage — many of them for the first time — of the theatre in the city centre, in the presence of the president's wife, the president of the Criminal Court, parents and many others, and performed a moving spectacle in the form of 'fierce' music, spoken word performances, dance and an exhibition of the results of their cooperation with a painter and a graphic artist. At the same time a (mini) CD and an artful booklet containing 'private' work was launched. The astonishing and moving surrender with which these students went public with their creations was incomparable to previous experiences with (professional) students undertaken in much more favourable circumstances. These students were — consciously and willingly — prepared to be themselves in front of 'the enemy' who had ordered their imprisonment. A comfort zone was conquered and, for once, not abandoned.

A day later, back in prison, I was silently offered a hand by one of the most 'impossible' rascals. That had never happened before. Touching, particularly with 'outsiders', was taboo for these children. They looked me straight in the eye with a look I will not soon forget. Even 'the enemy' (the Public Prosecutor) took a remarkable step; the students were allowed — as a test at first — to go home for the summer holiday. Ordinarily, there was a certain 'void' during this period due to the lack of school and/or family visits, which made excessively aggressive behaviour a regular occurrence, with all its (possibly fatal) consequences.

The Need for Alakondra People

Is art a means of getting rusty social processes moving again in a supple and contemporary manner? At first sight, not really. But, while moving from the comfort zone to the new context, you can meet or bring about remarkable things due to astonishment, almost in a religious sense, I would add, knowing I am embarking on a slippery slope here. I mean religious in the etymological sense of 're' — 'ligare': to reconnect. A bridge can be built, a ferry service can spring up between previously unfamiliar banks, to create new possibilities. It is not the 'holy place' that brings about the miracles, but the 'journey' towards it. Or, in the less spiritual words of the 'disenchanted' Habermas, 'For a democratic, pluralistic society you need more (than tolerance). In their daily life, citizens have to make an effort to understand each other's arguments. For that, they need to learn each other's vocabulary'.

Compare this sentence by the then seventy-eight-year-old philosopher to the concluding argument of the young DNA student cited earlier: 'You don't have to feel admiration for the religion or political point of view of another person, not even appreciation; only understanding is necessary to get down to business. That is simply the only way to go in a free society where EVERYONE has equal rights'. These might have been the words of an Alakondre human.

The Advantage of Elephants

Building a Community of Artists One Trunk at a Time

Lionel Popkin

My recent choreographic work, *There is an Elephant in this Dance*, is an evening-length quartet, set around a comically overlarge, plush elephant costume, worn in pieces or as a whole.[1] Within these pages, I will do my best to avoid discussing the artistic dimensions of the work, and instead focus on two elements that have more to do with its practical development. When choreographing this piece, I developed a model for touring that specifically addressed the problem of how my work can, firstly, have a meaningful dialogue with artistic communities in a number of different cities and, secondly, still be desirable and affordable to presenters.

The dance is built around a series of solos that I perform. The other three performers come in and out of the piece with solos and duets that offset and guide the narrative, resulting in a sectional and episodic structure. Parts of the elephant are always evident on the stage through the presence of the afore-mentioned costume. From a compositional standpoint, this serves as a core image for the dance, helping to link its various parts. In a more personal way and in one of the main premises of the work, it also signifies how a simple visual object can be used to reveal a multiplicity of meanings and interpretations.

In 2007, when I first started work on *Elephant…*, I had recently relocated to take up a full-time university teaching job at the University of California, Los Angeles (UCLA), and I was determining how to continue my creative life from my new geographical position. I wanted to make a work that furthered my connection to other dance-makers. I suspected that there was a community of people making work scattered across the United States, who did not have many chances to interact. We only saw each other at conferences, and, for the most part, those scenarios are designed for us to be able to chat to presenters, rather than to each other. There were also a lot of people across the States, in many different cities, with whom I wanted to reconnect. We had known each other in the past, and I missed them. I sensed that a trans-geographical arts community was being developed, made up of dance-makers, in different cities, with overlapping interests that could be cultivated and encouraged.

My new location and employment had put me in a relatively isolated place, so I sought ways to both build and access a national community of dance artists. I thought it was important to engage in a conversation about work being made throughout the country in a way that differed from just seeing the work that toured through the venues in my city or that was shown at conferences and festivals. I also wanted my work to tour more.

When starting the project, I had to contend with the fact that my dancers and other collaborators lived all over the States. The first step in working with this dilemma was to build the choreographic structure around my solos. Having these as the backbone of the work gave me confidence in the work's realization, even as I tried to negotiate schedules and rehearsal time with my out-of-town collaborators. This served two important purposes. Firstly, during the early phase of the work, it allowed for short bursts of rehearsals with the rest of the cast in whichever city we could gather, which is not unusual. Secondly, it created a sectional piece, so that the substitution of one cast member or another was a built-in possibility during its touring phase. Having a flexible touring model as part of the design and intent of the project was essential to my goal of identifying and fostering a trans-geographical community.

In its final form, *Elephant…* is an intimate piece housed within a modular structure. As the piece tours, the presenter and I identify one, two or three local performers to replace the original cast members.[2] I travel to the city in advance and meet dancers, attend performances, rehearse with the artists selected to perform. We share a process, get to know each other better; I learn about another city's dance scene, share information about where I live, and the artistic divide across cities shrinks. In a normal touring situation, this is not possible because everyone is too busy. In this scenario, there is a connection between people who would normally see each other only briefly. Also, the presenter gains in two ways. The touring fees go down because of reduced travel and housing costs and per diems, and the audience draw increases through the hybrid structure of local and touring artists performing together.

At this point, it is important to provide some background, to give a sense of why these particular ideas developed and go some way towards explaining why they are included in this volume. I entered the arts as a professional in the early 1990s when the term 'arts in the community' was prevalent. In the United States the NEA crisis of the

---

1 Thanks to George Lugg from REDCAT in Los Angeles for the bulk of this sentence describing the piece.
2 The original cast for Elephant... was Carolyn Hall, Ishmael Houston-Jones, Peggy Piacenza and Lionel Popkin. To date, other performers have been Mary Buckley, Adrianne Fang, Mark Haim and Morgan Thorson. There have been performances in Los Angeles, Minneapolis, New York, San Marcos, Seattle and Washington, DC.

early 1990s was in full swing and federal funds for individual visual and performing artists had dried up.[3] The National Endowment for the Arts (NEA) is the main federal agency for granting arts funding from the government. Grant application forms had started asking, and continue to ask, about the community outreach and impact of a project. More and more artists were partnering with community centres, homeless shelters and prisons in order to undertake residencies.

At the same time, the arts funding boom of the 1980s was evaporating, and dance companies started using local performers as they toured. The roles given to local artists tended to be simple in design and frequently used as a way to fill out a scene, to have more people on stage and create a mass group statement with greater impact than the average mid-size company could accomplish on their own.

These two working processes are still very much a part of the dance landscape, and this essay offers an alternative to these versions of an artist interacting with a community. It looks at the assumptions behind the concept of an artist serving a community other than their own, and it turns the question around to ask: what if the community in need was the arts community? Additionally, it asks how a touring project can interact with the local artistic community, and how that, in turn, fosters a sense of a trans-geographical community of artists.

Since everyone in the cast of *Elephant…* has a significant role, when a new person joins the cast, it differs from the more common model of the company that tours and utilizes community members to fill out the cast and provide a background chorus. This difference in the interactions at the core of the community involvement model means that every new cast member feels more invested in the dance's run in their city. Instead of being a complete overhaul of the touring model, this is an alteration in how it operates and how it puts local and touring artists into a stronger conversation with each other. Though less people are involved than in the earlier model, more is asked of those who do participate.

A legitimate question to ask at this point would be: how many of these changes are part of the normal vagaries of casting and touring, and how many are unique to this project and therefore represent a new model for touring? Or, put another way, why is this any different from a normal tour in which you have to occasionally recast for a number of reasons? I think it is a question of mindset, of willingness and desire to make the dance shift, and of building it in such a way to make room for that shift. In some ways, the results are similar — a new person dances the role — however, what is different about this approach is that the piece is actually designed and marketed to encourage that change as a way of becoming part, even briefly, of the local performing community in the cities where *Elephant…* is performed.

This process has both pros and cons. There is a flexibility that I gain, but a consistency that I lose by employing this casting carousel. Each new cast changes the work. We all bring specific meanings and reverberations, both known and unintentional, to a role. Some changes maintain certain choices, and some dramatically shift them. When recasting is built into the ongoing process of the work's touring life, all of these possibilities must be reckoned with. What does it mean to significantly change one of the characteristics of a performer, such as their race, gender or age? Here are some examples of how this plays out. The role of the elephant was originally played by a forty year-old white woman, and, in a recent performance, a white woman in her sixties danced the role. Changes were made. One section in particular had a series of repetitious jumping. The woman in her sixties very sensibly said to me that she was not going to jump that much. So, our task was to find new ways of maintaining the purpose and energy of that section, while making it easier on her calves. What I did was to give it a more legible spatial pattern and to work with stops and starts in the action rather than using a persistent rhythm as the motor. This maintained inevitability and drive in the section, both of which were important elements. The initial reason for the shift in recasting was that I wanted to make the elephant role older and wiser, in order to see how that would impact on the overall piece. I was convinced that I would gain as much if not more than that which I was losing, and wanted to see the results.

Other recastings have raised very different issues. A role which included being a watcher, originally performed by a black man in his late fifties in New York City, was danced by a white woman in her early forties in Washington, DC. As age, gender and ethnicity

3   In 1990, four artists (Karen Finley, John Fleck, Holly Hughes and Tim Miller – dubbed the NEA Four) had their individual NEA fellowships withheld due to the controversial content of their work. In the subsequent years, prominent government officials led a successful movement to severely cut the NEA's budget. Though they failed to completely dismantle the agency, individual fellowships for visual and performing artists were abolished. For an analysis of this time in US history, see Cynthia Carr, On Edge: Performance at the End of the Twentieth Century (Middletown, CT: Wesleyan University Press, 1993, rev. ed. 2008), Karen Finley, A Different Kind of Intimacy: The Collected Writings of Karen Finley (New York: Thunder's Mouth Press, 2000) and the useful summary of the legal battle by Julie Van Camp at http://www.csulb.edu/~jvancamp/doc4.html.

were redefined, many things changed in the meaning that was being conveyed. In this instance, there are two important shifts to note — one of power and one of history. Making the watcher younger and female in the Washington, DC cast deprived the role of the air of authority that the watcher in the New York cast originally possessed. In that cast, the man had an air of responding from both his own history and, particularly in the last moments, a sense of bemusement. With the younger performer in the watching role, these factors dissipated and the observation took on a more curious and usurping edge. There was also a sense that she might at some point replace the older woman playing the elephant, which had not been an issue when the watcher was older and of a different race and gender. Ethnicity and race realigns our perspective again, but plays out slightly differently in the piece, in part because of the dominant onstage presence of my own brown body.[4] As a result, with these two casts, in one instance we have the idea of a knowing and slightly amused observer, and in the other we get an eager watcher ready to pounce. The nature of the staring changes, but the idea of the monitor and onlooker is always there, and that is what was most important about that section within the arc of the entire dance.

To cite another example, in the three-minute opening section of the dance, I employ a different strategy. This is a funny, whimsical, slightly melancholy introductory dance by someone in a big elephant suit that fits most performers. While the specifics may change, as different people perform the work, its core ideas remain. It feels crass to admit, but when much of the force of a section is the result of an oversized elephant costume, recasting is far less complicated than in the previous examples.

The impact of recasting leads us to ask, then, how accommodations in the choreography change the dance, and we have partially answered this question already. The sections in *Elephant...* have very practical narrative purposes; it is, therefore, surprisingly easy to make the revisions necessary as personnel shifts occur. Individual moments and movements are not my objective, but rather the overall result of a section is what I must retain. As a result, I can shift the choreography according to the strengths and weaknesses of each new person as long as I make sure that the meaning of each section is maintained. In fact, I find this process to be enjoyable and informative; I learn more about how slight variations create shifts without changing the overall meaning of the work, which helps my own skills as a creator grow.

As a way to help me through this, I designed each of the roles to have very distinct skill sets. So, for example, one of the roles is made up entirely of structured improvisations; one is completely set; one is very tied to a known dance vocabulary; one is quite quirky and reliant on a theatrical sense of time. These different skills mean that, when I am recasting, I have a lot of options. At any one time for any particular role, I might be looking for a skilled and savvy improviser, a technically trained dancer with partnering skills, or a performer who has a comic's instinct. And, of course, there is the 'fifth' performer, the elephant itself, who packs into a trunk and always travels with me, a vital, though unpaid, member of the cast.

What I am doing with this project is different from the standard shifting of casts that occurs as dancers move on and a project continues. *Elephant…* seizes the opportunity to reconfigure the cast as a way of opening up artistic questions around how the work is read. If I am curious about what it would mean to the work if a particular role read as older than the others, then I can try it in one city without being wedded to the new meaning. I can shift how an audience makes connections between different roles in the dance and learn more about how those associations steer the dance's overall impact. In this model, recasting is an opportunity rather than an inconvenience.

I would now like to turn to a consideration of how this model fits in a book about community art. The typical template for community art is of an artist going into another community — we hope in a welcoming and welcomed manner — and making a difference. But I want to go backwards to an earlier stage in that process. My commitment to community with this project has less to do with where the artists are going, and more to do with where they are coming from. I am curious about how artists exchange ideas and build their own sense of community.

In most definitions of community art, the arts were being designed to go to a community that was categorized as underserved or underprivileged. Two of the admirable goals of the movement were to enrich lives and expand audiences. Yet, it has always struck me that there is a constituency of underpaid, under-insured and overlooked people in this matrix: artists. I kept asking myself,

---

4   I should say that the question of race in the piece extends beyond the exchange of roles. In particular, the presence of the elephant's over determined body incorporates a number of factors that are beyond the scope of this paper, including my own mixed race heritage, the figure of Ganesh and the ideal dancer's body.

'what about the community of artists — where is the outreach to them?'[5] Could projects be designed in such a way so as to foster and enrich the interaction between artists? Would there be a way to encourage an active discourse about work that allowed for deeper interactions than were usually available as projects travelled from city to city? *Elephant...* is a step in that direction; it has created a space that gives artists in different cities a reason to engage in a creative process together. Without the function of a specific performance, few US presenters would give over the resources of their theatres to such an interaction. In some sense, the piece serves as an excuse to bridge the geographical divide between myself and choreographers and performers in other cities.

This may be a problem singular to the United States to some extent;[6] the distances involved make it much harder to connect across cities than in European countries where proximity operates on a smaller scale. In the States, I have moved around a lot and have lived in Los Angeles, New York, Philadelphia, Seattle and Washington, DC. All of those cities have committed and diverse performance scenes, but there are very few opportunities for a shared conversation. I have friends in many cities but, if a friend of mine in Seattle has a show, it requires a plane ticket and an overnight stay to see it. Though time and funding are two major factors limiting conversation, the actual nature of interactions must also be looked at. Real dialogue happens when an active investigation is undergone. Putting people in a room with a creative endeavour forces them to interact and relate to each other. *Elephant...* does this as it tours, and, as a result, it expands how choreographers and dancers in different cities converse about their work.

In the US, geographic isolation is compounded by the migration of active choreographers to university teaching positions, and their colleges and universities may not necessarily be in large cities, which only increases the gap. This trend, of which I am a part, has been building for years, but it is more prevalent than ever before. From a funding standpoint, the serious depletion of government arts fellowships means that a university teaching position is one of the only contexts in which a choreographer can receive sustained support to make their work.[7] As US artists look for ways to sustain themselves, whether in different cities or in and out of the academy, it makes it even more important to find ways to create situations for choreographers and dancers to cross-pollinate in innovative and evolving ways.

As a result of the distances involved, it becomes important for me to draw on a less commonly used definition of community, which is not about locality but about shared interests. We often think of a community as constituted by geographic proximity. There are many current thoughts about how the internet and globalization are expanding that concept, some of which applies here but much of which does not. Most of the time, live performance still requires people to be in the same room as each other; travel is needed.

Another concern for me, in terms of defining 'community' within my field, centres on the role of the dancer. Compared to choreographers, dancers are less important in grant applications and in a project's life. Their invisibility throughout the process disturbs me. As I set about determining the structure of *Elephant…*, I realized that I needed to make sure that the ways in which the roles were taught off and the people to whom they were taught mattered. This may seem an odd point to make when the entire structure of this model is contingent on each role and each performer being replaceable. Still, the flexibility of the choreography takes account of each new performer. Space is consciously left for each new cast member to make the role their own. This is achieved partly through my approach to rehearsals, and partly, when casting in each new city, through looking for mature and capable performers who will bring their own skills and perspectives to the performance. As a result, this process represents a shifting idea of repertory. When a role is recast, the goal is not the reproduction of the outer form or shape of the role. Instead, a more fluid approach to reproducing an effect is summoned.

So how does an individual artist negotiate this territory? Admittedly, there are dubious aspects to my model. I am in charge. It is always me and my choreography that travel. People in the cast have to fit the needs of the work, so the process can only go in certain directions. I have mitigated these needs, to some extent, by creating a malleable structure, and by paying close attention to how the roles

5   The formation of this idea owes a great deal to the choreographer Stephanie Skura, for whom I worked in a number of capacities from 1990 to 1996. Her reframing of the definition of outreach, particularly through her 'Movement for Intellectuals' workshops, also pushed me to reconsider the concept of outreach.
6   Thanks to Marc van Loon from the Fontys Dance Academy for initiating this thought.
7   One of the oddities of my job is that I am employed by the state of California. My salary at UCLA is a form of government support for the arts and is, to the best of my knowledge, the only form of sustainable individual funding for an artist that the US government provides. A different paper could look at this trend in isolation and discuss its impact on the ways in which US artists are making work.

are recast and then reconstituting them around the skills of each new performer. During a particular performance, the characters you see on stage are distinguishable and not at all confused with each other. Anonymity is not an option. Still, the limitations are there.

Additionally, *Elephant…* is not about large groups of people. The cast is small, and never replaced in its totality. Contributing to its intimate scale, the venues chosen for the project are dance and performing arts venues, and the target audiences tend to be interested in artistic experimentation. The scope here is not one of massive social groups; instead, the project focuses on having a large impact for a handful of people. Beyond that, my goal in developing this community is a self interested one. I am looking for like-minded people beyond my immediate geographical region with whom I can connect. In that sense it is an unavoidably self-serving model.

On these pages, I have analyzed *Elephant…* from a social and economic vantage point. It is, however, important to remember that there are aesthetic and artistic needs that underpin the project, and what has been discussed here must further those artistic goals. By way of conclusion, I want to ask whether this model brought out different artistic choices. Did it change the work? The simple answer is yes. It is a more efficient work than I have made in the past. It forced me to be extremely clear about the purpose of each section, so that I knew what I could lose and what I had to hold onto when each new person took on a role; each new cast teaches me more about these parameters. It also pushed me to be very clear about what my solos were accomplishing. My own sense of embarrassment would have prevented me from making a work so contingent on my own dancing, but necessity trumped modesty and, because so much of the work focuses on me, I had to be absolutely certain why each solo was in the piece.

Finally, it is worth asking whether this is a viable structure that others might utilize. Artistically, it has allowed me to find a way of touring a work that keeps it growing. I can ask new questions of the piece and shift the ways in which particular roles influence the whole. This has been immensely refreshing. Even this article is a result of the modular structure, which lends itself to a variety of purposes. It does need to be acknowledged, though, that the dance's variability is just an outline within which the real piece lives and moves. For the work to transmit, the aesthetic content must connect. The very premise of this article would be irrelevant if the work itself was not of interest. But, in some ways, that is what makes looking at the model in isolation useful. Other works, with other enquiries, can incorporate parts of *Elephant…* that suit their own needs and desires. It is by no means a perfect model, but its ability to contain the actual content of the piece and facilitate more practical desires was intentional. One of the things that made it work for me was that it was designed for and around this particular piece. What has made it a valuable and pleasurable way of working is its head-on approach to the constraints that aesthetic, economic, geographic, social and personal desires place on the process of making and touring a dance.

This paper originated as a talk at the 2nd Annual Guongdong Modern Dance Festival Symposium in July 2010 in Gunangzhou, China. The topic of the Symposium was 'The Future of Contemporary Dance − Connecting Artistic Exploration and the Market Needs'. This paper was written in response to that premise and then revised for this collection.

Portrait of the Activist-Artist as an Ageing Artist-Activist

Ricky Seabra

Where I live in Copacabana, Rio de Janeiro, there is a stretch of sand in front of the Copacabana Palace Hotel where non-governmental organizations (NGOs) often stage protests. Protesters usually set up the installations at night. And, with the break of dawn, beach-goers and commuters might come across 1,000 black balloons, symbolizing some significant statistic having to do with street kids or 500 crosses, symbolizing some statistic to do with trees, or 300 blind-folded baby dolls, symbolizing some other cause. The installations are usually sequential in nature; the same elements are repeated in a grid-like fashion across the sand. It is clear that activism is appropriating an artistic style that has been in vogue since Ann Hamilton introduced repetitive elements on a monumental scale in the 1980s.

These images always make headline news, be it on covers of newspapers, reports on prime time news or images from traffic helicopters. This type of installation, or performative activism, seeks the media. And often the media falls for this kind of action just because it produces somewhat interesting images — artistic images. Activism has become not only about desired results but also about the amount of media coverage it can get.

While writing this piece, one more installation has gone up on Copacabana beach. After the floods that occurred here in April 2010, a group wanted to call attention to the plight of the poor living in the *favelas*. A *favela*-style hut was put up, with fake sewage pouring from it into a hole in the sand where there was a plastic rat. It made the news. *Favela* teenagers posed for photographs with gags over their mouths in a performance that didn't really go anywhere and didn't say much, beyond calling attention to itself. But did they provoke action? Did their actions seek results beyond appearing in the media? If you can answer yes to both these questions, such art can begin to have a voice rather than being a mere imitation of land art or installation art.

Observing these installations in the sand reminds me of my attempts to combine art with activism during various phases of my life. I will discuss three of these phases here.

Intactivism and Bad Art

In 1992, upon moving to New York for the second time, I became an anti-circumcision activist. I'm not talking about female genital mutilation; I'm talking about what doctors do to boys. For those of you who don't know, American males are circumcised as babies before leaving hospital. It is done without anaesthesia and parents are encouraged not to watch the procedure. It has nothing to do with religion. This unique American medical fetish began when doctors in the 1800s decided that masturbation was the root of all illness. They wrote books on health and encouraged readers to buy their cereals, which were meant to diminish sexual drive and keep adults and children from 'self-polluting' (masturbating). Masturbation was bad because it, allegedly, drained the body of its vital energies. Prominent among these authorities were Dr. Kellogg (of Kellogg Cereals), Dr. Graham (of Graham Crackers) and Dr. Granula (Kellogg stole his recipe and called it granola). Dr. Graham (of Graham Crackers) and Dr. Granula (Kellogg stole his recipe and called it granola). Anyway, it's a wacky issue, very widespread in the US and very taboo. Every two decades, since the 1890s, proponents of circumcision have been seeking justification to continue the practice. In the early 1900s, the rationale moved from the prevention of masturbation towards the promotion of hygiene. In the 1930s, it was done to prevent cervical cancer in women and, in the 1950s, it was thought to guard more generally against sexually transmitted diseases. Then came penile cancer, urinary tract infections and now proponents claim it prevents HIV infection.

All that said I became a prominent anti-circumcision activist. Most of the other activists lived in San Francisco but, when I, a New Yorker, joined, the movement started to take off. I thought the term 'anti-circumcision activist' was too convoluted and negative, so I coined the term *intactivist* (used in a headline about the movement on the cover of the *Wall Street Journal*, which made me quite proud). That might well be my most illustrious publication ever.

I worked very hard as an intactivist for five years. My friends and family were worried about me because I had abandoned my art. I treaded along calling, writing, meeting with parents, explaining the procedure which involves five brutal mutilations before they get to the actual circumcision (all without anaesthesia). I appeared on a few television programmes, but did mostly radio. Throughout this time, my fax machine and I in my little apartment on 93rd Street comprised the New York Chapter of the National Organization for Circumcision Information Resource Centers or NOCIRC. On the west coast, activists were very concerned about educating parents. I was interested in politics, in trying to change policy at the top. No one in the organization had really confronted the paediatricians and obstetricians directly. So I started to study the structure of the policy-makers; I mapped the committee structures of the American Academy of Pediatrics and the American College of Obstetrics and Gynecology. I called their offices, got names. I went to their conferences and I spoke at committee meetings. I met with the top brass, flirted with secretaries. (Secretaries are very important. Only they can forward your calls.) I was threatened by doctors and almost arrested.

After mapping the policy-makers' structures, I organized a massive letter-writing campaign and, in around three years, I succeeded in changing the policy of the American Academy of Pediatrics to 'we no longer recommend neo-natal circumcision'. The change in policy hit mainstream news and talk shows. Jay Leno and David Letterman made jokes about Hillary Clinton and how she was against the policy change… because she believed they should cut off more (Laughs from the audience) (these were the Monica Lewinsky days).

I then wrote a letter to the movement, wishing them well and saying that I needed to get back to being an artist. So I did. I moved to Europe, and was inspired and wanted to be an *artiste* wandering the streets of Amsterdam on my stolen bike bought for 20 guilders. Even though I was away from the US, the issue was still very fresh to me. I wanted to channel what I knew into something like a book or an art project. I made artworks, like a nappy with a plastic ring and a stain of blood in it, a reference to the little plastic ring around a baby's penis if the circumcision is performed with a Plastibell device which falls off a few days after the surgery; I hung a Circumstraint on the wall (the board to which babies are tied) with a huge uncut penis dildo stuck to it; I reproduced a baby's penis sticking out of a canvas with circumcision instruments attached to it. I made representations showing the amount of erogenous tissue removed from the penis. The only somewhat interesting work was a film in which I circumcised a Calla lily with all the proper medical instruments. But, in fact, these works were mere visualizations of the issues I had dealt with over the preceding five years. Even though I had used oil and acrylic paints, canvas, resin and mixed media, these works remained all issue and no art. I realized I had to retire the soldier in me. *(When you are an activist you are a soldier. You are willing to make sacrifices that the normal civilian wouldn't.)* So I laid down my weapons. I was relieved.

But, two years later, I met Dirk Verstockt of the Kunstencentrum Nona and told him about my *intactivism*. The Nona Theatre commissioned a piece from me for a Porn Art Festival, starring, amongst others, Annie Sprinkle. I started to write a monologue about circumcision. It was called *Weird Circumcision: A Masturbated Monologue.* The one thing that kept the piece grounded in the realm of art was the act of storytelling. I often find a song that sets the tone of my work; in this case, it was a song by Dinah Washington I had heard ten years earlier called *Big Long Sliding Thing*. The song is actually about a guy with a big uncut penis. The metaphor is that he is a trombone player who teaches Dinah how to play 'it' with a very explicit description of where to put the mouth, the finger and the thumb, 'Blow through here, Work my finger and my thumb, I slide right on, then I slide back again, then I get a lot of wind and slide it up again', she sings. (Observation: this song is NOT included on her complete works CD).

Weird Circumcision was very informative. I didn't mention my activist work in it, yet it is an oddly interesting work that makes a strong case against neo-natal circumcision. Just because it is about a cause doesn't necessarily make it activist. However, performing the piece as part of the normal theatre programme seemed odd to me. I only felt comfortable performing this piece in festivals with activist leanings. Maybe I hadn't really meshed art and activism yet. It would take another four years for me to gain enough distance to write an artistic text about the issue.

Art-in-Space Activism and the Isadora Module

There is a second chapter in my life during which I tried to convert activism into art. I have always been a science fiction aficionado, a futurist, having grown up in the futuristic city of Brasilia. I enjoyed designing space stations and lunar cities on the side. I continued being a space buff even during my intactivist years.

In 1999, after all the activism, I decided to pursue a childhood dream and become an astronaut. Being a US citizen as well as Brazilian, I wrote to NASA and requested an application; much to my dismay, the application contained a clause saying something to the effect that: *if you don't have a degree in physics, mathematics or engineering don't bother applying.* I was indignant. At NASA's application level, the arts and humanities were being discriminated against — I was denied access to space! Something must be done! This was clearly a job for Ricky the activist. The activist in me was easily rekindled and I applied to the Masters Programme at the Design Academy Eindhoven. Since there was no place for me as an artist in space, I realized that I must create a context for artists in space, so that I could go, of course. My thesis was to design an artist's residency module which would be carried into orbit in the Space Shuttle and attached to the International Space Station, a venue to which artist-astronauts could be sent to create works in zero gravity. I called it the Isadora Module after Isadora Duncan.

Two months into my Masters Programme, I came across a poster announcing a call for papers on 'Innovative Uses for the International Space Station' for a space conference. So I mailed in an abstract about the Isadora Module and, much to my surprise, a few months later I received a letter saying that my proposal had been accepted and they were inviting me to present my paper at the conference.

The conference was in Albuquerque, New Mexico. I paid my own ticket, stayed in a dive called the Star Dust Inn on Route 66 while everyone else stayed at the five-star Hyatt Regency. Once again, making sacrifices. I schmoozed with astronauts and lunched with people from various departments of NASA, Boeing, the European Space Agency and others. Once again, I was trying to understand the structures of these agencies and not waste my time talking to subordinates. I believed that art in space could be the next logical step in manned space exploration.

When my turn came to speak, I presented my design and all the concepts involved. Then came a special moment. I pulled out a sketchbook and placed it on the overhead projector and told the audience: 'In this book is a collection of the thoughts of artists I interviewed on what they would like to do in space. And I would like to share these thoughts with you scientists and engineers'. So I asked someone from Boeing to dim the lights and hit track 9 of a Nat King Cole CD. While *The Very Thought of You* played, I flipped through the book showing the phrases of artists I had pasted in the book, phrases like: 'I would take my piano'; 'I'd explore the human as a combination of chemicals vs. the magical being'; 'I'd take cigarettes, a chair, everyday objects'; 'At night I'd keep my door unlocked especially if they are Russians'. This brought a poetic and entertaining moment to an otherwise stiff scientific conference; the scientists and engineers were very appreciative and applauded this 'scene'. I became the art-in-space activist. As soon as I sat down after my presentation, a representative of the Japanese Space Agency and an astronaut who worked for Boeing simultaneously gave me their business cards. They wanted to talk (I later learned they just wanted to suck up ideas for their marketing departments).

While writing my thesis and designing my Isadora Module in Eindhoven, I attended space conferences in London, Toulouse, Amsterdam, Albuquerque, Los Angeles, Berlin and Paris, where I collected many business cards. I also collaborated with Daimler Chrysler Aerospace and the European Space Agency on art-related projects.

I eventually finished my thesis, with its design for the Isadora

Module. When I presented it, I performed the Nat King Cole scene, flipping through the artists' phrases again. I recall being enormously frustrated because this was the kind of quality I wanted to achieve for the entire project. But, at the time, the Design Research department at the academy was demanding a very hard science approach. They wanted an academic paper in which I collected qualitative data, analyzed it, discussed it, then concluded with design recommendations. And that's all I could do. For some reason, there was no room even within me for the artistic. A colleague of mine explained to me: 'Science and Art: It's two different coats that you gotta wear. Hang one up. Put on the other. That simple'.

Two years later, the Kunstencentrum Nona wanted another work of mine. I expressed my desire to make my thesis into a performance and it was accepted. I invited a long-time collaborator of mine, choreographer, Andrea Jabor, to work with me on the piece. And, after two residency periods in Belgium, we created a piece for theatre called *Isadora.Orb, The Final Metaphor.*

Isadora.Orb is a sort of lecture performance with live animation, story telling, music and dance. I perform images live and tell stories while Andrea mixes the soundtrack and dances. It's a pop-art space fable manifesto in which I feature elements from my thesis, like the first song written in space, the first poems written in space and the only sculpture to be placed on the moon's surface back in 1971. It is very informative, very visual and very moving.

Once again, the activism came first and served as a content supplier, a knowledge base for the artwork. This time, perhaps there was more of a mix between the two forms (activism and art) because Andrea and I enacted the results we hoped to see happening *within* the Isadora Module in orbit, effectively performing the poetic potential of space. I suggested that the Isadora Module should be coated inside with mother-of-pearl. We created a zero gravity dance scene with the help of a combination of cameras resulting in a live projection of Andrea floating and dancing in the air inside a mother-of-pearl shell in my hands. I wrote, 'something from the deepest depths for the highest heights'. This, to me, was the final metaphor.

I think the provocative, activist element to this performance came about because we communicated the concept of art in space as something extremely simple and logical, suggesting that this supposedly outrageous idea isn't that outrageous after all.

Brasilia

The third and final chapter I would like to discuss in terms of my activism and art, is a project I was working on for the fifty-year celebrations of the city of Brasilia, where I grew up. But, in October of 2009, the governor of Brasilia was arrested in a corruption scandal, so I wasn't about to continue seeking state funding for my project while public servants were being interrogated and replaced. I'm letting the fiftieth anniversary pass and I've shelved the project until we elect a new governor in 2011.

This project is not an artwork per se. It is an exhibit that will be called *Eu-meyer, be your own Niemeyer.* 'Eu' is Portuguese for I, so people visiting the project will be able to experiment with the idea of being Oscar Niemeyer, the architect who conceived the most prominent buildings in Brasilia. Visitors will be encouraged to design what they want for their future city, in particular what they would like to see built in an empty square kilometre in the centre, which has been designated for cultural institutions.

Unlike the previous two projects, I won't be doing any activism prior to making this work. The exhibit itself will get people to act, to create. But, before I continue, I must explain the need for such a project. Brasilia has an empty square kilometre in its centre called Setor Cultural Norte and Setor Cultural Sul (referring to the North and South sides of town). But, architects from Brasilia, professors of architecture and local designers have not dared to design museums or culture centres for this space. For forty-five years, the National Theatre (designed by Oscar Niemeyer) has stood alone in this sector. In the past five years, Niemeyer has designed a National Art Museum and a National Library in the South Cultural Sector. There is still room for three large buildings and nine underground facilities. It has the potential to be a sort of Museumplein in Amsterdam, Smithsonian Institute in Washington or La Défènse in Paris.

But the new National Library and National Art Museum don't have collections. The buildings were put up without knowing what their content would be. Government officials expected that the formal capital city of Rio de Janeiro would give up its National Library collection and transfer it to Brasilia. Rio said no way, so now they have a huge building for which they are slowly acquiring books. And this is why I find this project important: To keep politicians from imposing monumental structures on the city without first thinking about their content.

In 2009, the people of Brasilia rejected one of Oscar Niemeyer's projects for the first time. He had designed a one hundred metre sundial-like structure for this area with a building called the Pavilion of the Presidents. Ouch! Presidents? So now tourists could visit the likes of President Collor, who was impeached for a massive corruption scandal. Would our military dictators from the 1960s to the 1980s be featured as well? The people of Brasilia finally spoke up and rejected the project. The Eumeyer project will enable citizens of Brasilia to project their own desires onto the grand downtown space.

The Eumeyer exhibit will begin with a few examples of designs that were never built for Brasilia. Also on display will be unrealized architectural visions for other cities like Berlin, Chicago and LA. Technicians standing next to computers and drawing boards will help people to draw in three dimensions, to create the forms of new monuments amongst the existing Niemeyer buildings. Visitors will be encouraged to come up with names for these new museums as well as to write a few sentences describing the content of these structures. As museums and cultural centres are created, they will be projected onto the curved walls of the museum interior, a fifty-metre diameter dome. New content will constantly be uploaded to the surrounding curved walls as visitors finish their designs.

After creating their own museums, visitors will be given a pair of augmented reality glasses. He or she will then be able to walk out onto an impressive ramp that jets out of the museum and curves back into the dome in a truly genius piece of Niemeyer engineering. From the ramp, the visitor will be able to look out onto the grand empty spaces and, with the help of the augmented reality glasses, they will see the buildings they have designed inserted into the landscape in front of them.

During the final two weeks of this three-month project, debates and seminars will be staged to discuss the new designs, and the best works will be chosen. Directives about how to develop this final square kilometre at Brasilia's centre will be debated and established. This resulting manifesto of recommendations onto the exterior of the dome will be projected at night during the final week of the project, when what has been brewing inside will be projected outside for the whole city to see.

In a way, this is the opposite of how I have previously worked. In the anti-circumcision and art-in-space movements, I undertook the activism first; this time, the art came first. First, everyone creates, then the manifesto and call for action goes out. One can argue that the call for people to create is activism and, if that's the case, then I may have achieved something of a balance between art and activism.

Reflections on the Body's Participation in a Work

What these three phases in my life have in common is the desire to combine art and activism. My art is not just about art; it's about presenting solutions or spreading the idea of a solution. I don't let my audiences leave the theatre empty handed.

But I wasn't always successful; while I did activism I didn't make art, and while I made art I stopped doing activism. I always used to think that it was the designer in me that sought solutions for the world through my art, but it is in fact the activist in me that believes in communicating these solutions.

I may not explicitly call people to action in my theatre pieces, but there is a deep-seated hope that, one day, people will react to my work and act, that some day a little girl who saw *Isadora.Orb*, for example, may be so inspired that she grows up to be a high-ranking official at NASA and actually implements an artist–in–space programme.

Activism seeks action. Art seeks to move. Activists making art usually come up with inane installations, like the land art in Copacabana I mentioned earlier. Artists whose subject matters are those of activist groups often come across as zealously militant or *pamfletário* as we say in Portuguese.

Part of the success of artistic activism or activist art comes about when the body experiences the issue as a whole. A grandmother dressed up as a tree in a demonstration could be thought of as artistic, but a grandmother who climbs a tree and saves it from being cut down has the tree as proof — a small metaphor or representation of the cause's goal — and there is something artistic in that.

The World Wide Fund for Nature (WWF) developed a paper towel dispenser that incorporates the viewer's action of pulling a paper towel into awareness-building. The dispenser has a transparent map through which one can see the papers stacked inside; as one pulls the green-coloured paper out of the dispenser, one sees the colour green being emptied out of South America. Is this just clever or is it artistic?

The installation *A Clearing in the Streets*, by Julie Farris and Sarah Wayland-Smith, reproduces a fragment of grassland in the middle of an asphalt and concrete setting in Lower Manhattan. A ten-sided plywood structure houses a meadow, fifteen feet in diameter, offset by a panoramic interior mural of a vast blue sky. Eight-inch gaps, spaced throughout the structure, permit visual access to the enclosed landscape. The work has more impact because the viewer's body is excluded from the field that once covered the concrete landscape.

Artistic Activism, Activist Art, Artivism; it's a hard balance to strike. I believe the form doesn't necessarily have to get people in the audience to go out running to sign up for Greenpeace. Part of what makes the activist's work more artistic (or the artists work more activistic) is when the form leads to (even if just an iota) the results desired.

Finally, Dresden

I would like to conclude with yet another story from my life. During the period I was writing this piece, I fell gravely ill for two months and, for the first time ever, I wondered if I would even last two weeks. In bed, contemplating my future (or lack thereof) I got to thinking; if I could travel to one last place in the world, where that place would be. Immediately an image of Dresden's Frauenkirche (Church of Our Lady) came to mind. It wasn't on my list of places to go, like Havana, Istanbul, Petra, Shanghai, Rome or Wat Po. Instead, a church in former East Germany came to mind, and I recalled the significance of this image.

Growing up, I would occasionally leaf through a book that belonged to my father, called *Lost Treasures of Europe*, which featured palaces and buildings that had been destroyed during World War II. One image in particular caused me great pain to look at: a black and white photograph of the Frauenkirche that was destroyed in the fire bombing of Dresden. How could something so elegant and beautiful be gone?

Decades passed and, as a thirty-six-year-old man, I visited the Hanover 2000 Expo (on my way to a space conference in Berlin). I walked around from one pavilion to the next, unimpressed by most of them and tickled by only a few. In front of the German Pavilion, there stood a metallic gazebo, with black columns supporting a lattice stainless steel dome, which caught my attention. There was a glass cube which seemed to contain a maquette of a building. I approached curiously. In the glass cube was a model of the Frauenkirche with a little slot requesting contributions for its reconstruction. As I approached the model, sacral choral music started to come out of speakers. I looked up and the three-metre lattice dome began to unfold and rise above me to form the tall proportions of the Frauenkirche dome. The unfolding of this dome was so graceful as it ascended towards the clouds and the choir so moving, that the prospect of the dome being built again stirred me greatly. Almost without thinking, I reached into my pocket and slipped 10 Euros into the contribution box. The music ended and the dome slowly unfolded, shrinking to its flattened form.

In a way, this was a very effective combination of art and activism (fund-raising being a crucial component of activism). The artistry of the techno-sculpture rising above me had me completely in thrall, and the result it implied moved me to action. I contributed. Years later, I saw on the news that the church had been inaugurated. The builders mixed stone from the rubble of the original church with freshly quarried stone, resulting in a sienna-coloured church speckled with black stone — an artistic choice that embeds this church with a statement about the war and its destruction (I call it the Dalmatian Church). When I saw the inauguration on the news, I recalled that I had contributed; I had helped to rebuild this church. I felt part of a beautiful process from beginning to end, one that involved form, awareness-building and action.

So, in conclusion, I think that what all art and all activism have in common is the quest for resonance in their audiences; that dormant inner echo which, in my case, had spanned a lifetime, from leafing through a book as a child to standing in an art installation and contributing to a church's reconstruction. Was I having a religious experience when this church came to mind when I was very ill? If so, then someone upstairs was reminding me of what's at my core: my artist-activist nature and my long-winded need to bring them together. In this Frauenkirche episode, form, awareness-building and action all came together, and when you have this combination you've got something. But, if you can add resonance to the formula then you've got something really special, and maybe that's when the art-activist form puts on its best smile.

147

The Kids of Mitrovica

Bertus Borgers

This is a success story… at least so far. As the story is set in a highly unstable part of the world, this success could already beA history by the time you read these words. The odd thing is that this could actually happen, while nobody in the whole wide world wants it to…

A woman with an American accent called to make an appointment. Her name was Laura Hassler and she represented Musicians without Borders. This organization carries out international projects in conflict areas, where they use 'music' as a means of getting people together again. Naturally, the Balkans is the perfect area for such an initiative and Musicians without Borders had already carried out several successful projects in the area.

Over the years, Hassler has managed to build a valuable network of supporting and financing organizations. She wanted to talk about the city of Mitrovica with the Rockacademy, a four-year bachelor's degree programme in the field of music in the Netherlands. Before the war of 1998, when Yugoslavia was still a union, Mitrovica, a town with approximately 200,000 inhabitants, was the centre of pop culture in Yugoslavia. Rock music, concerts, bands, artwork, fashion, it all came from Mitrovica. When the province of Kosovo broke away from Serbia, Mitrovica became a shining example of a conflicted city in the Balkans. The problems of this provincial town are easily understood once you picture its geography — to the north of the river Ibar live Serbs; to the south, Albanians. The bridge over the Ibar is no man's land where the UN's military vehicles stand. Thus, an unnavigable river flows between two religions, two languages, two currencies and between two peoples who are unable to get along. Laura Hassler's question was simple: 'Can the Rockacademy contribute to a cooperation between adolescents on both sides of the river?'

As a representative of this organization, I offered to find out whether there were any ways of doing something meaningful around the teaching method called 'band coaching', which helps bands to develop by finding the right repertoire, making a demo, perfecting their performance, etc. This teaching method is very suitable for groups of absolute beginners; with the right coach, every member can discover music playfully and at their own speed. The beauty of band coaching is that it uses a group process that requires communication on very different levels and in very different ways: verbal and non-verbal, body language, clothing, choice of words, intellectual, intuitive — one way or another, each member of the group contributes by definition to the end result.

150

On 5 May 2008, after my gig at the liberation day festival, we convened in an outdoor café in Alkmaar and decided to start simply. Laura and her daughter, Wendy, who also worked for Musicians without Borders, suggested organizing a summer camp in neutral territory. They had a very useful contact, called Yabir, in Kosovo's neighbouring country, Macedonia, who could probably organize something like this. With the help of a few older musicians, Musicians without Borders would recruit a few youngsters on both sides of the river in Mitrovica and invite them to form occasional bands in the Macedonian capital, Skopje. Our students would help these bands decide on a repertoire and ensemble, and coach them towards a final concert at the end of the week in the park of Skopje near the grand soccer stadium.

The Rockacademy would send a team of five or six students, supervised by an education expert who would record everything professionally so that it could be sent to potential funders of the project. To this team, I added my brother, Ruud, not because he is family but because he has twenty years of experience in teaching pop workshops in community art projects in the city of Eindhoven. He is not merely an all-round musician but also a man who has become very streetwise through applying pop music to situations with considerable social tensions, and he would be well able to convert the tensions underlying this project into positive action for our students.

And everything went well, I have to admit. In the last week of August 2008, our students arrived in Skopje with two teachers and met a handful of professional musicians from Mitrovica who were accompanied by twenty-five teenagers from that city, boys and girls between the ages of thirteen and nineteen whose parents had allowed them to participate. Of course, during those first few days, we had to wing it a little; the rooms intended for the rehearsals turned out to be unavailable on some days, the equipment arrived in boxes and had to be unpacked, assembled, connected and fine-tuned, but none of this is a problem if you make situations like this a part of the project. Teenagers get to know each other well while assembling a drum set, and, during that week, something unfamiliar to them started to blossom.

By the end of the week, the Mitrovica kids were playing in mixed line-ups in the Skopje park. I was standing near the stage when a group of girls and boys came to me. They were excited. 'Sir, sir, thank you, thank you', they shouted. One of the boys, a singer, proudly told me: 'We want a concert like this in Mitrovica'. 'That is not possible at this moment', I said, at which point the entire group started calling to me, 'We want it, we want it, we want it!' 'All right, all right', I said, 'if you want it, the Rockacademy will help you get it.' They scattered away, loudly calling, 'Yeah, yeah, yeah', and I realized that the Rockacademy had started out on a rocky, long and winding road.

This initial success immediately generated new plans. The Kosovar musicians wanted to start a school in Mitrovica, a school for music in which the youngsters of the town could play in bands and develop a Mitrovica Rock School! Immediately after they came home, the Serbian and Albanian musicians started recruiting pupils and, on their 'own' sides of the river, went looking for a location. Wendy Hassler set up an office near the bridge and the Mitrovica Rock School was born.

The next time we met was at the Rockacademy in Tilburg, the Netherlands. In December 2008, the teachers of the new school, Serbs and Albanians, came to Tilburg, ten in all — nine thirty-something men and one woman, a classically trained singer. Our education expert, Gerdien Visser, had set up a tight schedule for that week. It contained some tough subjects for the self-taught musicians from Kosovo, such as how to compile a curriculum and what the consequences would be for the new school for music. With the success of Skopje in mind, the Kosovars opted for a curriculum based on band coaching. Their pupils would start out as members of a band before receiving individual musical tuition and theory lessons. First, they learned how to play together and how to select an appropriate repertoire before definitively choosing a discipline or instrument. This form of curriculum also fitted in well with the goals of the project, namely getting the new generation of Mitrovica to work together.

While preparing for this training week, the Rockacademy team had decided to focus on the development of musical education and to ignore the ethnic and political problems that had given rise to this project. We intended to treat the Kosovars as a single group. With that in mind, we had rented a small van for the five Serbs and five Albanians so that they could move about, and we housed them in a single large bungalow in a safari park. It had a shared kitchen, there were plenty of beds and, fortunately, two bathrooms (it ended up, not surprisingly, with one bathroom for the Serbs and one for the Albanese). We had also supplied them with a keyboard and a few acoustic guitars so that they could make music. All of this was intended to give them the chance to interact on neutral territory and to work toward the same goal — the Mitrovica Rock School.

Our teachers and students took the group to visit interesting places. During the evening programme, the Kosovars were introduced to various regional organizations in which pop music was practised and taught. First, the Factorium in Tilburg, a trendy centre for amateurs in the performing arts, well equipped and with modern views. Next, the music school in Waalwijk, a rather traditional regional music school in which several of our students now teach. And, lastly, they visited PopEi, the pop collective in Eindhoven that was once set up by squatters to provide services for local pop musicians, which had grown over time into a large organization with rehearsal rooms, administrative and fiscal support, a recording studio and a maintenance service, where around 180 bands are registered. This pop collective made a particular impression on the Kosovar teachers and fuelled their ambition to build something against all odds.

We also planned an evening to make music on a Tilburg stage with students from the Rockacademy. That evening it became clear that it was too much to expect the Serbian and Albanian musicians to play spontaneously in the same line-up at this point in time. The Serbs clustered together on the stage and the Albanians also formed their own little group.

The time was right to draw this project into a broader Balkan debate. On 2 December 2008, we organized a panel at the Hogeschool voor de Kunsten in Tilburg, entitled 'From guns to guitars: rock music in Kosovo'. This panel included a good complement of 'hands-on' experts and other people who were somehow involved, including a diplomat from the Balkans, NGO representatives and the Serbian coordinator of the Kosovar teachers. They all took part in a lively debate in which the central question was: 'Do cultural projects contribute to the positive development of the Balkans?' The final conclusion was remarkable. All parties shared a mutual distaste for the bringers of culture who organized a project quickly, let themselves be photographed in a successful pose, holding a glass of champagne, and then left forever, leaving the target group without means or plans. That night, everyone agreed that this project shouldn't end this way. And, since the Dutch support couldn't last forever, there was only one possible conclusion after reaching such a noble resolution: the end goal had to be that the Kosovars would eventually have to run the school entirely without support from the Netherlands. Not an easy thing to do, maybe still far in the future but certainly doable!

In January 2009, the Kosovars started the Mitrovica Rock School on both sides of the river. Wendy Hassler settled permanently in Mitrovica and inserted the project into Mitrovica Community

Building, an organization that promotes the unification of Mitrovica every way it can, financed by the IKV-Pax Christi peace movement (amongst others sources). Wendy devised a structure for the development of the school with coordinators on both sides of the river and gave the teachers official work contracts. In short, using only modest means, she set up a working organization.

In May 2009, the Rockacademy visited Mitrovica for a week, with a team of five students supervised by Gerdien and Ruud. We were curious about how the 'school' was doing. We had had an intensive e-mail correspondence about the wishes of the Kosovar teachers in which they made it known that they specifically needed songwriting lessons, vocal coaching and workshops for the rhythm sections. And so, our students had a busy week teaching their skills to Kosovar youths of Serbian and Albanian descent. This was the first time we had actually visited the city in question and we couldn't help feeling slightly astonished. North of the river Ibar, anarchy rules; the Serbs refuse to acknowledge the authority of Kosovar police, politicians or government. They drive around without license plates, stubbornly conduct trade in dinars, curse anything that looks American and refuse to clear away the rubble of the war. The Albanians on the south bank are clearly glad to be out of the underdog position; they are rebuilding their surroundings, want to be part of Europe and have a positive cooperative attitude. On the bridge, the NATO-led Kosovo Force (KFOR) military from several countries sit, heavily armed, ready to deal ruthlessly with any serious confrontation. Our students were the invisible people in this situation; they could walk across the bridge without any trouble and made friends on both sides of the river.

Everyone on our team was thrilled with the level of interest in the workshops and the commitment shown by the teachers and pupils working together on the Mitrovica Rock School. On both sides, more had budded than a mere school of music; it was a place where young musicians gathered, even when they had no classes.

In the meantime, Wendy had been busy fundraising and had secured enough funding to continue the following year. We decided that, for the coming season, we would stick to the cycle that had developed naturally; we would teach a summer school in Skopje in August, have a training week in Tilburg in the winter and a project week in Mitrovica in May, when our students would give workshops.

Skopje, August 2009. A year ago, we started this project in Macedonia on neutral territory and all the people involved felt that the summer school in Skopje was a key function of the success. Actually, it is the most important moment of the annual cycle because the target group — the teenagers of Mitrovica — can make music together unhindered. There was, however, a noticeable difference from the previous year, when our students gave band coaching to the teenagers while Kosovar teachers observed or played in the band; this year, the teachers were capable of coaching the bands themselves and the position of our students became less obvious. We also noticed considerable differences in expertise among the Kosovar teachers, both in teaching and in music. The school had acquired a few highly skilled instrumentalists as teachers, who were able to teach our students a thing or two. The relationships were shaken up soundly! And here, one of the dangers of projects in the community arts reared its head: before you know it, artistic values become dominant in a project that started out with social goals. Obviously, musicians have to be given some time to juggle their instrumental skills, but now was the time to re-stress the goal of this mission: the pupils were to experience a week they would never forget. Artistic tours de force, different tastes in music, they all had to be subordinated to the simple goal, to make sure these children give a memorable performance in Skopje park on Friday night.

And, once again, it was a heart-warming concert.

The official opening of the Mitrovica Rock School was set for Saturday 26 September 2009. My colleague and fellow director, Gerard Boontjes, and I were invited. As project leaders, we used this moment as a PR occasion because, frankly, we could do with a little interest and support. In truth, I had hoped for more support from the European politicians. After all, they had embraced the creation of Kosovo as a separate state and they would benefit from cooperation between the two peoples. Besides, they always flaunt Mitrovica when they need a positive example of the Balkan situation, but there was not a peep out of Brussels, so maybe we didn't know which doors to knock on. Mitrovica still looks gloriously derelict. The Ibar flows but is obviously not maintained, nor are the small gardens on the Serbian side. There are few women on the Albanian side, a lot of men waiting for something or someone, dinars on one side, dollars on the other, a combined unemployment figure of 75%. And, on the bridge, soldiers from the rest of the world with a few worn out jeeps and a tank, fortunately have nothing to do. Hills in the distance, a beautiful country, it's just a pity that the people don't get along.

On the Albanian side, the Mitrovica Rock School has nestled

itself into an old school building that is part of a small sports stadium. The playing field is covered with asphalt and the lines make it clear that games like basketball, volleyball and perhaps a few more sports are played here. On the bleachers at the head of the field is a stage, a reasonable PA system has been installed and the field is nicely filled with families. I notice that all ages are present — mothers, children, a lot of teenagers, young couples, middle-aged folk and even a few old people. The programme starts at 19.00 hours and it is followed attentively, songs are sung along with and the young musicians are loudly encouraged by their friends. It is a beautiful summer evening that darkens slowly. The music performed is mostly the 'decent' side of contemporary genres. The volume is checked and whenever anything happens that even hints at decadence, it is immediately undone by the innocence of the performers. Amy Winehouse is imitated by fourteen-year-old girls with teased up hair, and boys play Guns 'n' Roses, pressing down a distortion pedal and waving their guitar in the air, but everything is done with a lot of flair, in a pleasant atmosphere and appreciated by the audience. The teachers play too. They like proper and somewhat complicated music like fusion. Even traditional jazz makes an appearance.

I had told the organization beforehand that I would bring a mouthpiece for a tenor sax; if they could arrange to have one present, I would gladly play a number at the openings on both sides. It was highly appreciated and they prepared a sax piece for me. Very sweet, of course, but I am not a jazz player per se. Fortunately it was a Duke Ellington tune, a number from my late father's repertoire. I was impressed by the whole event, primarily by the broad acceptance the school had managed to gain in the Albanian Muslim community, and I was certainly impressed by the musical level of some of the teenagers. It was all a bit too neat for our taste — no booze, no dope, a family event, decent and positive — after all, this wasn't the Bronx but a decent small Muslim town.

When the first performance had finished, teacher Ruud and his students took down the backdrop with the logo of the school because it would be needed for the stage on the north side as well. A remarkable detail was that the teachers had brought along the sax with them from Pristine as one wasn't available in Mitrovica, at least not in their circles. I was allowed to take the instrument with me to the Serbian side where the opening of the Mitrovica School was scheduled for 21.00 hours, provided I took the instrument back to the Albanian side the following day.

So, a little before nine o'clock, we lugged that backdrop and the tenor sax past the KFOR soldiers over the bridge and went looking for the location of the Serbian opening. During the day, I had already visited the school on the Serbian side and realized that we couldn't have the opening on their premises as it was a vacant building with bullet holes, partitioned into awkward, small rooms without any hint of mainten-ance, which was why we had the opening in a café with a stage.

It was a rough bar, full of noise, tattooed girls, boys in black clothes, loud music, a lot of beer (to put it mildly) and loads of enthu-siasm. The backdrop of the Mitrovica Rock School had to be placed behind the stage because these youngsters were just as proud of the school as the Albanians were, but the wooden supports on either side of the backdrop were too long for this low-ceilinged bar. Few words were wasted, the wood was forcibly cut down to size and, amidst loud cheering, the banner was erected behind the stage and the last deci-metre of space was filled with amplifiers, pedals, empty glasses and mi-crophones. The programme began and all I heard was hardcore rock with grunters, screamers gesticulating wildly and pretty boys trying to sing in the highest pitch that they could. There was only an oc-casional girl, but it was obvious that in this school power and volume had merged into a unique performance style. These youngsters were angry and militant. Bomber jackets with swastikas, fists in the air, this wasn't a pastiche of a TV culture; this was about their own life!

The teachers came to ask if I felt like jamming with them. Fusion. Sure. So, I stepped onto the stage with the tenor sax. It felt like going back in time by thirty years. They played the music we used to play in our jam sessions in the Melkweg cultural centre in Amsterdam, in the mid-1970s — themes from Herbie Hancock and Billy Cobham, long improvisations, a lot of energy, expression. I have to say that I had a marvellous time.

I knew that the two schools would be different but I hadn't re-alized that the difference would be so immediate and so fundamental. We would have to take this into account from now on.

At the end of February 2010, the Kosovar teachers came back to Tilburg, this time for two weeks — one week for training at the Rockacademy and one week during which they would perform to-gether in Tilburg, Eindhoven and Veldhoven and learn about each other's music. (This worked very well. It took a journey to the Neth-erlands to find a place and time to really get to know each other's music.) There are a few new faces, they speak no English, and, dur-ing the first briefing they receive on the academy about this week's programme, a funny scene is played out, one that I will see time and time again during this project. I say two sentences in English, then a Serb whispers to his friends what I just said in an incomprehensible language, while, at the other side of the table, the Albanians do the same. When both 'interpreters' sit up straight again, I continue. Later, when a Serb wants to ask me something, another Albanian translates the Serbian question for his side of the table while the Serbian 'interpreter' translates it into English for me. I wait until everybody looks at me again and answer in English, after which the chatter in the Balkan languages begins again. Many Serbs don't understand Albanian and vice versa, or they don't want to understand it. The teachers have come across a mutual problem during the development of their school; how do they handle the great diversity in talent and ambition among their students?

The children all came to the school a year ago, to play informally in a band, but opinions have begun to diverge. Our educational expert, Gerdien Visser, who has designed and supervised all didactic processes from the start, is happy with such a well-defined problem. The training week is spent on devising an assessment system with which to measure and coach the students. We impressed upon the Kosovars the importance of establishing an assessment system that is easy to explain to the parents of their students. It will ensure their continued involvement with their children's progress and reinforce the authority of the school.

For once, the extra week we planned this time was not intended for study but for making music and we really hit the mark. Our guests hung around together like friends and, during performances, they played a set together in an ethnically mixed line-up; something that will not be possible in Mitrovica for some time to come.

The next get-together was early May 2010. We went to Mitrovica with the same two teachers — Gerdien for the didactic supervision and Ruud, who was to coach our students in making music during this project. Both had been involved with this project from the outset, and had witnessed, and often initiated, all the developments. Through e-mail, we knew exactly what the school needed and we had recruited four new students that would be giving training in the required areas: bass lessons, singing coaching for boys and girls, song writing and recording demos.

I decided to go too, mostly because Laura Hassler, the manager of Musicians without Borders, would be there. I thought it would be a good idea to meet in the place where it was all happening. After all, we had started this whole thing, just the two of us, so we thought we were entitled to enjoy ourselves a little. There was, however, less enjoyment ahead than I had hoped for. When we arrived, project leader, Wendy, reported that the Kosovar teachers had made no progress at all in taking responsibility. They were getting paid by an international NGO and they were quite content with that. The targets we had set for the development of the school were simply not being met, whereas Wendy had promised the donors that they would be. If this continued, there would be no point in starting a new school year in September because the money would inevitably stop flowing. The things that were supposed to be arranged by the school were, for example, a shared website, house rules, a strategy for handling parents, class schedules, etc. etc.

There was nothing for Laura and me to do but to call on our management skills and spend our days there trying to solve this problem. We drew up a schedule, talked to every teacher, and, at the beginning and end of that cycle, we had an additional meeting with the Albanian and Serbian coordinators. Laura and I would much rather have watched our students perform — we are both musicians after all — but it boiled down to doing management duties such as holding performance interviews, motivating people and brushing up our organizational responsibilities.

It was somewhat amusing that, during each talk we had, the teachers failed to see why they had to achieve these goals. Agreements on maintaining house rules and keeping in touch with parents worked just fine on both sides of the river; they had mutual solid agreements on reporting absences to the parents and about maintaining order. Everything went just fine, so what were we complaining about? Each time, we had to convince such a teacher that the organization paying their salary wanted to see all of this in writing. The message we kept hammering home was: 'Go and sit behind your laptop, type the required letters and mail them to Wendy. If not, you will be without a job in September. It really is that simple'. This seems to have helped because Wendy let us know about a month later that the mentality had completely changed and now everyone assumed their responsibilities full of energy. We assume, therefore, that we can go ahead and organize the main events for the school year 2010/2011 after all: Skopje Summer School in August, training week at the Rockacademy in Tilburg for the teachers in the winter and practice for our students in Mitrovica in May. As I write this, it is 29 August 2010 and I am receiving text messages from Gerdien, Ruud and our students, wildly enthusiastic about the concert the teenagers of Mitrovica gave last night in the Skopje park. I am curious to see what happens to the project this coming year, because the marginal side-effects that a simple plan can generate are fascinating. A Macedonian conflict area has been added to the project, and Ruud has already made two small musical tours through Serbia, Macedonia and Kosovo, accompanied by a Serbian band. A female Rockacademy student, who went with us the very first time and has graduated by now, is taking a course in Serbian because she is moving in with a Serbian bass player. A different female student that went with us last year has now put together an accompanying band in Kosovo, and has included six months in Mitrovica in her study plan so that she can teach and play there. In an internet café, the teenagers maintain e-mail contacts that have to be hidden from their own parents, neighbours and social surroundings. The Bourbon brand, Jack Daniel's, wants to sponsor our students to continue work at the Mitrovica Rock School because they think it is a cool project. So, will the money from a liquor factory in Tennessee end up with Albanian youngsters who aren't allowed to drink and with Serbian youths who hate the Americans who bombed their parents? Is this, perhaps, new justice? And I read the blogs, look at the pictures and read the texts the participants have posted:

1. 'The Rock School makes all of us forget the problems of Kosovo, and we have the chance to talk and chat with the other students from the other part of town.' (Visar, a sixteen-year old singer)

2. 'Our parents didn't have the chance to speak with them or to meet them, and now we do and it is great.' (Vesa, 15, drummer)

3. And that, ladies and gentlemen, is why we go through all the bother.

Additional Information

Website www.mitrovicarockschool.org
Blog http://skopjesummerschool.blogspot.com
YouTube www.youtube.com/user/hasslerforest
MySpace www.myspace.com/mitrovicarockschool
www.musicianswithoutborders.org
www.rockacademie.nl
www.bertusborgers.nl

Part III
Rethinking Basic Concepts

Art and Common

A Conversation with Antonio Negri

Pascal Gielen
& Sonja Lavaert

One of the most noticeable things about the oeuvre of Antonio Negri is that he often publishes works that echo multiple voices. Books are co-written, essays are produced in the form of letters. Texts assume the shape of dialogues as if they actually occurred as normal conversations. The conversation is, therefore, the perfect site at which the common takes shape. A conversation teaches us much about the common, not least through the fact that its formation presupposes a multitude of perspectives, differences, people, products and thoughts. The conversation teaches us that the common is formed in lively interaction and is constantly reconstructed. The common is a subject close to Negri's heart; this is immediately evident in the titles of his recent works. By contrast, he never mentions community. He prefers the adjective that moves, shapes itself into something different and, most importantly, encompasses many undertones. 'Common' is an ontological and logical category that presupposes an internally contrasting multitude of singularities and brings them together. Common is the social collective. Common is a cooperation, a product that is created as if in a laboratory. Common is also ordinary, everyday, from everyone, intended for everyone, a concept that echoes communism. Apart from common, imagination and art are also distinctive themes in Negri's publications. And, what is more, interest in the workings of the imagination and the nature of creative production is interwoven with the common theme.

Talking about art also means talking about the multitude. Furthermore, the political philosopher experiments with art forms in which he puts his political-theoretical reflections into practice. That is why, in 2009, within the space of a few months, he published *Trilogie de la différence*, a bundling of three plays, *Art et multitude*, a reflection on art and the multitude, and *Commonwealth*, a philosophical essay investigating the common, written with Michael Hardt. In the US, far more than in Europe, this focus on the problems of the common resulted in a lot of publicity, intellectual success and maybe even the beginning of a movement. For the first time since Foucault, people in the US feel that we are dealing with a body of thought that offers us an ontology of the current context. Colloquia have been organized with the title *Commonalities: Theorizing the Common in Contemporary Italian Thought*, in which people conduct transatlantic video conversations with Negri and, most importantly, reflect on the rising forms of the common and the fertility of the concept for a progressive policy. This is reason enough for our conversation with Antonio Negri. We met him in the two cities he alternately inhabits: first Paris, then Venice.

166

Pascal Gielen
& Sonja Lavaert

In Art et multitude, *you mention a recent visit to the Venice Biennale, during which you were struck by the immense lack of formal renewal. It was like a graveyard, you write, and it made you think that these days we are facing a crisis in which production, including artistic production, is empty and dead. Can we deduce from this that you have certain expectations of art, make certain demands of it? Can you describe these demands a bit more precisely? What should art do, according to you?*

Antonio Negri

I connect art to a very elementary experience. When I enter the exhibition of the Biennale, I want to find a description of reality. I want to understand something of the reality in which I am usually submerged, in my life and in other ways. An exhibition is a place where you are being submerged in a new element. That is the way it always is for me. Should this sense of submersion be lacking, no one would go to an exhibition anymore. An exhibition is a place you enter and become submerged, like water you dive into. It is not merely about a new vision on things but about a genuine insertion, an entering, a connection. It is about physical contact, hence the image of entering the water and submerging oneself. The concept of 'submersion' is very important as experience. For example, I remember the biennales during which this submersion occurred — and this also always means that a very direct and, in that sense, elementary relationship is created between imagination and reality — the one with Pollock shortly after World War Two or the one in 1964 with Rauschenberg. Those were two very important biennales for me. The two periods were important as well: the early 1960s and, in the case of Pollock, shortly after the Second World War when the world, reality itself, had completely fallen apart and yet contained a new solidity and, at the same time, pointed in a new direction. People started to discover grand analogies between, on the one hand, the artistic freedom that caused scandal and made the scandalized audience ask, with every innovation, 'Is this art?' and, on the other hand, the massive rebuilding of the world. I had a similar impression with Beuys; he, too, is an example that clarifies what I mean by 'submersion in a new element' and there were others as well. To me, art has always been something material, something that is very strong in its new reality, something you can touch. The submersion I talk about refers to a strong materiality. From an elementary point of view, this is art to me. And when I speak of a graveyard, it is because I do not feel this experience, this submersion. I say it rather brazenly; my judgement is based on whether or not I experience this feeling; it has no internal profundity, neither is it based on study and education. It is about a first impression, an immediate feeling, a snap judgement. The graveyard feeling is caused by an unsuccessful submersion. Like when you go fishing under water; there, too, you dive into a new element, the water. If you leave the water without having caught a fish you feel a chill, you get cold, whereas after a successful catch you are content and get the impression that the water warms your spirit.

P.G. & S.L.

Is the image of the graveyard confined to that one biennale or are you talking about a tendency that overshadows the entire art world these days?

A.N.

I was disillusioned by this latest biennale because that immediate experience was lacking completely. But that doesn't imply the tendency these days is absolute. For instance, not long ago, I had a grand experience of a completely different nature in Madrid, at the Reina Sofia Museum where *Guernica* was exhibited. The people who work there, friends of mine like the director, Manuel Borja-Villel, reorgan-

ized the museum: it is no longer structured in historical terms but aligned with political history. This means that the works are no longer exhibited chronologically by period but that they have constructed a completely new route. They have constructed a cycle, ranging from Goya to *Guernica*, in which they confront the visitors very directly with violence and political struggle. This exhibition was an extremely strong submersion experience for me. This initiative was, of course, a huge scandal in a Spain that has lived through the Spanish Civil War. It was a true political reconstruction of the organization of an artistic discourse in which the classic periodization was completely torn down, which, in this case, boiled down to the destruction of the nineteenth century as a systematic period. After all, art history is made in periods but at the Reina Sofia you have this political reconstruction and relating of past and present, a mixing up of chronology. To this end, they showed cinematic material between the paintings and interspersed the route with all sorts of curious and unexpected objects, but everything was placed very coherently in a discourse that infused the aesthetics with history, with a well-defined political history. This reorganization or exhibition method has started a continuous debate because the discourse is naturally connected to a very specific episode within Spanish history.

P.G. & S.L.

Is this a necessary criterion for you — that art has to communicate, grab time and say something about that time?

A.N.

Yes, but the stories are infinite. There are also other stories. It isn't like a dictatorship where they only tell a single, always identical story. For instance, I remember a different event that touched me deeply. In Munich, they had an exhibition on the exact spot and in the same museum as the exhibition in which Entartete Kunst [Degenerate Art] had been proclaimed and condemned. I went there with Hans Ulrich Obrist, a friend and curator in contemporary art, for a lecture on the same themes as the ones we are discussing now. There was some sort of construction, in wood, at the exact spot where Hitler had proclaimed Entartete Kunst in 1937. That too, was done beautifully, very powerfully and skilfully. At the entrance of the neoclassical building, they had installed loudspeakers that blared the sound of barking dogs, but this caused such a scandal in Munich that they quickly took the loudspeakers down again. This exhibition,

and what was happening there, made a huge impression on me. Not so much the anecdotic loudspeakers with the barking dogs but the fact of entering this room in which historical and political charge was actually happening — that is something laden with meaning. You see, this word is very important to me, 'meaning'. It is important to give meaning, and there is such a thing as continuously giving meaning to the artistic experience. Considering an event or fact at the historical level and clarifying, with such obviousness, what its meaning is – that is what art is all about.

P. G. & S.L.

The two examples you give have a political characteristic. Is political meaning a necessary criterion?

A.N.

In these cases, it was necessary but there may be other circumstances as well. Let us say that my vision is rather bio-political and that, to me, all forms of life are political. In other words, there are no forms, no art forms without political meaning.

P.G. & S.L.

In an interview, the Italian philosopher Paolo Virno stated that art is only an exploration of form and that the substance that is reported as a result is not really relevant in making art either art or political and that imposing new criteria is dismeasure. So you don't agree with this then? Art is not merely an exploration of form?

A.N.

My friend Paolo has changed his mind about this; he used to think the substantive dimension of art was extremely important. Now, however, he fundamentally reasons based on criteria of form and naturalism and searches for the common, or the general, and its expression in purely linguistic forms. Art is, indeed, essential in linguistic forms because it is through art that renewal happens, that new elements are inserted. We agree on that point, but Paolo now assumes a naturalistic structure, a natural generality as a basis. This is a Chomskyan supposition I disagree with. Even when he speaks about potency or dismeasure, Paolo keeps referring to a naturalistic presupposition. For him, potency is something that, in order to exist, has to transform itself into an action in an Aristotelian manner and, as a result, he thinks potency is no longer free but predetermined; it is fixed.

P.G. & S.L.

He probably wouldn't agree with that himself. I am referring to the debate between Foucault and Chomsky in which he explicitly criticizes Chomsky on this point.

A.N.

His thinking is perhaps not completely Chomskyan but, one way or another, he starts from the idea of a naturalistic presupposition. There is a natural structure that he feels cannot be changed. I see things differently. For me, art is an expression that follows the historical ways of being. Art is one of the bio-political relationship forms between people. Art is one of the forms of the relationship people anticipate.

P.G. & S.L.

Seen from a system-theoretical and functionalistic point of view, think of Niklas Luhmann, art has a specific function in society. The role of art is to create a sense of possibilities. The message from art in society is that everything is neither necessary nor impossible. Or, with a wink to the novel Der Mann ohne Eigenschaften *by Robert Musil, everything that is, can also be different. Do you share this opinion about the role of art in society?*

A.N.

I agree with the view of art as a sense of possibilities but only within a certain reality that has formed historically. Art is an historical reality in itself, one that opens itself to possibilities but is also determined itself. It is not a reality without contours. It is a bio-political reality that is determined and in which the forms of life, the political balance that connects the forms of life with each other, the associations, the relationships etc., express the possibilities.

P.G. & S.L.

You use the term 'bio-politics' not 'bio-power'?

A.N.

Certainly. In imitation of Foucault and Deleuze, I use the term 'bio-power' to mean an imperial force that permeates everything and controls the lives of the people from above, while the term 'bio-politics' stands for the possibility of resistance, disobedience and self-determination, from the bottom up. Of course, art is bio-politics, in the sense of the subjective act of the artist, but also in the sense of the social conditions that allow the artist to perform his artistic act and to produce art. An artist is never merely an individual but is also always a person like everybody else, and one who manoeuvres, moves, shows and produces in relation with those others.

In that sense, the concept of 'dismeasure' that Paolo Virno uses is completely correct, because we can no longer talk about value and about production unless it is in terms of dismeasure; value is no longer a valid measuring stick. In that sense, it is an absolutely correct concept. This dismeasure, however, has no statistical references. It is an immaterial dismeasure and that is why it has potency. Paolo Virno, however, often talks about dismeasure as having the characteristics of a transition between two different orders of language usage. Those language usages pile up and there is supposedly dismeasure because two different language usages cannot be measured against each other. This reduces dismeasure to a concept without any potency. If that potency is described as transition to the act, it is an Aristotelian concept, narrowed down to a physics concept that lacks any potency because of its prefiguration. When I speak of value or invention, it is in a different manner. I use the term the way Spinoza does, as creative potency.

P.G. & S.L.

Let's go back to Luhmann for a while. It is clear that you usually disagree with him, but how about this point: can art create possibilities, bring about changes?

A.N.

The problem with Luhmann is that there is always a legal schema behind his considerations. Or rather, there is always a legal anthropology behind everything, a causal way of thinking that sees every effect as derived from a unique cause and vice versa. In short, there is always a mechanical scheme. Even behind the most relativistic considerations, you will find this legal, formal and mechanical scheme. What does change mean to Luhmann? He sees change in a new possibility that pops up in any situation. This is a purely formal definition. However, the problem lies in understanding not only that change is possible and that it might be something different from what exists now, but also whether and how this different thing is shaping itself. The dimension of being is fundamental in any type of language usage, particularly in legal language usage. There exists a certain internal transcendence that is inherent to reality. I think that Luhmann sees this sense of possibilities, in art for example, as entirely undetermined whereas the determination is always there. We do not exist in an undetermined world. Everything is determined in the sense that everything is unique.

P.G. & S.L.

You place the weight of reality and ontology in opposition to the emphasis on the formal nature of, for example, Luhmann and Virno. Nevertheless, you too talk about the 'lack of formal renewal' in Art et multitude.

A.N.

I think we attach too many meanings to words. As I said at the start, with that lack in formal renewal I mean the absence of that elementary experience. If you ask me whether I have an aesthetic model, I think back to the lessons of Sergio Bettine, who undoubtedly taught me the most when it comes to art. This Italian art critic was one of the great experts of Late-Roman and Byzantine art, a pupil of the Vienna art-historical school, of figures like Alois Riegl and Max Dvořák. The Vienna school studied the transition from Late-Roman to Byzantine art through a study of the construction techniques. Take, for instance, the San Marco Basilica in Venice, probably the most perfect or complete work of Roman Byzantine art. San Marco was built with and through the continuity of material and of traditional techniques and of materials research. It also incorporates what they call, a 'Kunstwollen', an artistic will. This could be anything — the will to honour God or to express the human capacity for potency. However, what is really important and what it is really about is that one determines the relationship between the substantive and formal element, particularly in relation to the material, and even mechanical, aspect and in relation to the work experience. Art is always work, collective work that is inserted into a whole made up of historical factors. The artistic will, if it exists, is the constant factor throughout this series of substances. For example, what one sees in the San Marco Basilica is a study of the arch, a study of the dome, a formidable machine of people and materials, the mosaic, the decorations, the images the mosaics have to express, all these elements together, the entirety of these experiences, that is the art.

P.G. & S.L.

And also the collective? Do you imply that art is the result of a general intellect?

A.N.

I mean that as well. Around the individual artist who has made a work of art, we must always construe a collective intellect, a mass intellect. I don't imply that an objective, Averroistic general intellect exists somewhere as an object. What I mean is that the general intellect is a sort of subjective machine in motion, formed through the interaction of a great many singularities, of their ideas and products. It is an active collective, a multitude. Whenever we find a general intellect, we also discover a multitude of subjects who form this intellect, in the immanence or in the historical situation. This is the way in which we have to imagine the general intellect — as a multitude of subjects. I am convinced, by the way,

that this is what one ought to do when writing art history. With Caravaggio, we must go back through his work, through his paintings, to what surrounded him: the invention of oil paint, the study of characters in a particular work, the study of social relationships, for example who was the patron of a particular work, etc. All these relationships together create a work of art; this is how art history is created and this is how art is experienced, this is the way to actually see it. Art is always a bio-political phenomenon.

P.G. & S.L.

Is it like Pierre Bourdieu who reads Flaubert in Les règles de l'art *and sees social reality at work there?*

A.N.

Yes, but as it also is for Bakhtin. Both Bakhtin and Bourdieu base their work in a purely materialistic context; the first one does it from the bottom up and in a creative way, since he identifies the productive and collective engine of the artistic process, while the latter does it from the top down, in a classifying way but without losing sight of the creative element — he rather reduces it to parameters of expansion and of the production of dismeasure. Anyway, I think the great renewal of art history began with the Vienna school, this post-historic German school.

It is very important to the history of philosophy as well. On the one hand, the Vienna school already has all the techniques of historicism but, on the other hand, it also has the capacity to develop formal techniques. People like Wölfflin, Riegl, Dvořák possess this refinement of the instruments and of the technological analysis of history. It is historical positivism, you might say, that is completing its discovery function. Of course, there is also psychology; everything comes together in this silver period of German culture at the end of the nineteenth century.

P.G. & S.L.

You see a significant parallel between art and work, to such an extent that you occasionally interchange them. Art is work and work is art. You are familiar with relevant theses, such as that developed by Boltanski and Chiapello in Le nouvel esprit du capitalisme, *namely that, since the 1970s, capitalism has embraced artistic production and artistic critique and, most importantly, has integrated their values — think of flexibility, communication, creativity, etc. In those analyses, as in Virno's, a certain causal connection is proposed between art and work, a diachrony. You, on the other hand, propose a parallel in history, whereby the manner of artistic production and that of general labour occur simultaneously. What really happened in the 1970s, according to you?*

A.N.

In the 1970s, work changed — that is correct — but the question is: *why* did labour change in the 1970s? I think labour changed because the old system could no longer be preserved. The capitalists found they could no longer succeed in accumulating value within Fordism. So, firstly, you see that capitalism was forced to change its production system. Secondly, you get a new kind of labourer, one who is gifted with a production capacity in the linguistic area and in the area of imagination that is undoubtedly bigger than that of the labour class within the Fordist system. This transition is a result of generalized work refusal by the factory workers. On the one hand, work refusal can be understood as the actual refusal of the Taylorist organization of labour as mass labour and, on the other hand, as the attempt to reinvent production and its dignity, and it is precisely at this second point that we can connect art to work.

P.G. & S.L.

What do you mean by greater production capacity?

A.N.

We have to assume that workers want production, but not that which is based on the current capitalistic development. They want a more productive, more intellectual and more artistic production. They do not want their children to follow in their footsteps, to repeat the tragedy of working in a factory. For that reason, the paradox of work refusal gains the upper hand, and by that I mean that one is productive only in conflict. However, we should be very careful with introducing a quantitative criterion into productivity because it is a very ambiguous criterion. When you say 'more productive', you say that the labour force, subject to capitalism, produces a dismeasure and therefore breaks the measure. In the past, labour was considered and evaluated with respect to the time it took to produce the goods. Today, this relationship has become impossible because the labour force being used to produce the goods excessively or immoderately is intellectual, communicative and cooperative. The measure of value has gone, and, talking about that ambiguity, what does more or less mean in this context? It actually means 'different'. It is very difficult to determine relationships with the past when the production methods have changed.

P.G. & S.L.

Does this mean that labour is dismeasure?

A.N.

Labour is dismeasure against the law of value. These days, much more is implied in monetary units, and these monetary amounts are extremely uncertain and changeable. Added to that, financial measuring criteria are about social work, rather than the work of a singular worker. This huge change regarding labour that occurred in the 1970s is obviously connected to radical changes in the art world. Just like art, labour becomes freer and more intellectual. There are, in fact, two new circumstances. Firstly, labour is disorganized. Secondly, from the moment labour is disorganized it becomes easy prey to capitalistic subsumption. However, this does not mean that labour is not autonomous; on the contrary. In a way, work has become more autonomous than ever before because it is mental, intellectual, etc. So we have the simultaneous phenomena of a more realistic capitalistic subsumption of labour and a higher capacity for resistance. And this announces itself as a potency, as a free and open possibility.

P.G. & S.L.

Does this also mean that you believe in social engineering? Or, to put it another way, do you see yourself as an optimist concerning the organization of society? How does this optimism relate to your statement, for example, in Pipe-Line, *that the adage of Gramsci should be reversed to 'pessimism of the will and an optimism of knowledge'?*

A.N.

I am not an optimist; I am a realist. The statement you refer to was made against terrorism because the phrase 'optimism of the will and pessimism of knowledge' is a terrorist statement. Optimism of reason means that people are capable of building the common and that every hindrance against this potency comes from an irrational and parasitical command. It also means that people won't be able to resist the excess of producing and of knowing. A pessimism of the will, on the other hand, means that there isn't an organization yet and that people acknowledge and understand the difficulty of acting. That is why we speak of pessimism of the will, as acknowledgement of the difficulty of acting. Pessimism of the will is a translation of Spinoza's 'caute' (caution), of the tension we create when we open up to reality and to the clash of the passions, knowing full well that all this will lead us to the common. For me, this transition in the 1970s is a very important one — from the optimism of the will to the optimism of knowledge — which is necessarily also a pessimism of the will. Optimism of knowledge can also be expressed in terms of transcendental formalism. For me, Spinoza has played a part in that transition, with his dynamic perspective of the three kinds of knowledge that are being thwarted by indignation. Even Kant's formalism has merit here — the transition from the analytical level to the constructive level, from transcendental schematism to not merely aesthetic but also reflexive and ethical considerations about building specific communities that are a form of the common. The assumptions of what Michael and I call 'the lesser Kant' in *Commonwealth* — assumptions of a utopian finality and the construction of a common world — that is what I mean by optimism of knowledge. This general future-orientated knowledge that Kant so strongly developed is hypothetical and has a constructive nature.

P.G. & S.L.

In Art et multitude, *you write that art is 'contra-nature'. Nature stands for tiredness, death, dependency and repetition, while art stands for collective poiesis and love: it is the productive side of life. In* Commonwealth, *you and Michael Hardt introduced a specific opinion about love. To use your own metaphors, you are not interested in the love between bees and flowers but in the love between wasps and orchids. It is about the kind of love that enables us to escape individualism without locking them back up in the private sphere. Only then does love have political power that can focus on producing the common. How exactly do you relate this opinion on love to art and politics?*

A.N.

The first time Michael and I spoke about love was during an introduction to the book *Multitude* in Madrid. The first time this theme came up in the discussion with the audience, we were completely unprepared; everyone started laughing. 'What's this?' the audience seemed to think, communists, Marxists talking about love? To Michael and me, this hilarity, this laughter was a sign that we had hit upon something powerful, something that sticks, so this was a point to pursue. So what was the problem in *Commonwealth*? We wanted to determine a series of conditions in which the common could be constructed, not the natural common of the water, air, mountains etc. but the productive common. What is this productive common made of? It is the common produced by people. Meaning none of the water, air and all the other things we found, as the Bible says, at the moment we were born but all the things that were made by humans. Nothing in the natural common still belongs to us. From the very start, capitalism's accumulation process has gradually appropriated all the natural re-sources. We are, however, mainly interested in the man-made common since this, like the natural common, is usurped in the structure of capital but still shows up as a lively, expropriated human common. The entire environment we humans live in has been expropriated. Capitalism presents itself these days as the Capital of the common. It is a cognitive capitalism, of global finances and bio-politics. What capital has not been able to appropriate, and never will be able to appropriate, is the energy of the labour force or, in other words, the energy of that productive force we call these days the power of invention or, still differently, the multitude of individuals that produce the common. After all, the common is not merely the whole of produced wealth but also the productive force par excellence. One can safely say that there is no production these days that has not been built by the common. The problem we faced was: how do we make the transition from this produced common to human co-operation at the level of relationships and community? And there we found ourselves — in opposition to the classical tendency like Spinoza's — as part of a construed solidarity that is not peace-loving, not sweet-voiced, but a solidarity that arises from conflict, through and in the clash of passions, one that enforces its naturalness and enforces itself in its strength. We have called this multiple and conflict-laden tendency 'love', a love clearly distinct from the religious love — let there be no misunderstanding, there is a fundamental atheism in this opinion of love — and also clearly distinct from any form of bourgeois love that is always based on identity and on a union of identities. The love we envisage enforces its naturalness and is a common tension of passions. Love is also something that people construe and that we renew or remake today. Its naturalness was overwhelmed by new affective and cultural attitudes. It is no longer possible to free nature from the massive shock love underwent and it itself has so often reproduced. Nature and love have been changed by the social practices in which they are reproduced. Nature and love have responded positively with regard to these changes and have construed new shapes of sexuality, pleasure and life itself. From feminism to biotechnology, love has renewed itself. The common is renewing as well and is therefore renewed by love. So this is the new way of looking at the love we are trying to develop. As far as the imagery we use in the preface in *Commonwealth* about the love between wasps and orchids, this imagery was copied from Deleuze and Guattari. Bees make love to flowers for the sake of pollination, with a defined function, as 'identity' and in a fixed pattern of natural efficiency that cannot be tampered with, whereas the wasp also makes love but with a love that has no function or identity. The wasp makes love with an orchid flower simply because he enjoys it, just like that, without other thoughts, and, while he does it, the wasp creates a community but it is a contra-natural community. What Michael and I envision, therefore, is a solidarity that has nothing to do with religion nor with the bourgeois family or with identity in general. The love of the wasp and the orchid is naturally a metaphor for a contra-natural love and for a fundamentally atheist idea of love. In contrast to a bourgeois union of identities, our idea of love is about a community being formed by the meeting of passions, a community that arises from contradictory passions and from conflicts. It is about a common beloved by the many singularities or by the multitude.

Our reflections about love are an example of what I call hypothetical thinking, but I would also like to emphasize that we very emphatically talk about love as such, ordinary love. On the one hand, we have romantic bourgeois love, leading to the construction of families, with all its accompanying disasters and all the catastrophes flowing from it. On the other hand, we have the religious, Christian love that is the basis for all sorts of fanaticism and is, therefore, also a guarantee that a community will not be created. In fact, Christian love has changed into something transcendental, on which people base social hierarchy and, next to that, all we feel is the opposite of love. Christian love is a love of sacrifice founded in the destruction of real love between people. To visualize our opinion of love, we could have made an apologia of St. Francis of Assisi. He is a true wasp. He stands for everything the church resisted. Poverty and love are unthinkable for and inside the Christian church. Next to this atheism, criticism of the family is essentially the basis of our idea of love. Hegel thinks that society is shaped on the family, the civil society or the market and the state. I feel these are the three institutions — family, market, state — that we have to take action against if we want to build a collectivity, generality or common.

Something else needs to be said too — the fact that we need to differentiate between art and non-art, between what is art and what is not art. To me, non-art is essentially seen in the naturalistic and individualistic reduction of the collective working that is produced by art. Non-art is where this naturalistic reduction to the individual takes place.

This can be fully compared to the romantic and religious love that is locked up in the family and, as a result, completely reduced to a function and therefore an identity, which equals non-love. Parallel to that, art is reduced to non-art to the extent to which it is reduced to individual, natural identity.

P.G. & S.L.

Then you probably have a problem with the concept of individual genius, like the one that took root at the end of the nineteenth century and is, for instance, now being constructed around Van Gogh? I am not talking about Van Gogh himself but about the discourse that was constructed around him that made the painter out to be a sort of individual genius. Do you think this romantic view of art and the genius is problematic?

A.N.

The concept of the genius in general is not a problem, but, at a certain moment, it becomes a mercantile and propagandistic concept. Obviously, there are real geniuses. Michelangelo and Picasso are effectively geniuses, but they are so because of everything they manage to produce, their abilities and what they bring about. Contrary to that is the genius as a purely commercial concept. We are being overrun with geniuses who accomplish nothing, make nothing and are nothing, who are a void. The majority of the art market today extols this 'nothing'.

P.G. & S.L.

Do you also believe that the authorship of the artist is merely a product of the art market? Does this mean that the oeuvre will be reduced to something through which we can anticipate and predict market value? In other words, do you see authorship as a necessary tool for the marketing of art?

A.N.

For me, the art market is the most despicable and lowest thing in existence. If you go to Venice, to the Punta della dogana or the Palazzo Grassi and view the permanent exhibition of the François Pinault Foundation, you will see it. These days, the great production of value does not take place via the accumulation of singular objects but through the accumulation of social labour and, in the Punta della dogana, you can actually see this. Accumulation is, as it were, represented by these museums and by these great mercantile art exhibitions, in which works are exhibited of completely different value that form a symbol of this ubiquitous and extremely violent capitalist accumulation.

When I was younger and came to live in exile in France, at first I held jobs in the fashion industry. In Italy, I came from a region with many specific fashion districts and the French were mighty interested in that back then. In France, there were and still are fashion districts that are also entirely based on authorship, which relies on the repetition of a brand name. It was very amusing to speak with French art sociologists like Boltanski and Chiapello. We immediately agreed with each other. The art market is absolutely uninterested in knowing which expression of knowledge or invention lies at the basis of an artwork. The artwork these days is aimed at exploitation of copyright, extolling the virtues of the individual so that (s)he is transformed into a marketable commodity, into a genius, which can generate an ever-growing series of profits and, this way, create a collective that only exists as an auction market.

P.G. & S.L.

In the speech you gave at Tate Britain about art and immaterial work — the text was incorporated in the new edition of Art et multitude *under the title 'Métamorphoses' — you end with the proposition of a programme, a road that consists of phases and that can determine the style of an artistic production. But you seem to want to go beyond the artistic production. You even mention explicitly — after you have made a connection to Virno's expression of labour as performance — that we have to go a step beyond Virno. You argue that the 'commune' that was developed in artistic forms has to be incarnated through a collective decision in a common government and in free forms of life. How should we do that concretely? Do you mean common institutions, decision-making procedures or merely forms of life?*

A.N.

A bit of everything. What interested me most, when I made those statements, was in underlining that there will also always have to be institutions of which you can say: institutions we will be happy to have. There is often an illusion that we can live without institutions and that free forms of life can be developed without any rule or order, forms of life that need no institutions. I don't think that is true. Not all institutions necessarily imply a lack of freedom. As in the connection with capitalism, I would say even more; I am inclined to differentiate between capitalism and the functioning or the attitude of the market. The current market is completely usurped by capital, but that doesn't mean that the market necessarily has to be usurped by the capital. The form of market exchange, like the form of institutions in general, has an autonomy that has to be conquered time and time again.

P.G. & S.L.

In Commonwealth, you and Michael Hardt state that a neoliberal society will try to completely privatize the common. The private stands in opposition to the public that is guaranteed by the state. According to you, the common, however, wants to break through the exclusive dichotomy of public versus private. How are we to understand this common then? And who guarantees free access to the collective? Which institutions and mechanisms can protect the common?

A.N.

You don't ask for much! Only a hundred thousand dollars!

P.G. & S.L.

Can you give examples of strategies used to transcend the false dichotomy of private versus public in the common?

A.N.

There is a fundamental problem, namely that of a legal definition of the collective or the general. These days, there is no such definition. Only international law has a sort of definition, which concerns the delineation of spaces in which the state rule is invalid whereby a trans-national space is delineated or one talks of unattributed spaces such as deep water, Antarctica, the moon etc. In other words, what exists as a definition for the 'collective' is purely negative. The collective is that which is neither public nor private. It is called *res nullius*, the right of no one. However, in the past, there have been different definitions of 'common right', especially in the seventeenth century when the occupation of the American continent began. There were great schools of Spanish Jesuits to whom we owe a profoundly positive definition. So, for example, the common included areas inhabited by the indigenous population, areas collectively assigned to the Indian autochthons. I hardly need add that this definition has never been realized. The conquistadors utterly destroyed the positive definition. The land has been privatized or become public government or state property. The strong resistance, that was generally organized by the Spanish church, to the genocide of the American native population by the conquistadors and European occupiers is based on this positive definition. How can we define the common these days? First and foremost, we already have everything that is naturally communal and general, like air, water, the mountains. Furthermore, there are language usages, legal rules, etc. and they cover everything that falls under the public state protection. The question is how we make the transition from public to common. We know how to make the private public; there

are the experiments of real communism — like that of the Soviet Union — the socializing of the private goods that was carried out in a totalitarian way. How to privatize the public is demonstrated continuously. The main problem for us today is to define the common institutionally and administratively and that is, of course, a very complicated matter. I lean toward a radical democratization of the socialization of goods.

P.G. & S.L.
Who can protect these radical democratic institutions? Who protects the laws and the legal apparatus of a common government?

A.N.
One can add to your question: who can and is allowed to use force? Because I think that there are already whole series of phenomena and activities that can be analysed — phenomena on which to build and from which to move forward. What we are debating here is not a programme but a tactic or an analysis of ways to build a programme. These days, there is some reflection on the notion of the common and there is a growing awareness of the fact that the dichotomy between private and public is false. There is not enough research into how the transition could be brought about. It remains a difficult problem. Next year, we

will organize a seminar in Paris with a few friends to discuss this very question; how do you make the transition from the public to the general or collective? In other words, we want to, and have to, debate, look for answers to this question. The question of how to valorize the public for the general or collective good is undoubtedly a tactical question. Let's take an example. Today the public domain valorizes the private and, what is more, the public serves the private. Maybe we should imagine the transition as a reversal of the function of the public. In this area in the fifth district (of Paris) and especially if you walk in the direction of the Pantheon, one square metre costs €25,000 on the real estate market. In the same neighbourhood, the French public sector maintains several primary schools, public swimming pools and a variety of institutions or initiatives that serve the common. So there already is a common function that goes against the logic of profit and concrete profits of the private real estate sector. The point is, of course, to increase these examples, as we say, from the water to the university. The goal is to make natural goods collective, in the face of any attempt to privatize even the cultural and intellectual wealth, to make any copyright or any appropriation of the common impossible.

P.G. & S.L.
But this community effect is protected by the state?

A.N.
No. Very rarely, but hardly ever. Marxist theoreticians of the law have shown how the right wing public is subordinate to private law and, therefore, to the functions of what MacPherson called 'property individualism'. Let us rather ask how to build a world in which the general or collective rules over the private and the public. I think we should reverse the function of the public, which is currently in the service of the private. This is a moment of transition in which we can launch a radicalism of the collective again in a democratic manner. Of course, one can make all kinds of objections at this point. But that is what we have to do, transit to a political radicalism of the common. As an old man, and I speak only for myself now, I am and will remain a communist and think that being a communist means precisely that these days. What could communism be but the recovery and re-discovery of the function of the collective and general?

P.G. & S.L.
We might all agree on the general goal of the common but the question remains about how to make the transition.

A.N.

You are enthusiastic because the possibility is real. The history of the twentieth century has shown that taking the state and changing its structures is possible. A radical change that denies private selfishness the chance to develop is actually very possible. It begins in the education system and continues at all levels. We have no choice, by the way. The alternative is permanent economic crisis, the destruction of all the common achievements we have made so far, having to work without pay, the precarity, increasing unemployment, working till you're eighty. Where did retirement go these days? Any reality opposing the common exposes itself as total madness these days. Madness is having to acknowledge that it is art that is being shown in Punta della Dogana by Pinault. But, as Brecht used to say, there are three of us now, we can start a cell!

P.G. & S.L.

At the same time as the biennale boom, we have seen that, regarding content, people often refer to radical political ideas. The books written by you and Hardt but also by Virno and Agamben frequently resurface in catalogues and exhibitions. At Tate Modern in London, by contrast, the bookshelves only hold books on a single 'philosophical movement', namely critical theory. Here, we discern a paradoxical, almost cynical movement. This proposes that while, on the one hand, neoliberalism envelops the entirety of the art sector, it also simultaneously offers the opportunity to criticize it from within. How do you see this? Your theories are becoming very popular and are used in the art world, which is strange considering that you really talk about reality and do not produce fiction at all.

A.N.

These kinds of phenomena obviously embarrass me. But... and yet... there is also another side. I remember the times when speaking up was difficult. This book [points to *Art et multitude*] was published in the original version by Politi: the publisher of *Flash Art*, a somewhat bizarre publisher with a famous art magazine which is well known for its publicity role in the art world. But Politi was the only publisher in Italy willing to publish *Arte e multitudo*. After I went into exile in France, no one in Italy was willing to publish my books anymore. So, on the one hand, there is this embarrassment about being used by the commercial art world; on the other hand, and from the standpoint of a circulation of discourses, this being used is also useful. It suits me fine, since I live off it. I survive and make my living by publishing, just like an employee. I serve a master. Paradoxically I can say, therefore, that I am a worker, no more no less, a cultural worker who lives from what he writes. But what is this all about, really? The heart of the matter is the capitalist necessity to appropriate all knowledge because intellectual labour has become the focal point of production. With that, we return to the problem we were just talking about and the big art markets that are forms of capitalist appropriation, to 'enclosure' and the way collective grounds were fenced in and taken into private possession in the early period of capitalism. From this point of view, the problem becomes one of conflict, of how to form resistance and how to create alternatives. These are problems about how to make the transition to the common, how to engage in this conflict now that the labour unions have become so weak and no longer carry any weight. The major problem of today is, therefore, also the organization of intellectual work. This means putting work into the transformation and/or sabotage of those big art centres, from the inside out.

Alienation and idolization are obsolete concepts that are no longer valid today. My books on the shelves of art market shops? The entire history of civilization is riddled with it; there are thousands of examples. Take, for instance, Machiavelli and Spinoza, whose revolutionary

ideas were read by the same lawmakers they warned about and revolted against. But, yes, these days things are done far more subtly. Only last night, I was invited to a high-end party organized here in Paris for the opening of a new wing at Tate Modern in London. That is real functionality. The same name, Antonio Negri, serves to make publicity for the curator and the new wing of that art temple. The invitation is not really meant for me, a friend, but for Antonio Negri, the author's name that becomes a brand name in this context and with which they can create publicity. You know, I always keep a great example in mind, of Tito to be specific. After he had participated in the Russian Revolution, he came back to Belgrade in the twenties, as an agent for the International, to surreptitiously organize the revolution in Yugoslavia. Tito then posed as a big livestock trader and travelled all over the land with a gold ring on each finger, and, as is proper in the Balkans, a mouth full of gold teeth. In the end, he succeeded in forming the largest Communist party in Europe and he recruited mainly from the leading classes, at universities, etc. This is the right road, according to me, go and visit those exhibitions and use biennales to change things from within.

P.G. & S.L.

But isn't resistance neutralized that way? To quote Bifo, the intellectual is an outlaw in both the right and the wrong sense. There is no room anymore for intellectuals to operate in the places you would expect, at universities, in politics, in the media, etc. The only places the intellectual is still welcome is somewhere at the margin, in the art world. Is this not ambiguous? Look at Sloterdijk and many other critical thinkers; they were all given asylum in the art world, where they can still make their voices heard. Their voice is, however, reduced to fiction this way.

A.N.

The discourse is always the same. This is about the organization of refusal, of movements. It was no different in seventeenth century Holland. Then there was a genuine school of social change organized by small movements and sects who resisted absolutist power tendencies to act against the administrative oligarchy and ecclesiastical authorities. Or remember pre-revolutionary Russia, where a strong populist resistance movement operated against the autocratic power structures that stayed in power through cruelty and made themselves felt under the Czar's regime. It is simply impossible not to act like that. It is simply impossible not to erect new alternative schools every time and with all the risks it entails. Also remember Italy in the 1970s with Bifo, by the way, who was active in the movement with Radio Alice and the magazine *A/traverso*. One has to be disobedient. Resistance occurs through disobedience. Producing art occurs by resisting. These sudden unbelievable twists and enormous transformations are, by the way, typical of the art world. A long time ago, Christian Marazzi — a friend who writes marvellous books about the economy like *Il posto dei calzini* — lived in New York with Basquiat, a young graffiti artist who was a total nobody at first. They were poor, possessed absolutely nothing and, from one day to the next, Basquiat was picked up by the art scene in which a whole lot of money circulated. Those were the circles in which Andy Warhol moved in the early 1980s. From one moment to the next, Basquiat's work was being sold like hot cakes for a whole lot of money and he became filthy rich. Some people failed to understand how Basquiat could surround himself with that environment, with those people. How can you suddenly start living like that and forget everything? That is the whole point; the commercial mechanism in the art world is like that: it turns a poor slob into a rich man overnight and of course, tries to change his ideas in the process. Christian decided that the whole challenge was to refuse to allow these ideas to be stolen from you and to maintain a continuum in the revolutionary process at any given time.

P.G. & S.L.

Does art as a social institution have potency, subversive power? Does it have a possibility to change things? Or is it only discourse?

A.N.

One sees that nothing is happening these days, nothing at all. Sometimes there are global, all-encompassing phenomena through which institutions change. An example is 1968. The 1960s, when the biennale and the film festival of Venice underwent enormous transformations. That was formidable, back then. Art can run ahead in the sphere of knowledge while at the same time following in the practical sphere and institutionally following the movement and limping behind. In other words, institutions that are formed around art, like the biennales and great exhibitions, lag behind when compared to resistance movements but when it comes to knowledge, art leads and often runs ahead of the resistance movements. The 1960s and what happened in both the US and in Italy are an example of this. Or we could point to the fourteenth century, with St. Francis of Assisi and Giotto, whose new artistic realism often anticipated the democratic policy of the Italian 'comuni' [city states]. The examples are endless.

P.G. & S.L.

A specific art form that explicitly aims at the common is community art. This form arose in the 1960s and seemed to go underground in the 1980s and 1990s, only to surface again in our times. What do you think of this form of artistic and/or social production? Community art often intends to improve social cohesion and integration through art or collective art processes, sometimes also to emancipate people, to make them politically articulate, etc. Do you think art can serve such social goals? Do you believe that art like this has the potency to change things, in contrast to the singular artist?

A.N.

Of course, I am highly doubtful about those possibilities. On the other hand, I still think that initiatives of community art can produce moments of solidarity and cultural education and that, on top of that, they can provide support for young people and older people from socially weak population ranks. Every kind of change belongs to a form of community art, if you will. I know of several kinds of initiatives here in Paris, of big cores of squatters who, for example, attempt to introduce art forms connected to working collective allotment gardens. Those are interesting initiatives, all the more so because these squatters contain many population groups, many immigrants, illegals etc. They are pockets of resistance. But it is also true that no major social changes will be brought about this way nor will any great works of art be created. There are the multifarious initiatives of the social centres in Italy. Or in Montpellier, there is a group of sociologists, with Pascal Nicolas-le Strat, which focuses on precisely these transversal and hybrid creative experiments and occasionally succeeds in producing social phenomena. I think it would be a very interesting analysis we have to make.

P.G. & S.L.

Both in Empire *and in* Multitude, *you and Michael Hardt describe certain concrete forms in which the multitude starts to form and starts resisting, like the manifestations of the alter-globalists and the gay movement. We noticed your attention for their aesthetic, sometimes theatrical approach: the dressing up, the happenings, the staging. Sometimes these descriptions remind us of what Bakhtin says about the carnivalesque — a form of symbolic inversion. Symbolic inversion, however, is also problematic; it is merely symbolic, it is temporary and therefore actually confirms the existing power constitution. Do you think that the use of artistic forms in resistance strategies could really lead to political shifts?*

A.N.

What you say is completely true. It is clear that these phenomena are completely absorbed by the capitalist structures and by the power structures. But they do lead to an alternative spontaneity. It is more or less the same problem you see in the French *banlieues* [suburbs], where the youngsters wear typical hip-hop clothes: low-riding pants, sweaters with upturned hoods. These are phenomena that, in themselves, are not determinant factors but they have an important function in the communication and construction of a basis. You see, they construct identity. Personally, I am against identities but these are identities that resist and can have a significant value during a certain period. I am against identities because they are organically absorbed and incorporated in the movements in the capitalist spirit. The agility and transformation of identities, in contrast, forms a subversive element. Police officers and reactionary parties sense this perfectly; they can tell immediately. Roma gypsies were hated because they are nomads; Jews were hated because they travelled around; immigrants are hated because they migrate. The command worships identities. Identity is only positive when it transforms and keeps moving. To name only one example: feminism didn't take long to move from identity to difference, and from difference to the equal.

P.G. & S.L.

Then what is the role of the artistic in all this? Because these groups often use those artistic forms.

A.N.

They function as aggregation, as binding, bringing together. This is extremely important. They allow for immediate recognition of a friend, of one who thinks and rebels just like you.

P.G. & S.L.

In your own work, the artistic plays an important role as well. Alongside the philosophical work, you wrote the autobiographical Pipe-Line, *in the form of an experimental, epistolary novel. You use figures from Shakespeare's Tempest in your Spinoza interpretation in* Anomalia selvaggia *[Wild Anomaly]. Finally, you also write theatre pieces like Trilogie de la différence. Why do you sometimes opt for narrative elements in a philosophical argument or do you explicitly choose fiction? Can you express and clarify other things in these more artistic forms than in your philosophical work?*

A.N.

You have to know that, for more than ten years, from the 1960s until 1979, I was active in resistance movements and exclusively wrote texts about Marxism. The best known work is *Marx* *oltre Marx*, but I published an entire series of books and political texts then, a lot in the papers and magazines I often supervised as well, from *Quaderni rossi* to *Classe operaia*. I churned out books about state rule, sabotage by the proletarians, a Marxist method for bringing about social changes, etc. Political pamphlets too, the most important ones have recently been republished as *I libri del rogo* [The books of the stake]. In 1979, this life and activism came to an abrupt halt when I ended up in jail and, at that moment, I needed a change in style. That change in style began with a book about Spinoza that I wrote in prison. *Anomalia selvaggia* is a turning point, it marks a major shift.

Before that, I wrote mostly in political terms; after that, I wrote mostly philosophical works, in philosophical terms. Now that I have completed the great work I wrote with Michael Hardt, the trilogy of *Empire, Multitude* and *Commonwealth*, the time has come to change again and so I am looking once more for a different style. The theatre experiment is very useful in this. I would like to work on an autobiography. I am trying to achieve a level of writing that is much simpler and more direct, quasi novelistic, without all the cultural references characteristic of a philosophical text. Writing theatre is very useful because you have to write in terms of dialogue and invent daily, ordinary and yet strongly expressive forms. I wrote six plays, the first three of which have been performed and published as *Trilogie de la différence* [which will become *Trilogy of the Resistance* in the English edition]. The next three plays will be published as *Trilogie de la critique* and the performance of the first play is planned in the Reims theatre in November 2011, while all three plays will be performed in Théâtre Gérard Philippe of Saint Dénis in the autumn of 2011. I don't want to publish the plays in Italy because my reputation is too negative there, so they are only played in French and the English translation is on its way. What I want to say is that theatre allows me to achieve a daily, ordinary and general language usage. In my life, I have spoken about politics and, after that, I have spoken about philosophy. From now on, I want to speak in a general form, in a common way. I see theatre as an experiment that is useful in searching for this new form of writing. After all, writing is hard.

P.G. & S.L.
Has the change in style connected with a change in the content of your thinking?

A.N.
But of course. Changes in style are, after all, accompanied by great changes in my life. Before I became active and wrote about Marxism, I published academic things as professor at a university. There is a huge difference between the university Negri and the militant Negri. And the difference between a free Negri and a Negri in prison or exile could not be greater. I wrote my book on Spinoza in prison, as I said. After that, I lived for years in exile or semi-imprisonment, a nightmare that lasted until 2002/2003. When this whole business was finally concluded, I had already begun my big work with Michael and was, therefore, caught again in the mechanism of a philosophical style; I was stuck in the same habit. And there is a continuity that goes from *Spinoza* to *Commonwealth*, a continuity of almost thirty years of work. And now there is yet another turning point. Now the years begin that I write as a retired man, as a common old man.

P.G. & S.L.
Is the play La Mandragola *by Machiavelli an example for you?*

A.N.
Oh, well, *La Mandragola*, that theme is laughter. Laughter has always been extremely important for me. In *Il lavoro di Giobbe* [The work of Job], I have dedicated an entire chapter to the effect of laughter. I

continuously collect material about laughter, have collected a whole stack of index cards by now, and planned to make a book of all that for years but, so far, I have not succeeded in bringing all the material together. The theme of laughter as a potency is also very much present in Spinoza. It can be connected with what we said earlier, with regards to the carnivalesque laughter of Bakhtin. In *Commonwealth*, too, we finish with a reflection on the revolutionary power of laughing. Its importance cannot be stressed enough. For example, I am extremely fond of Ruzante, a less well-known author from the sixteenth century. He came from Padova and wrote in the dialect of this Veneto region — the same area I come from — grand tragedies about the farm workers' poverty and misery, real tragedies but interwoven with extraordinary comical moments that cause great hilarity. Laughter is always knowledge and resistance. Too often, definitions have reduced laughter to a linguistic phenomenon or to a consequence of language rules, I mean to mere linguistics discrepancies, breaches, inappropriate comparisons, etc. That is absolutely not the case.

Laughter is an ontological expression, a form of ontology, and the disproportionality the laughter refers to is always real. In the biblical Job, people laugh or, better, the being laughs when the monsters Leviathan and Behemoth taste defeat and collapse when faced with a new natural order, due to the actions of humans. This also happens in Aeschylus, when Prometheus laughs at the gods from whom he has stolen the fire. Or people laugh in Shakespeare when, for example, King Lear disapproves of the sovereigns and condemns the order they stand for, or with Caliban when he praises the nature over which he has more power as a slave than Prospero does over the delusions of power. In short, laughter is both realistic and tragic. It is observing people and their uniqueness. Laughter is a materialistic view; it has retained the joy of the early materialism of the beginning of modernity, as found in Bacon, Giordano Bruno, Spinoza and also in Chaucer, Boccaccio, Ariosto.

I have always lived close to poetry and close to literature in general, and close to the visual arts too, by the way; lots of reading, lots of books, a submersion in literature and art. In that sense, my upbringing in literature and art has helped me enormously in my life; what a good fortune and privilege to have known that. I could mention so many examples. Like the other day, with the ash cloud and Iceland, which brought to mind Leopardi, his inimitably funny *Dialogo della Natura e di un Islandese* [Dialogue of Nature with an Icelander], comical, appropriate and illustrative in the current situation. Leopardi targets all the problems regarding human control of nature — the contrast between overconfidence and the limitations of modern man — with irony, causticity and mild indulgence, and all this in a few simple sentences and pages. Having a direct relationship with our culture, even though we know its boundaries, is of the utmost importance.

193

Revolution from Within:
A Grandson of Government Changes Chinese Art Policy

An Interview with Zhang Changcheng

Alison M. Friedman

In the Talks at the Yan'an Forum on Literature and Art delivered in 1942, Chairman Mao Zedong outlined the role that literature and art were to play in his revolution: 'Literature and art are subordinate to politics, but in their turn exert a great influence on politics. Revolutionary literature and art are part of the whole revolutionary cause; they are cogs and wheels in it'.[1] This talk helped define the role of the artist in the Chinese republic as one to further the political goals of the Party; 'art for art's sake' was deemed bourgeois and, therefore, counter-revolutionary.[2]

This philosophy reached fever pitch during the Cultural Revolution (1966–1976), when all performances were outlawed except for eight 'model dramas' known as the Yang Ban Xi. These were adapted from traditional Chinese stories, and, with Socialist-realist clarity, 'all the good guys were farmers and revolutionary soldiers [...] singing and dancing in the broad spotlight. All the bad guys were landlords and anti revolutionaries, who wore dark make-up and were poorly lit'.[3] Two of the works were ballets — *The Red Detachment of Women* (National Ballet of China, 1964) and *White Haired Girl* (Shanghai Ballet Company, 1965) — the former of which depicts the liberation of a peasant girl and her rise in the Communist Party. After the end of the Cultural Revolution, when the Yang Ban Xi fell out of favour, these ballets were revived and *The Red Detachment of Women* became part of the National Ballet's repertoire, performed regularly in China and on tour internationally along with the company's contemporary ballet and classical Western repertoire.

After the 'reform and opening-up' attributed to Deng Xiaoping took effect in the late 1970s and 1980s, China began allowing the first slow trickles of exchange in the cultural arena. In 1986, the American Dance Festival[4] invited four choreographers and educators from China to attend that summer's festival in New York City, including the then-principal of the Guangdong Dance School, Ms Yang Meiqi. While there, Yang observed her first modern dance class, and immediately approached the director of the festival, Charles Reinhart, to ask 'Why do those students roll on the floor in class?' Reinhart considered explaining the physical concepts of fall and recovery, of momentum and grounding the body's weight into the floor in order to release upward. Instead, recalls Reinhart, 'I asked, 'Why not?' That was the moment she looked at me and said, 'We need this in China'.[5]

With support from the American Dance Festival, the Asian Cultural Council[6] and the Guangdong provincial government, Yang organized China's first four-year modern dance training programme at her school in 1987. Teachers, including Sarah Stackhouse (US), Ruby Shang (US), Douglas Nielsen (US), Claudia Gitelman (US) and Lucas Hoving (NL/US), came for three- to six-month periods, and graduates of the programme founded China's first official modern dance company, the Guangdong Modern Dance Company,[7] in 1992.

Since then, several more such companies have emerged, including:

Living Dance Studio (1994), Beijing Modern Dance Company (BMDC) (1995), Jin Xing Modern Dance Theatre (1999–2000), Zuhe Niao (2005), BeijingDance/LDTX (2005), brand nu dance (2007), TAO Dance Theatre (2008) and Beijing Contemporary Dance Theatre (2008).[8]

This includes companies with a more established reputation and experience of performing abroad, but it is by no means an exhaustive list of modern dance practitioners in China, as there are individuals, collectives and school groups operating throughout the country with varying degrees of consistency and exposure. This list also excludes choreographers teaching and creating work in the academies full time.

The styles of the work these different companies perform vary from more classically trained, technical dance to more multimedia performance art. Content of the works is also quite diverse, yet rarely is it explicitly political. What *is* unexpectedly political about these companies, however, is the way in which their organizational

1   'Talks at the Yan'an Forum on Literature and Art' (May 1942), Selected Works of Mao Tse-Tung: Vol. III (Beijing: Foreign Languages Press, 1967), p. 86. Prepared for the internet by David J. Romagnolo, June 1997. www.marx2mao.com/Mao/YFLA42.html#t.
2   Ibid.
3   'An Educator's Guide to Yang Ban Xi', Shadowdistribution.com, 2005. www.shadowdistribution.com/study_guides.html.
4   ADF is an annual six-week programme of classes and performances for students and professionals from throughout the US and abroad. See www.americandancefestival.org.
5   Telephone interview with Charles Reinhart conducted by the author on 21 June 2003.
6   www.asianculturalcouncil.org/.
7   GMDC, www.gmdmdc.com.
8   Living Dance Studio: www.ccdworkstation.com
    Beijing Modern Dance Company (BMDC): http://blog.sina.com.cn/bmdc
    Jin Xing Modern Dance Theatre: no website
    Zuhe Niao: www.kkleeart.com/niao.htm
    BeijingDance/LDTX: www.beijingldtx.com
    brand nu dance http://nunu.we23.org/
    TAO Dance Theatre: http://blog.sina.com.cn/taoye1026
    Beijing Contemporary Dance Theatre: http://www.bjcdt.org.

models defy existing classifications of artistic organizations, thereby challenging the status and definition(s) of art in Chinese society.

By the late 1990s, culture and arts organizations had two official options: they could be established by the government as state-owned enterprises (SOEs) or be registered independently from the government as a commercial enterprise. Individuals could not register their own enterprises — arts/culture organizations or otherwise — until 2005, at which point individuals could officially establish their own enterprise, although this was still under the commercial classification. Art was, therefore, either political or commercial, at least according to official registries. Performing groups and artists' collectives, like the Living Dance Studio, which did not want to conform to either of these categories, chose to exist unofficially and underground, without any registered status.

In 2006, the process of changing the law began, to allow arts and culture groups a third option — that of registering as not-for-profit organizations under the Ministry of Civil Affairs, creating a category that is distinct from both state-run troupes and commercially classified troupes. Mr. Zhang Changcheng, Director of the Beijing Modern Dance Company (BMDC), was instrumental in lobbying the government for this monumental policy change, and BMDC became the first artistic organization in China to be officially recognized as a not-for-profit entity.

Zhang Changcheng may not be what the West expects when it thinks of a rebel in China. He speaks with the flowery, evasive language of a classical scholar, which perhaps comes from his upbringing as the child of an elite political family who expected him to enter business or politics rather than the art world. A nonconformist in his family, perhaps, but hardly the typical dissenter in the artistic or social world, Zhang feels it is more effective to work within the system to change it, rather than to fight against it or shun it by existing underground or on the fringes.

This interview is not an academic exploration of the roles or relationship of politics and art in China; rather, it is a glimpse into the perspective of a professional arts manager who believes in working according to the letter of the law in order to change that law — in much the same way as a martial arts master uses his opponent's *qi* against him — and thereby create a revolution from within.

Alison M. Friedman

Tell us about your family background and your education. Were they closely linked?

Zhang Changcheng

My grandfather was a very high-level government official. His situation was quite strange — he was the son of a capitalist family, the kind that should not have been welcome in the Communist Party. He was educated at St. John's University[9] in Shanghai, and could speak foreign languages. But he gave up his leather shoes to join the revolution. He felt society had too many problems so he joined the army to fight the Japanese, and rose in the ranks to become a general. Then, in 1949, with the founding of 'New China', he was promoted to a high-ranking official position, a member of the first generation of the Communist Party.

His influence on me was profound. Not a daily influence, but towards my spirit. He taught me crucial values about how to live my life. Let your actions speak louder than your words. If you do things well, that speaks for itself; you don't need to go around bragging. People will always talk, but don't use words to answer, use actions. Things may not go smoothly, but you can't control what is external, you can only control yourself. You must maintain your own standards, not just abide by other people's.

A political family makes you understand that your life has certain requirements on it, and you must face your responsibilities. You can't escape them! A political upbringing also taught me how to hold my tongue. When you must speak, you speak. But sometimes it's better not to say anything at all, than to speak irresponsibly. You must be clear what you are and are not capable of doing. If you can do ten, only promise eight because something might happen to prevent ten. And whatever you do, don't promise twenty!

My grandfather always made me read the newspaper, read those government publications, very official things I didn't understand when I was young. He made me explain what I understood from the words I read, and slowly taught me to read between the lines. He wanted me to know that there was never something empty on the page, there were always reasons and back stories. You had to know the

9 St. John's University was an Anglican university located in Shanghai, China. Before the Chinese Civil War, it was regarded as one of the most prestigious universities in Shanghai and China. In 1952, the university was broken up and its faculties were joined with similar faculties from other universities to create several specialist universities. See http://en.wikipedia.org/wiki/Saint_John's_University,_Shanghai.

context behind the words, so he always made me read, read, read, read things that had nothing to do with my life.

Now, when I read a news story, I can see the full picture behind it — I have a sense of why that story was chosen to be reported, and what it might portend beyond itself. I always question: why is it this and not that being reported, what is the reason for this news coming out? Is there a new policy coming out and that's why they want us to think about this topic now? What might that policy be? What are the official agendas and how might they affect things? There's the surface story, and then there's the whole machine operating behind it. If you read carefully, you can start to pick up on how this system operates and what might be in the works. It's right there on the front page for you to find if you look for it. Many just see a clear crystal ball, but in it I see the future.

A.M.F.

You studied business at university. When did you first become interested in art?

Z.C.

I was always interested. Art was different, it allowed you to transcend daily life and enter another world. When I was little, art was just a curiosity. Then it became a habit. Then it became a passion. Then it became a part of my life, and finally it became my destiny.

I got involved with Beijing Modern Dance Company around 1996 and officially became director a year or so later. At first, my family was really against it. They thought art should be a hobby, not a profession. So this was a big pressure, but I still insisted. Because I feel one can choose a job but one can't choose their profession, because that has to do with destiny. I didn't choose art, art chose me.

A.M.F.

What were your family's objections?

Z.C.

They thought I was just playing around, being a playboy hanging out with all these dancers, not really working or doing anything. They thought that someone with my background would have so many opportunities; they believed I just chose something 'fun' to play around.

I faced a lot of pressure about how to measure 'success'. Success in art is not so quantifiable. I watched as my classmates and other contemporaries rose to more prestigious titles in their companies, received increased salaries, other measurable benchmarks of success. But with art, it's harder to quantify. So this is where my grandfather's education was most important, about how you must maintain your own internal standards that are not reliant on external validation.

A.M.F.

How did your political family background play a role in your work with Beijing Modern Dance Company?

Z.C.

Because of my political upbringing, I was more sensitive to how politics worked and how one could work within that system. I therefore knew how to protect BMDC from potential political pressures in the late 1990s. I was able to give them even more creative space and freedom. BMDC was, therefore, able to do a lot of pioneering and avant-garde performances for its time, but never underground. We were able to do them right out in the open.

For example, by the end of the 1990s, every performance had to be vetted by a government official. Since I was familiar with the government, I would already have a sense of which part of a piece might cause alarm or be an issue. I then knew how to explain to the cadres, before they watched the rehearsal, how they should view the piece, what they should notice, etc. I could ex-plain so they could understand, in their own terminology. And, in the end, they would always say, 'I see what you mean! No problem. Just don't have any nudity' [laughs]. Not once in those days did an official tell us to change or edit anything.

So they slowly began to trust BMDC. And then gradually, they would start to be our supporters in the government, speaking for us, testifying that 'I've seen it, there's nothing to worry about'. These officials whose job it was to censor us became our own best supporters!

We began to exist on the fringe of the mainstream. We were able to push the boundaries of the mainstream, without becoming populist and without having to hide underground. This was the balance.

A.M.F.

In 2006, the Chinese government initiated the process to develop policies to allow arts and culture organizations to register as not-for-profit organizations. You were instrumental in making this happen. How did you do it?

Z.C.

You must be clear about what you can compromise on and what you can't. Whatever you can compromise on, do, so that you can then focus all of your energy on realizing that one thing that you will never compromise.

Originally, I thought that, for art to flourish, you needed funding. Then I realized it wasn't just money, but good management systems to help manage the funding. Then I realized it wasn't just management, it was the entire environment that needed to change to allow art to flourish. And, for the arts environment to change on a mass scale, you need good arts and cultural policies in place, so that everyone understands the rules of the game.

The more international conferences and festivals I attended, the more I started to wonder why there were so many contemporary performing companies abroad but so few in China. I realized it was because those countries had systematic arts and cultural policies in place that affected the management models of these different arts organizations. So I started doing some research, about how clearer rules could be developed for the game so that more people could start to play.

But you can't just wait for the policies to change. You must engage with policy-makers and give them advice and information so that they know how to change the policies.

A.M.F.

So how did you start? Did you criticize existing art and culture policies (or the lack thereof)?

Z.C.

I am not a critic. I never came out and said 'You are wrong, you are stupid, you are mistaken'. My way of thinking and working is to first understand from the other perspective, to understand *why* someone would do something from that perspective, and let the policy-maker understand that *I* understand why they do it that way. Then, I can suggest, 'Hey, I have a new idea, since I see your perspective, maybe you can look from my perspective'. Just a slice, just a tiny space to try my way. We see how that goes, see if the results are interesting or not with this small trial. If the small trial succeeds, we make it bigger and bigger, and then totally change the system.

A decision-maker, a policymaker, they are not machines. They are people! You can talk to people! You can make a person see something from your perspective. Many people in the cultural bureaus who once criticized us are now our friends. You must have faith in yourself, and in people in general, to be able to do this.

A.M.F.

Why did you choose non-profit status as the important policy to focus on?

Z.C.

In China, we always put business and art together. We

use business to talk about art, we use art to talk about business. I knew they needed to be separate. If you want to do a commercial project, talk about it in commercial terms. But if it is not a commercial project, if it's purely art, we can't use commercial values to judge it. I say 'Render unto Caesar the things which are Caesar's, and unto God the things that are God's'. You must clearly separate!

Not every great artist will become a great product; Van Gogh died starving! Just because you can't sell it doesn't mean it's not worth something. So you must have ways to help those people create. And also, it is not wrong to do commercial and entertainment things too. They are both right, they just must be clearly distinguished.

So I first had to start with the people around me, the team around me, then slowly figure out how to expand this group, to get more people to see from my perspective. I feel everyone has a responsibility to make the world better. You can't just be there criticizing and not *doing* anything. I'm a doer, not a talker. So I decided to do something.

A.M.F.

Did your political background help you in changing the policy?

Z.C.

My background wasn't a direct help, but it might have given me some opportunities to meet with and speak to some decision-makers, to talk about things they'd never thought of because they'd never had the opportunity to be exposed to such ideas. They get official reports, not details. So, if you can go and talk to them about details, they might start thinking about things differently. Everyone has the ability to consider and think about things. The big decision-makers are truly intelligent, but they need *information* to make better decisions. If someone does not have enough information, of course they believe they are right because, given the facts they have access to, they *are* right. So if you talk to them like a person, a friend, you understand from their perspective what *their* problems are with an issue, then you can help them solve their problems and get the result you want!

You can't change it completely overnight, it must be gradual. And if you criticize, it becomes antagonistic, and the issue is lost. It becomes about two people fighting, about who is right and who is wrong, no longer about how to deal with an *issue.*

You must consider *how* you deliver the information. You must tell them *how* to do something, and you must tell them that, if there are mistakes, they will not take the blame. You must make them feel safe. We always talk about how Eastern cultures are about relationships, trust, helping each other. If there's no trust between you and the decision-maker, how can they help you to do something new?

So, when I was dealing with this policy, we decided to make BMDC a trial case. That way, if it failed, it was BMDC's failure, not the government officials'. They felt safe with this. We established trust, so then when our case succeeded we could then expand it slightly larger and then larger, until we succeeded with the overall, full policy change that would benefit everyone. It takes time, and happens by degrees, not all at once. But if you start it with an argument, then it won't go anywhere and the decision-maker with all the power is most likely to win.

A.M.F.

What were the initial opposi-tions to changing this law?

Z.C.

Most people don't want to try something totally new because it's a risk, and no one wants to take a risk. So you must find a way to say that *you* are the one who will shoulder all of the risk, and that you are *able* to do this, and show *how* you are able. This is where my family education

came through. I was honest and direct, and promised only what I knew I could deliver, nothing more. Then I left the final decision up to them.

A.M.F.

How did you change their minds?

Z.C.

You must give choices. Do your research so that you can offer options, Option A, B or C, each with varying degrees of risk. They will most likely choose the option with the smallest risk, but at least it's one of the options you put forth. If you insist on a Yes-or-No confrontation, the most likely outcome will be 'No'. No one really wants to say 'No' to anyone, but, given no other choices, 'No' is always the safest. If you offer choices, they will consider the options.

In 2006, BMDC was the first trial company to be a not-for-profit arts organization. The second one to try was in 2008, the Beijing Contemporary Dance Theatre [founded by Wang YuanYuan]. Then, just before the Olympics, it became an actual legal policy. In the end, it wasn't even me who went to argue for the full policy, it was a government official who came to *me* and said, 'You've done so much groundwork on this, why isn't it just an official policy already?' So *he* went and did it!

In the end *they* were the ones that went and made it happen!

I believe you must do things legally, according to the law. The biggest risk is being outside of the law. If you want to change a policy, you must first respect the policies in place.

A.M.F.

Artist Ai Weiwei is one of the most outspoken critics of the government and current social situations in China. Some people say that the things he does are just publicity stunts. Others believe there should be more outspoken critics like him. What is your opinion of Ai Weiwei? Do you think his methods are effective?

Z.C.

China is big, 1.4 billion people. There's room for different ways of doing things. There's nothing abnormal about people criticizing the government, or their bosses, or their parents… This is normal. That's his choice. I just have my own choice, and I have chosen not to be an outspoken critic. I don't derive pleasure from that. This is just the method I've found to work for me, which I choose for my life. But I also believe this world needs critics, this world needs people doing things in their own way, diversity.

And just as this world needs critics, I need people to criticize me. But generally speaking, people criticizing me won't really change me. I'll listen patiently, sometimes I'll see they have a point, but mostly I feel like they're not me, how do they know why I do what I do, how do they know this is worth criticizing. The hardest thing in this world is making others understand why you are doing something. I can't know why he's doing what he is doing, I can only see the result his actions bring. And it is the same with me; people will not know why I do what I do, but I must be clear with myself. As I said in the beginning, actions (results) speak louder than words.

A.M.F.
What is the situation now for art and cultural policy?

Z.C.

The government has a new cultural development policy and they are investing large amounts of money to support it. As a result, all these business people are suddenly artists. Before, there was not enough money for the arts. Now, there is too much! The policy development and the financial development are uneven. If you have so much capital being invested, you need better policies and management models. But those things take *time,* while money can come quickly. So this is causing a lot of problems.

It's such a messy era we

are living in, this current era of commercialization, all this capital influx into art and culture, from the government, from investors, from buying and selling the art itself. Everything is chaotic, we need time to find the balance. The next big change won't take ten years; I think it will be sooner. I think China will soon have clearer cultural policies to differentiate art and industry. Right now, it's all mixed together.

Culture is about spirit, industry is about flesh. A healthy society, like a healthy person, has both a healthy body (material life), and a healthy spirit (psychological life). The way you develop these two aspects of a person or a society are also different. Right now, I think China is confused about this distinction, and its development is all material, all about the flesh. But many of the problems we are now facing are about the spirit, not about our material lives. So I think very soon people will start focusing on that.

A.M.F.

Some critics both in and outside of China have suggested that anti-government criticism in art sells, and so artists are just creating so-called critical work to sell it abroad. What's your take on this?

Z.C.

Right now, criticism is a good business [laughs]. It doesn't cost much to criticize, but you can sell it at a high price. So, China is in a very interesting situation; everyone is criticizing the over-commercialized situation but, as a result, they are able to sell more work and contribute to the increasing commercialization! All these rich artists are still criticizing! I had dinner with an artist the other night — platinum credit card, young girlfriend, but his art was still critical, he said he couldn't keep up with what his gallery rep was able to sell. This is such a hilarious thing, criticism becomes a business.

Performing arts are always the most difficult to sell. You can't auction it. It's never 100% perfect. Every performance, there's something you can do better. It's temporal. It's an experience, not a product. So its weakness is there is nothing left to sell afterwards. But, for this reason, it avoids a lot of the pollution of money. Performing artists are always the poorest ones in the art world, but the ones who really persist are really strong. People who can't handle it change careers.

A.M.F.

What do you see as the 'next frontier' for art and politics in China? Do you think things will continue to get more commercial, or do you think there will be a rising artistic revolution?

Z.C.

In the performing arts world, I'm sure there are critical works out there, I believe there must be, but there really aren't that many; really very few. I don't know why, I haven't thought about why. Are these performers too friendly? Too kind?

In the rest of the world, rock 'n' roll was often the most critical art form, and in the early days of Chinese rock 'n' roll this was also the case, but not so much anymore.

Before, criticism could be focused toward a group, like the government or other people in power, but now it seems our critical focus is more towards complex issues like war, terrorism, pollution. The things we are paying attention to aren't right next to us, they are bigger global issues. Because we are in an age of the internet, people's focus is starting to shift away from our own immediate lives toward global issues. So, when we criticize pollution, we aren't criticizing ourselves or the way we live that contributes to pollution, we are criticizing an abstract situation.

A.M.F.

During the 1989 Tiananmen democracy movement, music and art played a significant role. What happened after? Why is art not such a political tool anymore? Where are those artists?

Z.C.

The artists didn't change, the times changed. That was a different time period. In China, you can feel that every day things are changing, it's like sprinting a marathon. You can't use unchanging methods to change a changing world.

1989 was a major moment in China's history, but for people born after that, it is far away from their lives. The people born in the 1990s are more cognizant of, say, the Iraq War, terrorism, the fact that Obama is the US's first black president. Each generation has a different focus. To those of us born in the 1970s, 1989 influenced us in a big way, but for those born in the 1980s and 1990s, that event is just something they might have heard of somewhere. There are so many things they might have heard of these days, thanks to the internet. There's no point in bringing it up with them. 1989 is really only brought up among other people who were born in the 1960s and 1970s and remember it and its impact on us.

I think the whole world's biggest problem right now is the environment. Is the world we live in safe? This is bigger than all of us, than any government. Have you seen the movie *2012*? Do we really just have two more years to live? All these natural disasters in China in the last few years — earthquakes, floods — people need to be considering whether their lifestyles are sustainable. So maybe this is what people are paying attention to.

My attitude toward government and money is the same — they aren't inherently good or bad, they are just *tools* and the good or bad result depends on how you use these tools. You can do something beautiful or dirty, depending on how you use them. The most important value is respect. Everything I've done, which people said couldn't be done, came from respecting others and finding ways to live a life so that others would respect me. And this is something I learned from my grandfather.

The author conducted this interview in person with Mr. Zhang in Beijing, China, in September 2010.

209

'We're in a Cage, but it's a Very Big Cage'
An Interview with Richard Schechner and Carol Martin

Klaas Tindemans & Karel Vanhaesebrouck

What possible role could the avant-garde play in the twenty-first century? And, perhaps even more importantly, can we still use this category to describe current artistic practices? Is the avant-garde still a genuine practice or is it mere discourse, a way of describing and selling one's art on the neoliberal market? How can an artist be truly innovative in an era in which innovation and creativity have become neoliberal commodities? Artists and critics alike now live and work in a world in which the classical antagonistic model of centre and periphery has totally disintegrated. What, then, can an artist do? What is his place in the surrounding world? What role should or might he play? Is resistance possible or superfluous? And, most importantly, is there an 'outside' — can one act and work from a perspective outside the predominant presence of the neoliberal market?

The American scholar and artist, Richard Schechner, whose name and reputation are undoubtedly connected to the rise and fall of the American avant-garde (the title of his seminal essay is 'The Decline and Fall of the (American) Avant-Garde: Why It Happened and What We Can Do About It') is highly critical of the current — self-proclaimed or otherwise — artistic avant-garde. Schechner (born 1934), theatre director, editor and playwright, is Professor of Performance Studies at the Tisch School of the Arts, New York University, in the Performance Studies department which he co-founded to establish performance studies as an autonomous academic discipline. He also founded The Performance Group[1] in 1967 and directed milestone performances with this ensemble, such as *Dionysus in 69* (1968), Bertolt Brecht's *Mother Courage and her Children* (1975) and Jean Genet's *The Balcony* (1979). He is also editor of *TDR: The Drama Review* and the author of several seminal publications within this field, such as *Environmental Theater* (1973), *Between Theater and Anthropology* (1985), *Performance Theory* (1988) and *Performance Studies: An Introduction* (2002), many of which have been translated into other languages. From 1992 until 2009, Schechner was artistic director of East Coast Artists.

For scholar, Carol Martin, questions on the position and social relevance of contemporary performing arts are equally important. Through her work on documentary theatre and what she calls 'theatre of the real', she has critically investigated alternative strategies of theatrical representation. Martin is Professor of Drama at Tisch School of the Arts, New York University, a Senior Fulbright Specialist, Head of Arts Area Panel, Regents Awards to Louisiana Artists and Scholars, General Editor of the book series 'In Performance' published by Seagull Books, and serves on the Advisory Board of the American Theatre Company Witness Relocation. As an editor, she has published several books including: *Dance Marathons: Performing American Culture of the 1920s and 1930s* (1994); *A Sourcebook of Feminist Theatre: On and Beyond the Stage* (1996); *Brecht Sourcebook* (2000, co-edited with Henry Bial); *Global Foreigners* (2006, co-edited with Saviana Stanescu in English and Romanian), and *The Dramaturgy of the Real on the World Stage* (2010). She was the guest editor of special issues of *TDR: The Drama Review* on contemporary Japanese performance (Spring 2000) and documentary theatre (Fall 2006). Her essays and interviews have appeared in numerous anthologies, academic journals in the US and internationally and *The New York Times* and have been translated worldwide. Her book, *Theatre of the Real,* will be published by Palgrave/MacMillan in 2011.

In our e-mail correspondence prior to this interview, Schechner and Martin asserted that they have very 'separate professional lives'. The truth is that both are ardent theatre and performance lovers, who have continually advocated the need for critical and socially relevant reflections on performance and theatrical representation. Moreover, Richard Schechner continues to develop his own practice as an independent artist with the East Coast Artists, through the Richard Schechner Center for Performance Studies at the Shanghai Theatre Academy, and elsewhere. Not only as scholars but also, and perhaps more so, as enthusiast defenders of art and of artists, Schechner and Martin travel the world to participate in academic conferences and networks, to meet colleagues, to work with artists and scholars. But, more than anything else, they are very eager and highly critical spectators. Wherever they end up on their global trips, the first question you will hear coming from their mouths will be: 'can we see something?' Schechner and Martin are experienced as scholars, spectators, and, in the case of Schechner, in artistic work. They are constantly rethinking and re-evaluating the position of art in general and of theatre and performance in particular. This interest in all types of contemporary practices and their historical antecedents allows them to address complicated questions regarding the position of performing arts vis-à-vis the omnipresent logic of neoliberalism. Their work is an enduring attempt to rethink the position of performing arts in a world that differs in a very fundamental way from the

---

1   The Performance Group, with Elizabeth LeCompte and Spalding Gray among its members, was the forerunner of The Wooster Group.

one in which they started their careers. It is in this shift, during which words such as 'creativity', 'experiment' and 'innovation' have become mere commodities, that we find the challenges that face artists and scholars today. Recent publications, like *The New Spirit of Capitalism* by Luc Boltanski and Eve Chiapello or Paulo Virno's *Grammar of the Multitude* — to name just two haphazard examples — have shown how this major mutation into post-Fordist creative economies has affected arts and artists, and, moreover, have pointed out the ways in which artists have been implicated in the development of neoliberal globalization. It is exactly this development which constitutes the driving forces behind the work of both Schechner and Martin who now feel stimulated to rethink categories such as 'representation' or 'avant-garde' — albeit from a fundamentally different perspective.

Klaas Tindemans & Karel Vanhaesebrouck

The arts seem to be increasingly engrained by the rhetoric of innovation, flexibility, excellence, etc. What do you think of the hypothesis that the (performing) arts functioned as an experimental ground for the neoliberal economy?

Richard Schechner

In a strange kind of way, the actual positions of right and left have flipped. Up to the 1960s, the classical avant-garde and the classical political left were in harmony with each other. Their programme was to bring down an ancient order and to establish a new one. This goes back, of course, conceptually and artistically, to the Renaissance, philosophically to the Enlightenment and politically to the French and American revolutions. The military term 'avant-garde' was picked up by social activists and artists and reworked again and again through the nineteenth and twentieth centuries. There were many, many manifestoes saying 'destroy the old, bring in the new' — at a nihilistic level, just destroy the old and, at a utopian level, a brave new world. 1968 wasn't the only moment, but it was a big year with enormous consequences. Not only were there huge student manifestations in Paris, Mexico City and at the Democratic National Convention in Chicago, all within the period of a few months. There was an enormous incidence of this spirit.

Also in 1968, in the US, there was the double paroxysm of the assassinations of Martin Luther King and Bobby Kennedy, which followed the 1963 assassination of President John F. Kennedy. The 1968 murders put an end to a certain kind of hope: the hope that mass action and mainstream politics would change the world. Robert Kennedy was actually much more radical than his brother and King was a true revolutionary, the American Gandhi. And so, when both were killed and after the people took over the Odéon in Paris and then, sooner or later, the police were sent in, what happened then was that — and this is a much conflated summary — a lot of radicals went into colleges, myself included. I had been there before — I was never fully outside the university — but, after 1968, the university became even more a place where radical thought occurred, in France in particular — think of the French post-structuralists: Foucault, Derrida, Deleuze and Guattari, Lacan, you name them. The English-speaking world had comparable people, though many were influenced by the French. This movement of thought shifted the locus of action to a certain kind of conceptual action, but it also reconfigured history — or, more accurately, it strongly introduced the idea that we are always 'redoing' history, constructing it, remaking the past in terms of the present and the imagined future. And I think that, without knowing it at the time — one of my essays, 'Restoration of Behavior',[2] is a key statement of this process — we began to see events as repeating themselves. This retreat — if we can call it that — did not happen all at once. If there was a destructive aspect to the classical avant-garde, there was also a constructive, utopian aspect. This kind of 'superman hope' — backed up by money and a national commitment — can be heard in John F. Kennedy's 1961 call for a sustained, focused, capitalist-state ambition, long before neoliberalism: 'I believe that this nation should commit itself to achieving the goal, before this decade is out, of landing a man on the Moon and returning him safely to the Earth'.[3] The 1960s displayed — before the crushing of the uprisings of 1968 — an enormous ambition everywhere.

But, at the same time or a little after, a different mode of thought was developing — a way of thinking that is now dominant among progressives (I will not call these people 'left' or put any other old label on them). A flip happened; progressive thought became, in a certain sense, very conservative, in the literal sense. The ecology movement fought against unlimited destruction/reconstruction, unlimited expansion. The ecology movement advocated: 'Do not rape Gaia, the mother earth', 'Do not exploit at every level', 'Protect species', 'Do not practice excess', 'Make a smaller footprint', 'Recycle, reduce, conserve', etc. This urgency to take care was combined with an awakened interest in a practice that conformed to, or enriched, theory — an increasing convergence of practice and theory, in fact. The interest in theory arose out of the fact that, increasingly, artists began their careers not as apprentices to other artists and not in the marketplace but at college. To cut a long story short, many of the newer generation of artists after 1968 no longer worked in art from the start of their careers.

And what did these newer generations of artists find at college? They discovered — that is, they were taught — not only post-structuralist theory, but also world views influenced by the uncertainties of the Heisenberg principle and the neoliberalism of Milton Friedman's economics. True, probably most student artists never mastered mathematics to the level necessary to manipulate physics or economics, but they were educated where they inhaled these ideas. The resulting clash of ideas in the 1970s and 1980s led

216

not so much to a dialectical debate as to a profound relativism. Certainty went out the window. After 1968, 'tenured radicals' taught ideas of post-this, -that and -everything: post-modern, post-colonial, post-structural, post-Marxist, post-psychoanalytic. At the same time, universities became breeding grounds not only of radical thought but also of avant-garde art. Before the 1960s, this wasn't the case. Many artists may have gone to college, but there weren't very many large art or performance departments, no less whole colleges devoted to the arts. That change is fundamental. These young artists, who now are very mature — even old, outdated or dead — were educated in the new theories. These generations of artists, even until today, were much more aware of concept and theory than those prior to them. They were also aware of the historical avant-garde. They didn't so much experience Futurism (Italian and Russian), Dada, Surrealism, and so on, as actualities but they learnt about these movements and sampled them — in retrospect and through the filter of scholarship. New art began to self-consciously quote, sample and — decisively — understand and theorize what had gone before. Earlier artists had theories,

of course, but they were not very theory-driven, and they learned more outside of school than within. For earlier generations of artists, school was a place to pass through, or maybe even avoid. But, as the tenured radicals took over, and notable artists accepted professorships, schools became kinds of post-modern monasteries (with sexual privileges).

As a consequence of learning these new theories — and also learning the history of avant-garde as well as classical arts — artists from the 1970s onwards increasingly got involved in sort of 'redoings' of older art. By the start of the twenty-first century, the avant-garde was being analyzed in terms of 'tradition' and 'repertory', a fact that would have been unheard of fifty years ago. It's not that there was no art history, but that older artists — those who the younger ones were taught constituted the 'historical avant-garde' — were not academically educated in art history, and often didn't care much about it. But from the 1970s onwards, artists did know and care. By today, of course, the re-production of an avant-garde repertory is common.

In 2010, Marina Abramović was celebrated at MoMA in New York with a retrospective show, called 'The

2 Published as a chapter in Between Theatre and Anthropology (University of Pennsylvania Press, 1985).
3 Address to the US Congress, 25 May 1961.

Artist is Present'. This was the first time that a performance artist had been exhibited in-performance at MoMA. Abramović herself sat in a chair for hours on end from 14 March to 31 May 2010 as crowds of people, many of them young artists, lined up for the chance to sit opposite. Her presence on the ground floor of MoMA constituted a pilgrimage as the artist became a kind of religious icon, a living shrine, a 'miraculous' manifestation. Meanwhile, upstairs in the museum, there were objects and documents from Abramović's long career (with and without her long-time partner, Ulay). And, uniquely for a museum that prides itself on displaying 'originals', several of Abramović's most famous pieces were enacted by others. Most of the models/performers cast were roughly the same age as Abramović was when she had first made the works they were simulating. But, of course, the enactments were not the same as when these works were performed the first time; the consciousness of many at MoMA was that of seeing an 'again', not a 'first time'. Even if a person had never seen the original, the setting at MoMA made it clear that what they were experiencing were works that had already been done years ago. Museums, after all, frame what is displayed inside them.

In this way, Abramović, so 'original' in the 1960s and 1970s, became thoroughly museumified (just a step from mummified). Her works which, when originally performed, invited participation — sometimes wanted, not as when spectators burned her with cigarettes — became thoroughly cleansed and protected by a phalanx of guards making sure that no one touched any of the (naked) performers. Works whose very essence was unmitigated endurance were played out within the time-frame of 'fair labour practices', with rest breaks for the performers simulating Abramović. The ambivalence of the MoMA show was most evident in the way Abramović's and Ulay's 1977 *Imponderabilia* was restaged. The artists stated their intentions back then: 'In a selected space naked we stand opposite each other in the museum entrance. The public entering the museum has to turn sideways to move through the limited space between us. Everyone wanting to get past has to choose one of us'. But, in the MoMA show, the performers playing Ulay and Abramović were positioned a little further apart than in the 1970s (getting past them did not require brushing against them). Even more decisively, there were two ways into the room. In the 1970s, you slid, pushed or squirmed your way between a naked woman and a naked man or you could not enter the museum. But, at

218

MoMA, this re-enactment was on the top floor rather than at the entrance to the museum. Moreover, if you wanted to avoid even this reduced test, you could enter the room through an alternative doorway. Granted, the MoMA retrospective was about a lot more than *Imponderabilia*, but at least, I thought, the MoMA curators, or Abramović herself, should have insisted that the only way into this particular room was by means of the naked passage.

Abramović is not alone in re-doing iconic works. Allan Kaprow's *18 Happenings in 6 Parts* was 're-done' (as Andre Lepecki, who oversaw the project, put it) in New York in 2007 and it was 're-invented' in Los Angeles in 2008 as part of a three-month retrospective of Kaprow's work. Anna Halprin's 1965 *Parades and Changes*, which was so radical when it was first shown in Stockholm, was 'replayed' in 2009 in Paris at the Centre Pompidou. Also in 2009, the Rude Mechanicals of Austin, Texas replicated The Performance Group's *Dionysus in 69*, basing their production on Brian De Palma's 1968 film.[4] I attended some rehearsals and gave some advice to the Rudes. The Austin Critics Circle named the produc-

tion the best of the 2009-2010 season, so old is new again.

These re-doings, replays and replications are not *Aida* coming back in new productions. The repetition of the avant-garde is an attempt to recover with some exactitude what the 'original' was. In quotation marks because an original is never original; nor can it be reconstructed exactly because audiences change and, even more importantly, knowledge changes. Once something has been done, knowing that changes the way any repetition is received, no matter how accurately the 'original' is reproduced.

So, to get back to your question, today's market economy is owned by the right, by the neoliberals. The market economy is free-wheeling (with the self-proclaimed freedom of 'let the market decide'). In point of fact, the free market is not free, either theoretically or legally; there are many laws regulating markets, but the rhetoric is that of 'freedom', of unbridled activity, unlimited possibilities. In this sense, the neoliberal market economy wears the mantle of the classical avant-garde, while the classical avant-garde has become, in its re-iteration, much more co-responsible,

---

4 Allan Kaprow was the first person to use the term 'Happening'. He organized 18 Happenings in 6 Parts, which required active participation from his public, at the Reuben Gallery, New York City, in 1959. Dionysus in 69, a radical adaptation of Euripides' Bacchae, directed by Richard Schechner, premiered at the Performing Garage, New York in 1968, on the day Robert Kennedy was assassinated.

much more conservative in the classical sense. It is the progressives who now advocate conserving resources — everything from population control to protecting species, from consuming less to establishing wildlife refuges, no-fishing zones, and so on — in a move to 'grow smaller' (enjoy the oxymoron). What many in the avant-garde now want, what the young people I talk to who are doing avant-garde theatre want, is a smaller population, less intrusion, less distortion of natural processes, more protection of species and the whole environment.

A question we are not discussing, but which also should be on the table, is the limits to enquiry, to experimentation, and the application of (Faustian) knowledge. I mean genetic engineering, the creation of artificial species, uses of atomic energy — a panoply of research in which human physical knowledge is outrunning human ethical wisdom. I bridle at advocating any limits. I have always been, and continue to be, an advocate of unlimited experimenting. But, frankly, I am scared about the consequences of messing around with fundamental processes. Knowledge needs to be guided by wisdom, and these two — though closely related — are not identical.

K.T. & K.V.
Does this line of thought apply to the maintenance of the welfare state too?

R.S.
Indeed, and this is what younger people — and older people, myself included — think is the right thing to do. This is not the classical avant-garde approach; this is really a profoundly conservative approach, in a good sense. I have to say 'progressive', but I should say 'conservative', yet this term is so attached to Ronald Reagan, Margaret Thatcher,[5] George W. Bush, and so on, and I don't mean them or what they stand for. The neoliberals, if you will, still act as if they are pioneers riding wild. I have not wholly theorized the flip I spoke of earlier. According to many neoliberals, every catastrophe is just an exception, or something that the market can take care of, rather than being an inevitable consequence of the system they created. This makes for a different kind of avant-garde, not an avant-garde at all in the sense that the avant-garde previously existed.

Or, to put it historically, the notion of art as value-added (art as objects or behaviours for sale) really begins in the West during the Renaissance and continues until now, but, in addition to value-added art, we have non-value art, ritualized arts, community-based arts, everyday life as art (what Kaprow called the 'blurring of art and life'). In relation to value-added art, these are earlier and co-existent practices. We are coming to the end of art as a sellable object. It continues, but there's another art there that isn't either truly post-modern or truly pre-modern. The emergence of this non-value-added art occurs at the same time as the classical avant-garde has ended. This has been my theme for fifteen years or so.

K.T. & K.V.

From an historical point of view, is it exaggerated to say that the avant-garde you're referring to functioned as a kind of laboratory for the post-Fordist economy?

R.S.

This is something that I haven't thought about, but it could very well be true. That would be something future historians — maybe you — would write about. If we are seeking intellectual cohesion, then definitely, yes, because one can see the continuation. So yes, I do think that certain of the energies of the neoliberals, several of their key ideas, were derived from the avant-garde. Yes, I think that's a very good idea.

K.T. & K.V.

Is the craze of re-enactment and historical reconstruction related to what one could describe as a phantasm about historical authenticity?

R.S.

Yes. One explanation is what I have been talking about, but there is also another impetus: the emergence of the digital archive. This makes recollection a different thing to what it was during the age of dark-room photography. The digital archive is inherently more 'democratic' than the dark room. Just about anyone can use Photoshop, and just about everyone has a digital camera, an iPhone or its clone or some means of recording and accessing images and actions. The separation between photography, writing, telecommunications, the internet and archiving is swiftly dissolving, if it has not already gone. Pretty much everyone has access to everything. Yes, I know there are industrial, military and government secrets, but the codes are decipherable; it is more and more difficult to keep secrets. This makes the world both more exciting and creative and more dangerous and threatening. I myself bounce back and forth from exhilaration to anxiety. But, basically, I am optimistic (in my

5   Former leader of the UK Conservative Party and British Prime Minister (1979-1990), the icon of the conservative (and neoliberal) revolution of the 1980s, together with Ronald Reagan, US President (1981–1989).

221

belly) if pessimistic (in my head).

An important consequence of the vast digital archive is that very young people are used to seeing things over and over again. They make their own archives; they access the archives of others; they use sharing platforms such as YouTube or Facebook to trade archives. At the level of distortion, this is advertising; at the level of art, it's the ability to use whatever materials are out there. Twitter is a parody of what used to be called a 'movement' (in arts, in politics). With Twitter, a person 'follows' someone else, one joins a very ephemeral movement, like a flash mob; but, instead of the movement being 'let's assemble to do something', it is 'let's assemble to assemble'. Let's follow to do the act of following, not following toward a political or social goal. McLuhan proved to be right; the medium is the message. To which I would add: the process is the product.

K.T. & K.V.

As far as reactions towards neoliberalism, there is apathetic acceptance or there is enthusiastic embracing. What would be the position of this — still to be invented — new avant-garde?

R.S.

A 'new' avant-garde? If one exists, I call it a 'niche-garde'. Because of digitization and the internet, one can get together with like-minded people and form a niche. I can put out on the internet that I'm a 'one-legged transsexual who eats only scrambled eggs' and ask for others who are like me to get in touch. Then maybe the thousand people around the world who are one-legged scrambled-egg-eating transsexuals will form a community. And I may belong to a number of these. A so-called single person (so-called because we are not individuals any longer, if we ever really were) can join any number of communities. Are these communities actual or virtual? Using e-mail, Skype and the like, the separation between actual and virtual is also dissolving; people can be co-present at a distance (another oxymoron). Each of these communities is a niche. Because there are so many niches, it's very hard to form a mass movement, a movement that brings together people of very different persuasions and habits to unite for a common cause. People would rather hang out with people they are really sympathetic to. We can now see and talk to others at a distance; how long before we can smell, touch and taste them? Virtually, through direct brain stimulation in the sensory regions? The touch screen is a move in that direction, the replacement of typing (an analogue process) with caressing or running the fingers over an image. That's a significant change, because these are really body metaphors. If I'm doing this (typing), I'm making the code, but if I'm doing this (touching), I'm stroking the other. Apple, and whoever runs YouTube, Google — these enormous corporations, who are, yes, empowering us, but also keeping us inside the cage of corporate 'whatever'. There is nothing outside the corporation. Within the corporation are a number of niches. The avant-garde is one such niche; and within that niche there are sub-niches, and so on. We are all connected but profoundly separated as well. Along with this is a new type of underworld, not people who hold up banks but people who steal identities.

Carol Martin

This theme of the stolen identity, of surrogation, of substitution, of replacement, relates very much to both documentary theatre and theatre of the real. Simply stated, theatre of the real is theatre that cites reality in the context of performance — however reality is understood — in the form of an interpolation in the creation of specific theatre and performance works with the understanding that secondary reality can now be experienced as primary, and primary reality can be experienced as secondary. Theatre of the real is in conversation with these other processes of the corporatization, virtuality and fluidity of identity. The thing that is interesting about YouTube is that professionals and amateurs are operating on the same platform. In documentary theatre, especially interview-based documentary theatre, the professional actor and the eyewitness, the person on the street, come together in a particular form. This form of documentary theatre many times uses very conventional dramatic techniques.

But in the case of theatre of the real, such as the work of Rabih Mroué or Gob Squad's *Kitchen (You've Never Had It So Good)*,[6] you see more complicated, post-modern techniques, more in the direction of constructivist post-modernism than de-constructivist post-modernism. Gob Squad's actors recruit spectators to replace the actors. The actors sit in the auditorium and, using microphones, they instruct the spectators, who are now onstage, behind a screen onto which their images are projected. The spectators have earphones, the actors whisper the instructions. The identities

6　The performance of Gob Squad is a re-staging of Andy Warhol's movie *Kitchen* (1965), an experimental film thematizing typical features of the 1960s avant-garde, such as the refusal to learn one's lines by heart.

of all involved are blurred. Gob Squad is reproducing Warhol; spectators are standing in for Gob Squad actors who are themselves substituting for Warhol film subjects. We in the audience can be aware of all these levels simultaneously. In other words, there are theatre-makers using techniques to explicitly create new kinds of meaning about history and reality and to reconstruct important performances and films in the live space of theatre. It is not nihilistic at all.

R.S.

There is no longer an avant-garde in the classical sense, there is the 'niche-garde', this identity thing. All this has positive and negative vectors. Yes, the corporations control it, but there is a great deal of 'freedom' inside that cage, that big cage which contains hundreds, if not millions, of smaller cages. We're in our own small cage, or a set of cages of our own making, but our cage, or set, is within other cages, and finally inside a very big cage. Actually, when you come to think about it, this is the same as theistic religion where all that is exists inside of God's 'creation' (God's cage). But even atheists agree that we live in a universe which is governed by some set of 'laws', whether we comprehend them or not.

Some of the restaging of old avant-garde pieces connects with borrowing (if not stealing) identities. Take Gob Squad's *Kitchen*. In this redoing of Andy Warhol's 1965 film, *Kitchen*, who is the author? Is it Andy Warhol, or is it the Gob Squad performer holding the microphone, telling the person what to say and do? Or is it the spectator-turned-actor? And what are the rest of us watching? A stage play, a film, a stage play of a film? The identities are really parsed out in a kind of cubist theatre of intended, complex deconstruction of the 'figure' (actor, person, past event, present event). Others, such as The Wooster Collective, use the earphone technique, but they are very highly trained performers who have rehearsed. The spectators selected by the Gob Squad are regular audience members, no plants, but when I saw them on the film, when I heard them speak, they were good, from an artistic point of view. We are used to seeing ordinary people speaking in documentary films, but they are representing themselves. In *Kitchen*, the ordinary people are … artists. Is it the case that so many people are on display these days, on YouTube or wherever, that our criteria of what constitutes 'good acting' changes? Warhol's fifteen minutes of fame has been expanded to the amount of time a person can claim the camera.

K.T. & K.V.

Given the fact, as you say, that the avant-garde has mutated into a sort of 'niche-garde', would you also say that it has lost its classical function of épater le bourgeois?

R.S.

That is because we — you, me — have become the bourgeois. Even the impoverished want to become bourgeois.

K.T. & K.V.

In the cultural system of the twenty-first century, there is a centre, which uses the rhetoric of the cultural avant-garde, and we live in a system where being critical is a criterion for subventions. But what to do then? What could be a possible option for our performing arts?

R.S.

I have spent a large time of my life being an advocate; I mean, that's part of what I do. But, right now, I'm trying to be more of an historian. I don't have 'the way'. At present, in New York at least, and from what I have seen in Europe and in parts of Asia, what we have are artists' groups who are very, very good at what they do. But what they do is not new; they're not trying to be new, they're building on things that were there before. This process is a very 'conservative' way — as I explained before. Gob Squad is very good, but The

Wooster Collective, long ago, had earphones and microphones. In 1992, Ron Vawter performed *Roy Cohn/Jack Smith* with an earphone through which he heard Jack's voice and he repeated exactly what Jack's voice said. Maybe there are earlier examples of this technique. And I don't know if Gob Squad knew about Ron Vawter's performance. But, whether they knew or not, that line of succession is there. I don't see anything in the current avant-garde that has not been done before, but I see a lot of what the current avant-garde does being done better than before. This makes me think of a see-saw; when innovation is high, excellence is low, when excellence is high, innovation is low.

C.M.

Gob Squad's work is very, very different from the work of The Wooster Group. In the work of The Wooster Group, I have seen something that I have seen also in the work of Josh Fox — in particular in *Surrender,* an interactive project developed by the International WOW Company. It is the device of training audience members to be performers in the context of the work on stage. What Gob Squad did, when I saw their performance of *Kitchen* in Ghent, was to ask for three volunteers from the audience. Those people were not trained but they were fed lines they had to perform in the moment. The unique thing is that we get to see the real in that moment, in which an untrained and unrehearsed person has to perform a role in public for the first time. In other words, yes, they are performing, and no, they are not actors. But they have to act and to answer questions from the resources they have at that moment. Yes, it is connected to that idea that everybody is capable of broadcasting themselves. In *Surrender*, about the Iraq War, which was performed in a warehouse in New York, audience members had to abandon their clothes, which were taken away and stored, and put on army clothes and boots. Audience members were then taken through a simulated basic training conducted by a real army guy. After that, each spectator was sent, with their assigned platoon, on a mission through a series of simulated Iraqi villages, complete with the overwhelming simulation of the sounds of the war — deafening guns, planes, bombs, explosions. Everyone had specific directions and a specific role to play. In my case, the role was to search insurgents for important information. I was given the instructions, 'don't touch women's breasts', 'with men you have to search their entire body'. I lived a situation that was totally fictional, but in a simulation that

was totally compelling and unnerving. We were screamed at by two men posing as the heads of our platoon. I searched and what I found was, in the realm of the theatre, important evidence, important information. The total simulation convinced spectators of its own efficacy. It is amazing what the participation did to me. At the end of the performance, on the simulated plane ride back to the US, the process of re-inscription to American culture began. We were shown *Friends* on a monitor above our heads. Slowly, the sitcom began to break apart, with images of blood and violence. We were looking at a screen with all these interpolations. The people who participated in the war simulations were asked to come forward and play a part in the play which was now before us. People were called by name as they had taken names at the door. When one was called, they went in front of the audience and read their lines from the screen that was now situated behind the audience. The performing that I saw in that situation, done by the spectators, was remarkable. Each participant was set in the specific milieu. One man had the lines of a war veteran who had no health insurance. There was something devastating and totally surprising about a person, not an actor, talking about how he fought for the country and now had no resources to care for his war injuries. These performances were entirely without any actorly patina; they were very raw. It all came across as a kind of unmitigated — although it was totally constructed — representation of ideas, from the mouths of those people who came to see this play. The audience became its own convincing mouthpiece for the point of view of those who constructed the performance. Surrogation, substitution, interpolation…

K.T. & K.V.

And is it interesting because it activates reflection or because it has an immediate sensory impact?

C.M.

It activates reflection and makes the subject not 'those people in Iraq', but 'this is us', 'this is what we do', 'this is what we live', absolutely in the moment. It was so interesting, disturbing and horrifying.

K.T. & K.V.

You said that the avant-garde ended in the 1960s, and still you are using words like 'disturbing', 'horrifying'. In what sense do these productions challenge mainstream attitudes, or at least differ from the mainstream?

R.S.

When I said that the avant-garde ended in the 1960s, I meant that there are no new techniques, not that there isn't a style called 'avant-garde'. The avant-garde in performance is one more stream of activity, no longer 'in advance', but rather a distinct style or set of styles that comprise the niche-gardes. Today's avant-garde is fundamentally different than André Breton's or Filippo Marinetti's. They wrote manifestoes calling for the destruction of the old and the invention of the new. These avant-gardists may have been at war with each other, but they shared a profound hatred of the 'what is'. That is no longer necessary — or even advisable. Avant-garde artists today seek government subventions, private donors; they tour to international festivals; they teach at universities. It's a whole different outlook on themselves, society and the future. Maybe you can understand the change I am talking about better if I refer to James Cameron's two blockbuster movies, *Titanic* and *Avatar*. *Titanic* is about the old world sinking; the romantic, glorious end of the Victorian era, and the love affair failed because Romeo dies while Juliet lives on into old age. It was a Marxist love affair: a lower class boy and an upper class girl. He liberates her sexually and conceptually, but she cannot save him physically. He freezes and she survives to tell the story from which the movie is made.

Avatar, on the other hand, is a whole different thing. It is about a utopian transformation in the future, an inter-species love affair that succeeds as he identifies with the people he was supposed to infiltrate. Nature defeats the machine; the human is morphed into a Na'vi. The moral is plain: nature is better than machines; humanist values are better than corporate-militarist greed. These two films are the largest selling movies in history; *Titanic* was, now *Avatar* is. So the corporations backing the movies say, OK, let's have a transformation, in fiction, as long as this neoliberal economy continues to actually generate the money. A nice, fictional, utopian, romantic cage fitted carefully within the larger corporate cage. But, if the truth be told, I — like so many others — enjoyed *Avatar* and vibrated with its good vibes.

K.T. & K.V.

Where exactly lies the difference? In the fact that, in the Cameron case, the transformation is hypothetical, while in the example of documentary theatre or theatre of the real it is not?

R.S.

It's more complicated. The hypothetical and the actual have blurred into each other — that's exactly the point. We live increasingly in digitized lives. And maybe, paradoxically, *Avatar* will lead to a 'greener' earth — can it be accidental that the Na'vi are green? Can we have greed, wealth and eco-do-the-right-thing at the same time? The utopians say 'yes'; the cynics say 'who are you kidding?'

C.M.

That's exactly what I would say is the new technique. There is pastiche, there is assemblage, there is deconstruction. But the thing that's new — I want to assert — is the way the real is being used. There is one new technique; it is the interpolation of the real into the fictional. Documentary theatre is mostly written about in terms of dramatic text.

In the US, the innovations of the group theatres of the 1960s and 1970s proceeded not only from linking theatrical narratives with political intention but also from revisions in the whole process of making and receiving theatre. Unmasking the hypocrisies concealed in the decorum of middle class life and the exposure of what were thought to be the lies of the American government helped to create theatre that was intent on social and political critique. Revisions of form, function and process in the theatre of this period are foundational for both documentary theatre and theatre of the real. Sea changes in set design, acting and dramatic literature in the late 1960s and 1970s were also important. Theatre practitioners of the 1960s and 1970s explored the practice of incorporating primary source material into dramatic literature in the form of documents, interviews and still and moving images.

In the US, many new techniques were triggered by a complete change within the idea of individual identity in relation to history — the idea that the individual story is as important as the story of the great man of history. So, for example, in a work like *The Serpent* by The Open Theatre, there is the story of the assassination of JFK, or more precisely, the re-enactment of the story of that historical event. It is not verbatim, but a physical re-enactment of the Zapruder film, performed and re-performed, forwards and backwards. In the US, this approach emerges in the 1960s — the physical, rather than verbatim, replication of what we can see on film and on television. Also in *The Serpent*, there are interviews with the actors about their personal lives, so there is an interpolation of the real both in physical and verbatim terms in that early work. What happened in the 1970s was a move away from activist theatre into the more formal work of The Wooster Group and Mabou Mines and eventually into solo performance such as the work of Spalding Gray. But Gray was absolutely using the real in terms of his personal story — the story of his mother's suicide in his autobiographical *Rumstick Road*. The same is true of the more text-based traditions, such as, for example, the work of Emily Mann and her use of interviews. So the techniques are shared across different kinds of theatre. But documentary theatre changes after 11 September, with the use of digital means to bring the real into the fictional.

R.S.

I would like to add another paradox to what Carol just said. It's another one of these inversions. What was also strongly called for, in the US after the 1960s, was increasing government support of the arts, including radical arts and artists. In the US, we have the National Endowment of the Arts, established by Congress in 1965. It's not that you don't apply if you are against the government; if you are against the government you certainly apply. That is because the government wants to show its dedication to free speech by giving dissident artists money. But there is a catch. First, most of the money goes to the established venues like Lincoln Center. Secondly, in 1990 after the NEA chairman rejected grants awarded to artists who became known as the 'NEA Four'

— Tim Miller, Karen Finley, Holly Hughes and John Fleck, whose work was felt by some to be offensive (sexually explicit and anti-religious) — grants were no longer made to individuals, but only to organizations whose job it was to make sure that government money was not spent on the 'wrong kind' of art. But this big chill has not prevented organizations that are progressive from applying, and winning, NEA grants. Who really knows how much NEA policy has stifled full artistic expression? The paradox is, of course, that, in the old days, individual patrons underwrote artists or artists routinely had day jobs to earn their bread. Patrons, both individual and corporate, are still very important — but so are box office receipts and lists of small donors. In the US, a donor gets some relief from paying taxes by donating to the arts. To cut to the chase: following the money means that artists take a big risk of losing all funding — public and private — if they *épater* too much or too strongly. And, given the acceptance of artists like Abramović by institutions like MoMA, what constitutes an outsider? Let's update Derrida who said that 'there is nothing outside the text'; today, there is nothing outside the corporation. The corporation is the state and the state is the corporation. In the US, the corporations really own the state even as the state tries to regulate the corporations. They are not separable. That's neoliberalism in action.

I cannot imagine any artist who is really outside that system, and, if they are, they are knocking on the door to get in. I do not know any young artist who is saying: 'I am not applying'. There is one that I know of: the Castillo Cultural Center in New York, a neo-Marxist group with a very particular slant on things, driven by the thinking of Fred Newman, a maverick Marxist psychoanalyst-turned-artist. The Castillo refuses any government money or big money from individuals. They work with box office takings and small donations. Most of those who attend Castillo events are not wealthy. These outsiders are so few and far between. So the idea of the outside exists, but the actual fact of it doesn't exist.

K.T. & K.V.
So the idea of subversion is rather problematic?

R.S.
It is and it isn't. The corporation in itself is smart; it wants to be changed, it wants innovation. It doesn't want to stop change or innovation, it wants to own it. The *Ancien Régime* before the French Revolution wanted to stop progress. What the elites

have learned in two hundred years is that they should co-opt, even use progress, not stop it. We are entering a period that can be called 'neo-medieval'. In the European medieval epoch, the state, the church and the landed gentry collaborated with each other. You had guilds that functioned in a certain sense as a niche-garde. Individuals were always owned by somebody; each person had a place in a hierarchy from which there was no exit. From the Renaissance onward, there were sporadic attempts to definitively overturn this order. New philosophies, new technologies, the emergence of the middle class, the colonization of the Americas, increasing global trade, and so on, all led to the end of the medieval system. Finally, the blood bath of the French Revolution provided, or seemed to provide, an exit, but the Church remained, even if fractured. And the notion of an interlocking hard-to-escape-from hierarchy was not extinct. Medievalism has been re-inscribed in the corporate world, with its system of interlocking agencies and authorities. The nation state, an imaginary of the Enlightenment, has now been subsumed into the corporation. The nation state is only part of the system. At present, the only challenge to the corporation comes from various religious 'fundamentalisms', which are in themselves very suspect and dangerous.

K.T. & K.V.

If you assume that there is no 'outside the corporation', what is an activist artist to do as an activist artist? Would the strategy of over-identification be a possible option?

R.S.

I am not certain what you mean by 'over-identification', but no matter how you slice the bread, you're still owned by the corporate system you're working in or even apparently working against. You're struggling at the boundary, but that boundary is flexible. I cannot break it because it is not really stopping me; it's resisting me but not absolutely. And it takes from the creative edge of artists what is useful for its own corporate entity-identity.

However, as I noted a little earlier, there is something outside the corporation: the religious states, like Iran; religious entities like Al Qaeda, and pockets of religious radicals such as the ultra-orthodox Jews of Israel, the fundamentalist Christians of the US, the Shiva Sen Hindu radicals of India, and so on. These are the last of the truly ideological states and non-corporate ideologies. Are they the 'last' or are they harbingers? These entities put what they consider

231

transcendent values ahead of economic logic, yet these people also make use of the technologies of the corporation — the internet especially. At the same time, they form their own niche-gardes exploiting those technologies. And, if they are states, they remain members of the United Nations; they trade with other countries; they make alliances, etc. So, at one level, they are outside; at another level, they are inside.

C.M.

I am not sure I agree with that. The US also puts ideological values up front. There are, of course, different levels of veiling.

K.T. & K.V.

Are the positions of the activist and of the artist irreconcilable? Is there such a thing as an 'artivist'?

R.S.

They are not irreconcilable, but artists are reformers not revolutionaries. For this, I think, we can be thankful.

C.M.

Theatre of the real offers certain opportunities to rethink this relation between art and activism. Because it uses the real, theatre of the real has different implications for critiquing political structures and historical knowledge. I don't know if this is revolutionary but it is important.

It is definitely a different kind of critical discourse that is looking to create something that is both formally new in artistic terms and conceptually new in meaning. To refer back to Mroué, in *Photo-romance*, Mroué and Linah Saneh have made a work about censorship, about the limits of imagination and about Lebanon and its future. The work implies that they are looking to create a future, a different future from the one that is currently imagined by the powers that be.

K.T. & K.V.

However, one important problem seems to be permanently absent from this new critical discourse: ecology, or, in more general terms, the state of our planet. It seems as if ecological activism is almost completely absent in the international arts scene. Why is that?

R.S.

Of course, a movie like *Avatar* is all about ecological activism, but that's a mainstream corporate product. However, I think that many artists are ecological activist, in the same sense that the Living Theatre was anarchist-activist. But this notion of re-staging things is inherently ecologically responsible, it is even saying that we could re-use, recycle these classics of the avant-garde. It is a model for a more general sense of positive recycling. It is hard for young artists to think outside the system; it is more and more difficult even to conceive the very idea of an outside. Artists, like most other activists, think in terms of evolutionary progressivism. An intriguing case is the Critical Art Ensemble. In their own words, 'The CAE is a collective of five tactical media practitioners of various specializations including computer graphics and web design, film/video, photography, text art, book art, and performance. Formed in 1987, CAE's focus has been on the exploration of the intersections between art, critical theory, technology, and political activism'.[7] The CAE is as important as it is unique.

K.T. & K.V.

How would you explain this renewed interest in documentary artistic practices? And how does it relate to this 'vogue of documentary' aesthetics? They are not the same of course.

C.M.

Both documentary theatre and theatre of the real are created, at least in part, from activist impulses. Most documentaries seek some kind of change, even artistically conservative documentary theatre seeks some kind of change. A tribunal play like *The Colour of Justice*, about the murder of the young black man by white racist thugs, is a reconstruction of the key events of the Macpherson Inquiry into the death of Stephen Lawrence. The goal of that play is to support the creation of a future in which racist killing does not exist. Many documentaries have that kind of objective, to create a future, by using a specific example as a means to launch a discussion that is generative, that creates a different understanding whether by summary or insight. This is why it is activist. There are two streams. One is the textual-dramatic tradition like *The Colour of Justice, The Investigation, Greensborough, The Execution of Justice, Twilight LA, Fires in the Mirror* — the other tradition, of course, is the performance tradition in which the performer himself or herself becomes the subject, with or without other textual material. When identity in the US — feminist, black, straight, gay, Latino — began to become politicized, all subject positions became politicized. For better or for worse, enunciating who you are on stage — as in *Coming Out!* by Jonathan Katz — became a very important political act in the public forum. It is the end of post-modernism as a technique that was used in and of itself. Now post-modern techniques have begun to be used to a different end.

7   **www.critical-art.net.**

There is a change in worldview since Obama. Obama's message is hope, hope for the future. I think, in a certain way, activist theatre has gained strength from that, and a voice, a very analytical and critical voice that was crushed. Unfortunately, war often creates a crisis that generates art, that pressurizes what we already know, creating an urgency for art that addresses the meaning of the way we live now. That is exactly what happened with Vietnam. There are many parallels between the 1960s and now in terms of urgency and the reformation of techniques that are already there but used in different ways.

R.S.

In the Vietnam era, one could get a mass movement into the streets. That period coincided with the Black Freedom Movement, when Martin Luther King declared his opposition to the war. From the 1960 Greensboro, North Carolina, sit-in onward, there was an ever-increasing presence of protest as a mass movement, as a 'demonstration', a performative act.[8] Those taking part in the sit-ins and anti-war activists practised civil disobedience in the tradition of Henry David Thoreau and Gandhi. But the times are different now. The government got smart and ended the draft. Poor women and men are in the American armed services;

college students don't have to go. No one is in the street protesting Iraq or Afghanistan.[9] They're not shouting because they don't have to go. The corporation, if I might use this word again, provided itself with an army of volunteers, killing two birds with one stone — reducing unemployment among poor youth and building an army to fight oil and ideological wars. The architects of the Iraq War and the Afghan War also made the public believe that they could have these wars without paying for them in terms of money or middle-class blood. People were urged to go on living their lives as usual. It all came crashing down with the economic collapse of 2007 and beyond. And, as the wars grind on, still there is no popular protest that parallels those of the 1960s.

C.M.

Maybe this resistance has taken a new form. In the 1960s, the war was visible; it was a television war; we saw it depicted in magazines; we watched it on nightly news. The Bush administration, however, created an intervention in the display of the war. What we absolutely knew that was going on became invisible for the most part. Theatre artists stepped in with works like *Surrender* — and this is largely what conventional documentary does, to make visible what is not visible.

Theatre of the real also does this, but in ways that approach meaning and truth through the self-conscious use and manipulation of both fiction and non-fiction. Platforms like YouTube offer *other* ways of seeing war, through individual postings. At the same time, we live in a culture of information which corporations are trying to capture. With the crisis in Iran, the *New York Times* launched a call to send them images and films shot in Iran. Of course, they immediately found themselves confronted with the question of the legitimacy of the images. Citation and legitimacy have become major problems. The internet in general and YouTube in particular have, in a certain sense, replaced the streets.

R.S.

The question, of course, is whether this new virtual community is an actual community. I think it is analogous but not identical. We participated in a demonstration in 2003 against the US invasion of Iraq. About 50,000 people came out in New York, but the crowd was highly controlled. In the Vietnam era, those people would have shoved their way through *en masse* to the UN headquarters where we were headed. But, instead, the police were easily able to siphon this huge group off into side streets, both breaking up the mass and short-circuiting the crowd's purpose. We were not a community. We were merely those who came together for this particular occasion, a niche-garde of anti-Iraq invasion people — more of a flash mob than a politically active ongoing community. The idea of the 'common' had vanished.

8   The first late twentieth century public manifestation was Rosa Parks' refusal, in December 1955, to give up her seat in the front of an Alabama bus and move to the rear as required by the laws of segregation. This led to the year-long boycott of the buses, a movement led by Martin Luther King, Jr. This was King's first move onto the national stage.
9   Before the Iraq War began, there were demonstrations, but nothing compared to what brought an end to the Vietnam War.

Part IV
Public Sphere and Activism

From Community Art to Communal Art

Paul De Bruyne

The 'ideal public space' — which of course never existed — is a space for exchanging news, for forming opinions, for seeing and being seen, for eating and playing, dating and courting, for showing the clash between poor and rich, legal and illegal, for walking the dog and cursing (or occasionally worshipping) the weather gods; in short, for living in together. This idealized public space is often thwarted by increasing (car) traffic which leads to increasing congestion, an increase in light and sound pollution, an increase in violence in certain areas of the city (including legalized violence) and an exponentially increasing commercialization that curtails the public nature of the space.

A rather remarkable semi-public space was created with the introduction of the shopping mall. Every effort was made to give the impression that it was an ideal public space (safe, clean, full of reciprocity and interaction, child-friendly, open, offering unhampered mobility, pleasant smells and sounds), while (legally speaking) it is a purely private space dedicated to maximizing profit. Community art has been deployed by various governments to fight these threats to the quality of living together in public space, not because politicians believe that the arts can solve the problems but they think they can strengthen community spirit, thereby creating a basis from which they are able to devise political solutions. This political concern is strengthened by the notion that the cultural economy should be bolstered. In an economy that has already evolved from an industrial to a post-industrial society and is likely to proceed into an attention economy, experience economy, creative economy and/or knowledge economy, the arts are potential sources of wealth and employment.

With its support of community art in the public space, the government wins back a movement the origins of which are fiercely anti-establishment, not to say revolutionary, in nature. The best-known example of a cultural-activist movement is Reclaim the Streets, which has taken the streets as its battlefield since the early nineties. The movement was founded by Earth First!, an ecological group that set up campsites in the streets to protest against government-implemented solutions to mobility problems in the London district of Brixton. The idea of 'reclaiming the streets' quickly spread across the globe, with the underlying thought being that it's cars, rather than pedestrians, that cause obstructions, and that occupying the streets *opens* up a public space in which political debates about mobility (amongst other issues) can be conducted better. The actions by Reclaim the Streets activists were, and still are, invariably spectacular, colourful and artistic in nature; artists and artistic means play a prominent part. The hippie atmosphere was never far away and, in combination with a tendency towards direct action that is not afraid of challenging and crossing the current legal, political and moral rules, it appeared as if the revolution was just around the corner ('our streets are as filled with capitalism as they are with cars and the pollution of capitalism is much more insidious').

Since the 1990s, in a not completely unexpected but still brilliant option for repressive tolerance — to use Marcuse's sixties concept — subsidizing governments began to support two types of community art that use the street as a pedestal, initially in the West but spreading worldwide. This gave rise, on the one hand, to neo-parades and, on the other hand, to art-in-public-space.

The most eye-catching example of community art in public space is the neo-parade. These parades deserve the prefix 'neo' because they are largely the successors of religious processions and national parades that slowly winked out in the cities of the sixties and seventies. Roughly speaking, they may be further sub-divided into city parades and identity parades. The Brussels Zinneke Parade, Notting Hill Carnival in London and Fêtes de la Saint-Jean in Montréal are all typical examples of city parades, among others on every continent. Neo-parades seek to turn the streets into a safe and creative meeting place, at least during the hours or days of the festival.

To study an interesting example a little more closely, the Brussels Zinneke Parade was organized for the first time in 2000 when Brussels became one of the Cultural Capitals of Europe, thus being introduced into the city from the top down. Since the first edition of the Zinneke Parade, the cultural policy documents made it clear that the goal was to have a cheerful parade with a theme that would emphasize tolerance of all shapes, colours and appearances. The criteria for participation in the procession were, and remain, remarkably ecological and aimed at renewal; the floats cannot have an engine, all movements has to be caused by human energy, all music has to be acoustic, all images and performances have to be original (existing stories are not allowed to be used or copied). The Zinneke Parade is constructed months in advance in about twenty ateliers spread across the city. About four thousand volunteers and amateur artists work on the images and music under the supervision of approximately 150 professional artists. The parade clearly shows what the government expects of (community) artists: they have to create a cheerful, politically correct (intercultural and ecologically sound), optimistic image that invokes pleasant feelings in as many spectators as possible, about the city, about themselves and about living together. The artists are used to create a situation in which the demons of the modern metropolis (noise, violence, unbridled commerce) are chased away for a few hours or a few days. It is a temporarily free, creative space, heavily subsidized by the government. It is a space with great symbolic value, signifying that this society is one of individual and collective freedom and happiness. (Terrorists who would want to inflict a symbolic blow to this society now know where and when to throw their bombs.) But it is also a space of great economic importance; many tens of thousands of spectators spend their money; economics, politics and art form a cooperative partnership.

The other branch on the tree consists of identity parades, of which Gay Pride is probably the best-known example. Identity parades are organized by groups that feel misunderstood or discriminated against by the hegemonic culture. They represent ways of becoming visible, both literally and figuratively, and of creating a distinct identity by screaming it out, by dancing it. Gay Pride demonstrates a way of reshaping public space from one in which homosexual behaviour is forbidden, and therefore invisible, to one in which homoeroticism, in many forms, contributes to the colour and experience of the space. These parades are also connected to community art because a community is quite literally being formed here. Added to that, identity parades use all sorts of artistic forms (music, dolls, costumes, dance, theatre, video, lightscapes) to make the party attractive for participants, for spectators and mostly for the media that spread the message of identity-forming far beyond the here and now. Gay Pride is a non-violent way of answering the countless violent crimes committed against homosexuals — the power of the gay multitude against the power of aggressive intolerance. Increasingly, governments actively support these parades instead of merely tolerating them. These parades also have the economic, political and cultural-symbolic added value that was so eloquently formulated by Richard Florida in *The Rise of the Creative Class*. However, they have the disadvantage of being one-off events. The possible change in the quality of living together in public space is very limited in time. The domain of the visual arts could bring relief here.

Just like the new parades, the interventions we include under the heading Art-in-Public-Space are a neo-movement as well, because countless monuments and statues from previous centuries are also community art in their own way; art erected to the greater glory of church, nation and capital. In its most recent form, the visual art

242

that is seen appropriated as community art has to create a cheerful, colourful, energetic public space.

In the Netherlands (but not only here), art is used to support the ambitious plans of city councillors and housing corporations seeking to give the city a lively, humane and contemporary face. The most striking thing is that visual artists increasingly use elements of performance and temporary structures in their work, through which they corrupt the permanent nature of intervention into public space while at the same time producing a continuously changing intervention (financially and organizationally). Enhancing the quality of public space is apparently a fashionable item, as if all the people involved are aware of the mercurial changes in public atmosphere. The Amsterdam-based project 'Love in the city. Artists who want to bring love to the city'[1] is a sugary and fun example. The Rotterdam-based design agency, Vollaerszwart,[2] creates projects that transform entire streets and districts into spectacular surroundings for extended periods. Between 2003 and 2010, the Dutch city of Tilburg had the long-running project *Huisboomfeest* (Earth and Hearth) supervised by the visual artist, Wapke Feenstra, who organized walks with the district's residents in order to encourage them to see their own surroundings with new eyes. The reports of those walks and talks found a home on the internet[3] and in a book. These and many other projects are, in the Netherlands and elsewhere, financed by the various governments who see them as a means of promoting social cohesion, city marketing and, therefore, economic growth.

Although, at first sight, this may look like splitting hairs, some fundamental critical comments on these usually cheerful and conformist practices may be offered. The contradiction in this work is that the government that organizes the community art is also creating the economic, legal and political conditions that make ideal public space seem so remote. Thus, a virus finances the doctor, who is called to the sickbed again and again without a cure in sight. Some artists feel abused by the current trend of community art in public space. They search for a way to provide an artistic contribution in order to make the contradiction of the hurting and healing government visible, or even to conquer it. They look for an intervention that has a certain subversive power or at least avoids subscribing to the politician's pathological optimism. They search for an artistic means of

1 www.liefdeindestad.nl.
2 www.vollaerszwart.com.
3 www.huisboomfeest.nl.

shaping the ideal (which they sometimes share with the government), of the public sphere as a meeting place beyond the over-economically determined and overly-conformist examples of the dominant community art. During the past decade, a number of mostly visual artists and dancers/choreographers have undertaken interventions that called the concept of public space into question. What is public space? How do you create meetings that make the contradictions of our culture visible? What is the relationship between public and private space? In a way, they strive towards community art that effortlessly integrates with hegemonic political and economic discourse, on the one hand, and with radical activists who want to revolutionarily reverse existing relationships in public space ('All power to the pedestrians, anti-capitalists, homeless people, lazy people', etc.) on the other hand. We could call them the artists of the third way, although it would be an injustice to their specific artistic contribution. The link with the theoreticians of the political third way, between liberalism and state socialism (Habermas, Giddens), is obvious, although the artists themselves seem to be unaware of it as yet.

A current example of the artistic third way is the originally Viennese Permanent Breakfast initiative.[4] Visual artist, Friedemann Derschmidt, and four collaborators organized an alternative to the traditional social-democratic May Day procession on 1 May 1996, by placing a table in public space and having their breakfast. The next day, each of the participants went to a new spot and invited four people to join them for breakfast. If, every day, each of these participants organized such a breakfast, millions of people would have contributed to the action within ten days. It didn't quite work out that way but the idea has lived on, continually and globally, with distinct characteristics and effects on several continents.

The breakfasts were usually organized autonomously by an increasing number of new people, who sometimes contacted each other on the internet and other times did not. For the initiators in Vienna, the stake of the action was, and remains, the double question: who is allowed to use public space? And who is capable of autonomously deciding how to spend his/her own time? The Permanent Breakfast initiative is, first and foremost, a means of stretching the imagination to consider what could be done in public space. The initiators want to displace the unwritten presupposition that everything is forbidden if it is not explicitly permitted in favour of a practice in which everything is permitted if it is not explicitly forbidden. This is understood as a political intervention; the question raised by the breakfast action is the question of flexible public spaces and their quality, a question about the hierarchies of power in public space. In the West, these breakfasts mainly raise questions about the growing expansion of private spaces which disguise themselves as public spaces — shopping centres, art quarters, etc. There, the participating artists/activists meet opposition (from private security firms) because they break the pattern of consumption. In any case, the Permanent Breakfast provides us with an interesting definition of what public space is: 'A space, at least a free space in which we cannot have breakfast is not a public space'. The authorities rarely disturb the breakfast; it is usually shopkeepers that make trouble because the free breakfast disturbs the logic of buying and consuming. The worst enemy of the public breakfast lurks within the participants themselves; it took all of them considerable effort to reclaim the freedom of the public space for themselves when it wasn't given by the government (as in neighbourhood parties with food on the street or the giant picnic on the Highway A40 during the festival, Cultural Capital Ruhr). As is the way of these things, this event was organized and implemented (financially and administratively) by the government. Political acts are, in the minds and hearts of many, either allowed or not allowed by 'the existing authorities'.

The second question raised by the breakfast initiative is about autonomy in our culture: how freely can we decide how to spend our own time? The people at the breakfast table sometimes ask passers-by to join them: 'To invite unknown passers-by as guests and to confront them with a gesture of trust is an exciting part of the performance'. It is the experience of the Permanent Breakfast initiative, particularly in the West, that it is mostly members of the new creative (post-Fordist) economy who have the time and the inclination to accept the invitation. However, in practice these options turn out to be limited; in principle, people may have the freedom and time to join, but there are a lot of ifs and buts… self-discipline is enormous since there is always something to do on the laptop which prevents them from consuming freedom and breakfast together. For the flexible, free new human, participating with the breakfast is a sign of so-called superiority, in society. But the hesitation to exercise that freedom is considerable. The workers in the Fordist nine-to-five economy are trapped in a discipline in which the public breakfast is either seen as 'stealing time from the boss' or as the uneasy transference of a private activity into public life. For the economically excluded, especially the

4   www.permanentbreakfast.org.

unemployed, the challenge to perform a public deed of togetherness is often an unwelcome reminder of excessive free time.

Worldwide, there is an enormous number of initiatives in which artists and activists call the boundaries, quality and meaning of public space into question, especially through the tidal wave of walks and guerrilla activities, interpreted in thousands of ways, to catch the eye: 'Urban exploration. Go where you shouldn't go' ('leave nothing but your footprints, take nothing but the photos'). Francesco Careri, Mike Pearson, myvillages.org are just a few of the names of artists and initiatives who seek to elevate the act of walking, running and intruding in forbidden (private) space to the level of (critical) art. All these initiatives hope to test the public nature of publicness and to chart its limits. In this way, they try to withdraw from uncritical acceptance of the limited quality of living (together) in real public space and from the conformist way in which the community arts are used within hegemonic policy that can easily be unmasked.

Another type of art initiative does not so much look for the limits and the (im)possibilities of discourse and encounters in the public space. It researches the possibilities of redefining one's own body in, and thanks to, public space, which, in the process, is revealed as privatized; the public sphere becomes a (semi)private sphere.

The French-Canadian project, In Situ,[5] by Martin Chaput and Martial Chazallon is a fine example of this art form. Chaput is a professional dancer and Chazallon is an anthropologist by training. Together, they have developed projects in which they examine urban spaces and the body's place within them. For the project *Do you see what I mean? A Blindfolded journey in the city,* In Situ organizes a tour through a city district lasting approximately two and a half hours and undertaken by individual participants. Each participant is blindfolded at the start of the event. The journey consists of three parts and the participants are only sketchily briefed on what awaits them. During the first part, a volunteer leads the 'blind' participant by the hand and takes him/her into the district where they visit a few people (a shopkeeper, a retired person) who explain how they experience the local area. In the second part, the 'newly blind participants' continue their journey with a genuinely blind person who tries to communicate how they experience the walk. In the third part, the 'blind' participant is literally put into the hands of a dancer who develops a kinetic track with, and in respect of, the body and energy of the 'blind' participant. In an after-course, the participants gather in a room with the volunteers, blind people and dancers and exchange experiences. The artists of In Situ regard their action as a proposal for the participant to start negotiating his/her own body, with other involved bodies and with stories and public spaces that present themselves. In spaces that the body (formed by biology, culture and age) experiences as familiar, a grey area is opened up, one of 'undefined spaces, open to any possibilities', as In Situ puts it. It is an artistic proposal to create a meeting between strange egos, strange others and alienated public spaces without a clear outcome; particularly the dance at the end has no other reason than to meet and influence the will of two energies.

According to In Situ, the meaning of the project lies in opening a potential road for the body, and therefore for the self and therefore for the public space, which may be transformed through movement and dance. The work of In Situ differs from the hegemonic community art because it looks critically at the 'cheerful acceptance' or 'temporary breaking up' of the existing situation. But the work of In Situ also clearly differs from that of artistic and cultural activists because it is not directly related in a revolutionary way to the social and political problems of the street (cultural diversity, pollution, violence, degraded public spaces). On the contrary, they accept reality as it is 'at first sight'. They observe more like an anthropologist than an activist; they experience that many parts of the city are off-limits at many times of the day and for many different reasons. They also see that the project elicits entirely different responses from the urbanites in Maputo than from the ones in Marseille. Their observations are thought to be interesting but they are not part of the project as such. To the artists, the project appears in the first instance to be strictly physical and private in nature. However, to In Situ, it is clear that their work actually changes public space; there is no space outside perception and experience. Changing that experience, to them, means changing the publicness. If one is willing to move with trust in other bodies and with openness to other bodies, the street changes and the whole public field changes as well.

Can the artistic practices of the third way be defined as community art? Undoubtedly in so far as these art practices are used in a search for the quality of living together in public space. Do the artistic practices of the third way have a greater critical potential than the conformist community art and the revolutionary-activist variety? That is doubtful. All varieties of art in public space struggle with the problem that the current economic, political and cultural regime

5 www.projet-insitu.com.

in the West (and increasingly worldwide) is so accommodating of criticism that any artistic intervention can be neatly fitted into its logic. The words 'critical' and 'changing' can, then, only be used in inverted commas. Those who want to work on changing public space in a fundamental way will have to practice politics, not art.

It is one thing to observe the impossibility of critical intervention by the arts in the West; accepting the situation is a completely different story. The question is whether the demand for critical art is all that compelling, whether accepting the impossibility of making critical art — as accusation, utopia or heterotopia — makes every art activity either complicit or pointless.

The community arts in public space indicate that we can accept our own responsibility towards others in an (artistic) act at any moment, and, at that moment, we find our own individual and political voice. That moment of trust and improvisation allows us, briefly and without being able to introduce any fundamental change, to abolish discomfort towards our culture without giving up self-reflexivity and without accepting or forgetting injustices and contradictions.

In the modus of trust and improvisation (the modus of the rehearsal room and the atelier) one can escape, temporarily and in a confined space, what Canetti described as fundamental(ly wrong) in our culture. He remarks that the people in our times:

> fear nothing so much as the touch of something unknown [...] everywhere people avoid the touch of a strange element [...] this repulsion against touch does not leave us when we mingle among other people. The way we move in the street [...] is dictated by this fear [...] the entire complex of inner reactions against the touch of a strange element proves by its excessive liability and irritation that it concerns something very vulnerable that is always on guard deep in a person and will never leave him once he has determined the boundaries of his person.

Artistic practices in public space can be an attempt to reconquer the right and the possibility of touch; an attempt to inject not only into the private domain, but also (even) in the public domain that which only seems possible in the private domain and at the moment of amorousness and of love.

In the modus of temporary trust and the improvisational we can, in the terms of philosophers Masschelein and Simons, approach the state of childlike dependency in which people are exposed to each other. That childlike dependency is a state which falls outside the autonomy and independence of the personality, restricted by the current culture. It is a state where the potential, the not-yet-shaped and the sense of possibility are still intact. There is evident criticism here on the injustice that 'our' current regime, for example, promises people freedom and equality and fails to fulfil that promise because freedom and equality can only exist in an atmosphere of childlike brotherliness that is absent in the dominant regime. That state of childlikeness is a state that makes exclusion impossible since it knows no human relationship other than that of surrender to each other; we are indebted to each other and we have been saddled with the burden of doing right by each other. In the improvisational encounter — and, evidently, it takes artists to organize such encounters (except in the domain of love) — a complete dependency is visible, with its vulnerability, reactivity and sensitivity for living together. Maybe this temporary community of improvisation is the closest we can get to a fundamental and/because fleeting criticism on the dominant cultural space.

In the exile of the present, in the exile of temporary trust and improvisation, lies the limited possibility of escaping the current economic and cultural regime. The most interesting moments of community art in public space, as a critical artistic practice, are those moments when the street is re-privatized — in a campsite with friends at a busy crossroads, on a square that has been turned into a breakfast kitchen, in a re-definition of one's own (blind) body, in a procession that celebrates one's sexual nature. The politicizing of public space, in the surroundings of flexible capitalism, seems to lie in its privatization, not for the sake of profit but for the sake of the loving mental and physical touch, human beings can perform upon each other. It is the way from the community to the common, from community art to the communal arts in which the political and the private merge by osmosis. Does that road lead to the Promised Land? Of course not, but it is a way of conforming to the slogan of the incorrigible Samuel Beckett: 'Fail once, fail more, fail better'.

Chief Robert Duncan's Transformation Mask

The Native Carvers of Alert Bay

Hein Schoer

Question:
So being an artist is synonymous with preserving
heritage and culture?

Answer:
That would be a big part of it, yeah, once you get
into it, that's your obligation.
Interview with Bruce Alfred, 8 October 2009

This essay leaves the Old World for a trip to the Pacific Northwest
Coast of North America. There we will pay a visit to the native carvers of Alert Bay, whose artistic activity naturally bonds with their
community involvement, not only through the artworks produced,
but also through their use in cultural re-enactment, which acts as
the glue that keeps the native communities going, giving them back
a piece of the identity that was stolen from them by the white colo-
nialists.

From the first contact with Spanish and British explorers in
the late eighteenth century to the enticements of commercial television, the history of the original inhabitants of the Northwest Coast
has been a constant fight against oppression and marginalisation.
Nowadays, tradition and modernity meet as ancient myths and *Oprah*
clash in their struggle for dominance.

Interlocking with a variety of measures — like cultural classes
at school, language courses and other activities — artistic practice is
one pillar of the Big House where the native peoples of the Northwest Coast can gather to live their culture, from the highly culturally
aware members of the community to the others, that profit from the
drip-down effect of the omnipresence of their almost forgotten past.

When I first arrived in Alert Bay for audio recordings, I only had
a vague idea of what I might find there. My luggage consisted of
a big black flight case filled with high-end audio equipment and a
handful of clothes. As part of my research for the *Sounding Museum*
soundscape project, I had been commissioned to make recordings for
a surround sound production that would be on display at the Sound
Chamber of the Nordamerika Native Museum (NONAM) in Zurich, Switzerland, a museum dedicated entirely to the presentation of
North American native cultures. The idea was to collect sounds in
traditional and contemporary settings that best present the indigenous

peoples of the Pacific Northwest Coast, to create a sonic illustration of the current situation of the First Nations of that area. For a time, I was accompanied by the NONAM's ethnologist, Heidrun Löb.

With the native-run U'mista Cultural Society,[1] and its exhibition centre located there, as well as the presence of numerous widely known native artists, we could expect to find many interesting individuals and settings, and we had contacts with the Centre established during former visits. We would soon find out that there would be much more to our task than just checking items off our lists, that I had developed from reading books, and talking to the NONAM people. Not being an ethnographer or a Northwest Coast expert, I would, on the one hand, rely on Löb's expertise but, on the other, this gave me the opportunity to approach this project with the most open and unspoilt ears possible.

Alert Bay is a small village (in fact the only one) on Cormorant Island, a small isle on the Northeast Coast of Vancouver Island, British Columbia, housing approximately 550 inhabitants, half of whom are of Caucasian origin, while the other half mainly belong to the Namgis, one of the seventeen tribes or nations of the Kwakwaka'wakw. Cormorant Island is governed by two principal jurisdictions, the village of Alert Bay and the Namgis First Nation. Reserve lands occupy about thirty percent of the island's area. Out of a total island population of 1,500, over sixty percent live on the reserves.

Despite its small population, Alert Bay (which, from now on, at least in this text, will include the reserves for reasons of simplification) is one of the cultural centres of the Kwakwawa'wakw, which is due in part to the afore-mentioned U'mista Cultural Society. Bruce Alfred claims that the village forms the heart of woodcarving on the Pacific Northwest Coast.

From the moment of our arrival, it became clear that recording the sounds that would be used for the composition would only be a small aspect of the overall experience — the most 'tangible' one (as selected

1   The U'mista Cultural Centre (U'mista: 'The Return of Something Important') was opened in 1980 in the course of the repatriation of a large collection of potlatch artefacts, particularly a great number of ceremonial masks that are now on display in a permanent exhibition. These had been seized by the Canadian government in 1921 during a raid on a secret potlatch, the most important ceremony in Northwest Coast native cultures, which had been banned from 1885 to 1951. For more information, please visit www.umista.org.

passages can now be listened to at the Sound Chamber and on CD) but by no means representative of the totality of our experience there. In order to make a cultural soundscape, you need to know a lot about the culture you are trying to represent,[2] and most of these things you don't learn from reading books. The real trip can only begin once you are there start to talk with the people. And talk we did. A lot.

On our first day, we actually met Bruce Alfred, who had made a bentwood box for the NONAM. He is one of the senior carvers, aged fifty-nine at the time of our visit, and he is also one of the few people who still possess the knowledge and the skill to create bentwood artwork. He is based in a workshop that is used by a number of Alert Bay carvers at St. Michael's Residential School right next to the U'mista Cultural Centre. When we first met, a very young artist was also present — Darren Alfred, who, at nineteen, was already quite advanced in his skills and working on a giant ritual eulachon[3] grease spoon as we came in.

We would learn that this bridging of three generations was not to be taken for granted, and that it is vital for the survival of the culture. We would also hear a lot about the tension between the bentwood box Bruce was working on for the NONAM and Darren's spoon, which would not be sold, being used instead during the most important festivity of the Northwest Coast peoples: Potlatch.

For the native peoples of North America, whose cultures had been almost wiped out (along with the peoples themselves), whether by the cruel system of residential schools, where violence, abuse, and the fiercely enforced ban of language and all other cultural expressions deprived whole generations of their cultural roots, or by the dominance of the imported so-called Western culture, and many other factors, the identity-sustaining power of art can make a major difference. This is confirmed on Bruce's website: 'Bruce began his career in the mid 1970s in an apprenticeship programme offered by renowned artist Doug Cranmer and it was here that he learned the elements of traditional Kwakwaka'wakw design, carving, printmaking, and the steam bent technique for making boxes'.[4]

It is obvious how important the traditional, one could also call it cultural, background is to Bruce and his work. He learned from one of the great masters of contemporary Northwest Coast native art, and he draws from these roots as well as from modern ideas. This becomes even clearer if we refer to another paragraph of his self-description:

'Bruce's approach to traditional art is within the context of cultural integration. The artist must have an ever-expanding understanding of their history, language, myths, songs and ceremony. And they must have a current relationship with their own community if they have chosen to relocate to urban centres to further their artistic careers. It is a challenge today — though not an impossible task — to find determined young artists who are willing to submit themselves to the rigorous and time-consuming task of learning art through mentorship, a process that honours the past and those who have gone before to clear the way for the next generation.'[5]

To adopt the stylistic elements of Kwakwaka'wakw artworks is a manageable task for professionally trained artists from any art school; imitation is not too difficult, and has been done many a time. To outsiders, such an imitation may well appear equal in quality and authenticity to the original. In an interview I undertook with Bruce, he complains about non-native artists selling copycat pieces, thereby not only challenging the economic position of the native artists, but also compromising the metaphysical context of traditional art. Bruce was very upset about these non-native carvers, because, on the one hand 'every dollar they earn is a loss to our communities' — not to the least because 'carving [is] all we got left. They've taken our logging forest, minerals, fishing…' — and, on the other hand, it is disrespectful to copy an art that has taken 'eight to ten thousand years to evolve'. Bruce claims that 'because we're artists, we have to know the legends, we have to know the copyrights, we have to be historians' in order to earn the right to practice these art forms.

2   There's no room to go into this here, but of course we do not claim to represent the Kwakwaka'wakw culture, as we are not members of it. The soundscape production 'Two Weeks in Alert Bay' (quadraphonic versions at the Sound Chamber/NONAM, stereo on CD) was released on Gruenkorder: Hein Schoer - The Sounding Museum: Two Weeks in Alert Bay - Gruen 082/10; www.gruenrekorder.de. This offers a representation of my personal impressions of my short visit, which is all that I can do. The finished composition was approved by the people of Alert Bay after a presentation at U'mista some months after the recording sessions, so it may be used for public presentation, and The Sounding Museum research project has been approved by the Swiss UNESCO commission as a contribution to the 2010 International Year for the Rapprochement of Cultures, but it remains the work of an outsider.
3   Eulachon, or candlefish, was traditionally caught for oil production due to their high body fat index. Because they were only caught during a very short period of the year, and not all Northwest Coast peoples had equal access to them, they used to be a valued trading good; to distribute the 'grease' to the guests in large quantities during a potlatch was a demonstration of family wealth, conferring esteem.
4   www.brucealfred.com/bio/.
5   www.brucealfred.com/the-bending-process/.

The carvers of Alert Bay do not only make their pieces to exploit (white) Man's lust for exoticism in the living room, but also as a way of expressing and advertising their cultural identity. This means that being an artist in the native community brings with it a great responsibility to that community. Bruce's website again shall serve us as an example:

— Ongoing countless talks and art-technique demonstrations to student and professional anthropologists, visiting elders groups, inquiring tourists and elementary school classes
— Donating several pieces each year towards various individual, community and provincial fundraising projects such as Cops for Cancer, Beverly Mountain Cancer Fund and B.C. Arthritis Society
— Donation of time, support and artistic skill to produce funeral crosses when there is a death in the community
— Sought out by families for assistance on potlatch pieces
— 2007 Donation of two pieces to fundraising dinner and auction directed toward exhibit honouring Doug Cranmer's legacy[6]

During our interview and in many private conversations, he would confirm the picture drawn of him and other artists from Alert Bay on their websites and bios on gallery sites.[7] 'If I was never paid another penny for my artwork, I'd still be doing that. I'd have to get a job, but I'd still be carving. I'd still be learning to sing and working the language, and passing it on. I try to teach my grandkids Kwakwala […]'

'One thing good about all the artists in Alert Bay is, when there is a potlatch going on, we drop everything; 99 percent of the artists drop everything, and say, what can I do. And that's powerful, you know, for you support that family and then, when you have a potlatch, they come and support you. […] It's a lot of work, and it's a lot of politics […], but once you are finished, and getting through all that, man, the pride you have after it's done, we did it, we pulled it off […]. It unifies, it makes your family close, it brings them closer […]'

Through many conversations with carvers and other individuals involved in different forms of native art, I began to understand that it is hardly possible to separate artistic expression and enterprise from cultural and community involvement. In many native communities,

there are heavy social fissures, related, to a great extent, to the encounter of the original inhabitants of the land with the European usurpers.
This tends to manifest itself in high unemployment, poor education
and nutrition (due to educational failure), alcohol and drugs, violence
and sexual abuse and high suicide rates. But I didn't see any of these
problems during my visit to Alert Bay, which makes it seem stronger
(or more intact) than many others of which I've been told. Of course,
I was not shown around to get acquainted with all the things that go
wrong; I was mainly surrounded by the most dedicated culturally and
socially involved members of the community, but I am also tempted
to believe that the fissure is smaller in Alert Bay due to the fact that so
many of the Natives here have such a high cultural awareness. And this
awareness very often expresses itself in artistic practice.

Almost everyone I met carves, paints, sings or dances, and, in
many cases, is involved in several or all of these activities. William
Wasden Jr. (also called Wa, as an abbreviation from one of his Indian
names, Wak'analagalis, 'The-River-Flows-Through-Him-Forever'),
leader of the Gwa'wina Dancers, is also one of the prime singers and
scholars of traditional lore, songs, family trees and mythology, which
are often tightly connected to each other. Many songs and dances are
family property, handed down as heirloom from one generation to
the next, expressing aspects of the (often mythological) family history, symbolizing privileges and supernatural powers associated with
inherited positions in the originally highly hierarchical social structure of the different bands (or clans or tribes). He also paints and
carves, his art combines ancient designs with modern ideas and he
handles the old songs as they have been sung for centuries as well as
composing new ones. I witnessed the rehearsal of a song he had just
written for a young girl who would perform it only a few days later
at a potlatch, that I was taken along to, in some sort of a coming-of-
age ritual (embarrassingly enough I do not remember the explanation Wasden gave me) that was, in its basic form, much older than
the song. This and countless other cases should illustrate the essential
meaning of art to the cultural survival of the Natives.

Let us return to the carvers, who have a way of integrating their
monetary needs with their responsibilities towards the community

6   www.brucealfred.com/achievements/.
7   For example:
    www.seanwhonnock.com,
    www.nativeonline.com/beau_dick.htm,
    www.umista.org/giftshop/item.php?item=456.

that is both simple and efficient. As Sean Whonnock, who is also based at the workshop in the old residential school, put it: 'I carve half the year for money, and the other half for potlatches'. I had spent some time with Bruce Alfred in the carvers' workshop at the old residential school the other day, made recordings of woodworking tools in action, and the long interview about the difficulty of finding apprentices to continue with the traditional arts and how the old ways can help the young to find their place in the world.

Today I am at Beau Dick's, to record him bucking a block of wood with a handsaw and one of his colleagues hollowing the back-side of a small totem pole. We go inside, where I sit for a good hour, talking and listening and watching the carvers at work, while the microphone patiently records the workshop atmosphere.

Beau Dick is one of the native art big shots of the Pacific Northwest Coast, with his pieces selling for respectable prices in galleries world-wide. On our first encounter, he gave an impressive demonstration of the art of storytelling that has always been of high value to the North-west Coast Natives. Traditional legends, in many cases identified with historic and mythic origins of the tribe, clan, or family, with references to current events or political discourses, are told in a way that suit the intentions of the storyteller as well as the expectations of the addressee. He also showed the qualities of a trickster, reminding me of the wily raven, when he started telling his story (it was his version of the legend of Dzunuqwa) at the moment I had to pack away my microphones because it was starting to rain. For the time I was recording, he had only talked about rather trivial matters, but, as soon as the machines went offline, he gave the most beautiful account of the story that I had heard (or read) so far.

Beau's house is the gathering point for a number of carvers who meet every day to work together. Being in this busy work atmosphere offers you a beautiful insight into the many facets and layers of a living culture with such ancient origins as that of the Kwakwaka'wakw. The masks talk of a mythic past and tradition, and some of them will be used in the spirit of that tradition. I saw one mask evolving from the first rough cut into a sophisticated piece of art — a deer head that, if you pulled a string, would open up and reveal a human face hidden underneath, symbolizing the idea that animals are people as well. This transformation mask was received as a present from Beau Dick and would be worn at his potlatch by Chief Robert Duncan a couple of days later, representing one of his supernatural treasures.

In a gallery, this mask might have been priced at over $10,000, but it was a priceless gift to the chief, with supernatural powers that only he would be allowed to display.

Beau talks about the ancient urges he feels when hearing the singing and beating at a potlatch, while some country pop is blaring out of the radio and a cell phone rings next to it. You have to be, as Wa puts it, 'in balance' for this tightrope walk, to master the tension between the call of the city and the need for roots and identity.

This balance doesn't come naturally, and Bruce has been looking for an apprentice for eighteen years. Young Darren seems to be rather the exception than the rule. Although many people in Alert Bay are interested in culture and art-making to some extent, only very few really devote their lives to it, like Wa, Bruce or Beau. As Bruce says, 'Alert Bay has the best carvers, but it could all be over in one generation if nobody steps into their shoes.' The wood-bending process that Bruce uses to create his boxes is a very cumbersome and tiring exercise, much more time-consuming than putting together a few standard shapes for a Raven t-shirt, and it seems nobody wants to master it. You have to decide if it is to become your passion, or if it will remain in the hobby state, says Bruce. If he passes away tomorrow, they will have to start from scratch.

It is almost noon now, and I have to move on. Heidrun and I have an appointment at the T'lisalagi'lakw Native School, where I have been invited to attend the classes in singing, dance, Kwakwala and science. Here we shall learn about the efforts that are being made to foster cultural awareness in the very young at the earliest stage possible, countering the effects of many decades of cultural deracination.

Probably the deepest gash you could deal to a culture has been imposed mercilessly and with devastating effect on the population of Alert Bay during the reign of the residential school system. Out of the 5,500 people that consider themselves Kwakwaka'wakw ('Those who speak Kwakwala'), today less than five percent, less than 250 individuals, are fluent in their own language. Now, teachers like Sandi Willie, Lina Nichol and Vera Newman teach the children not only how to read, write, count and about the different parts of the nervous system, but there are also daily classes on traditional song and dance and Kwakwala language.

We first meet with Sandi Willie at singing class, where the children sing the old songs in the old language. They could become the ones who fill Bruce's shoes in later times. Vera Newman is the language teacher of the school. Class today consists of games, in which the students learn some basic terms, such as the words for colours, and we listen to them sing a song in Kwakwala to a melody that sounds pretty much like songs we sing with our children in 'Western' culture. The children are obviously having fun, but also a hard time catching up, as they grow up with English at home and everywhere else; Kwakwala is not spoken in everyday conversation anymore.

We watch the girls dancing in full regalia, with their family crests on their button blankets, then we follow the boys to dance class. Sandi is there, providing voice and drumbeat, but today the boys have a special guest as well. Marcus Alfred, Hamatsa initiate and one of the finest dancers I've ever seen, comes to instruct the young ones in the art of Hamatsa dancing. Hamatsa is the name of a secret dance society in Kwakwaka'wakw culture that is traced back to some brothers who discovered the house of Baxbaxwalanuksiwe, the Man Eater at the North End of the World, whom they killed and thus acquired a share of supernatural treasures that could be handed down as an heirloom in their family.

To be initiated into this society is a great honour and privilege that is only open to members of certain families with aristocratic roots, a position which can only be claimed through a complex ceremony, usually during the course of a potlatch, in which the young man who will become a Hamatsa (cannibal) has to perform a number of dances representing his possession by cannibal spirits and his overcoming of these spirits with the help of senior members of the society. Most of the boys that Marcus is teaching will never be initiated, because their lineage doesn't allow it, but, as part of an attempt to preserve as much of their culture as possible (even by spreading traditions that originally used to be reserved for only a small group of people), the acceptance for 'outsiders' has been growing.

Not only youngsters are subject to the endeavours of the language community. At the U'mista Cultural Centre, language classes are held for the grown-ups as well. It is 3:30pm and we wait for Pewi Alfred to start teaching her language class. Classes are held in the main exhibition room of the centre, which is built in the style of a Big House and accommodates wonderful old masks from the Potlatch Collection. Mariah Wadhams is there — she is in training to become a language teacher following Pewi — alongside Don Svanvick, another native artist, who, as I learn incidentally, owns the Animal Kingdom dance, a very powerful supernatural treasure.

Wa has invited me to join him at Chief Robert Duncan's potlatch at Campbell River, two hours to the South. We leave early in the evening, in a pickup truck belonging to young Waylon Isaac, who will also be sitting at the singers' log during the feast. The following morning sees us at the Big House at nine o'clock. This potlatch is being held in honour of the chief's mother, who had died a year earlier. Mourning songs have to be sung before noon, otherwise they will invite the spirits to come and prey on more people.

Potlatch, roughly translated as 'to give', is the most important ceremonial festivity in Northwest Coast culture, with deep religious and ritual meaning. All cultural activity of the Kwakwaka'wakw culminates in the potlatching tradition. The event can last several days; dances, songs, masks and treasures are presented to the audience, which is also provided for with vast amounts of food.

To give a potlatch requires a special occasion, such as the birth of a first son or the death of an important relative, because its central purpose is to hand down or to claim positions, titles and privileges. This has to be witnessed and approved by high-ranking guests and cemented through the distribution of valuable goods, strictly according to rank and position. With the net worth of the distributed goods rises the position and thus the lineage of the host, for in West Coast societies ancestry is of high importance.

Being the central expression of aboriginal culture, potlatch was prohibited by the white government in 1884. Only half a century ago, the ban was lifted, and since then the Natives continue to bring back the original spirit of potlatching to life in a contemporary form.

While this potlatch lasts only one day, its impact on me nevertheless is profound. After having been around the people of Alert Bay for almost two intense weeks, getting acquainted to their world as much as is possible in such a short time, this event is truly the climax of my voyage.

I will not attempt to try to describe what happens here, one has to be there, has to watch and to listen, and even then an outsider such as me can only get a vague idea of what this all means to the people involved. Instead we shall listen to the fire, the speeches, and, most importantly, the singing. Two dozen men are sitting around a hollowed cedar log and beat it rhythmically. Someone starts singing and, after the first verse, the group joins in. It will go on until past midnight, countless dances and songs, most of which I do not know what they are about, a Hamatsa initiation, a clown's act. The chief will open his box of treasures to the guests, we will all eat and drink and have stripes of red cedar bark around our heads; many speeches will be held in Kwakwala and some in English, Wa will spread the eagle down…

I begin to really understand what Beau Dick meant, when he explained how you get caught up in the music and the sound and 'something takes over.'

At the potlatch there were some 800 people and, except for very few white faces, all of them were native. Despite being deeply moved, almost overwhelmed, I cannot imagine what it must mean to the people themselves to be part of such an event.

All these ongoing cultural activities at the U'mista, at school, in and around the carvers' workshops, and of course in the Big House, but also almost everywhere else you look, would obviously not be possible without the endless efforts and contribution of the artists, whose activities create the lifeline that connects the culturally active people and the community. And this lifeline is crucial, because by far not all of the Natives are devoted scholars of their own traditions. Quite the opposite, most have little knowledge of their own origins, apart from, for example, some stylistic elements in their clothing or on billboards that borrow from traditional visual design, and a rudimentary vocabulary in Kwakwala, being far from the ideal of one William Wasden jr., the ever-talking, ever-teaching living memory of the Kwakwaka'wakw, who knows everything about history, mythology, genealogy, and traditional lore. But as long as there is a strong group of people like him, Bruce, Beau, Vera Newman, and all the others, there is hope that enough of their teachings drip down to the rest of the community, helping their culture to survive. And hopefully they will be received as role models by their people, spawning enough successors for the next generation to carry on with it.

263

Michelangelo Pistoletto and the People of Corniglia

'We've Come a Long Way Together'

Luigi Coppola

To bring art to the edges of life, to test the entire system in which both are moving, was the aim and result of my **Mirror Paintings**... After this, all that's left to do is to bring art to life, but not as a metaphor.
Michelangelo Pistoletto

The whole story of Michelangelo Pistoletto as an artist is marked by his astonishing ability to relate and co-operate directly with the different social contexts in which and with which he acts. It is as if the dynamic interactions with the surrounding world, unleashed by the *Mirror Paintings* in 1961, can no longer stop.

As a contribution to the theme of community art, one could cite many of Pistoletto's artworks and actions as milestones in the history of a type of art that's capable of implementing open socio-political dynamics: the *Mirror Paintings* and *Minus Objects* (1965—1966), for example; the cycles of actions and collaborations with The Zoo (1967—1970); the Creative Collaborations undertaken with diverse communities and artists in Italy and around the world or the latest, complex experiences of Cittadellarte, the creative laboratory of the Fondazione Pistoletto that connects all the areas of human activity which form society, and the Third Paradise. The work that Pistoletto has organically developed during his long career begins with the individual (the self-portrait in the mirror) and spirals ever closer to the multitude, with all the political, social, cultural and spiritual implications this involves. As the collaborations which Pistoletto has established with the most diverse expressions of thought demonstrate, the spiral bears a strong force of attraction. Their progress tends to be characterized by risk and complexity, and they may not always run smoothly. Nevertheless, one cannot fail to recognize the compulsion towards an art which, as the most sensitive and complete expression of human thought, should be at the centre of social transformations.

Among all the possible insights that could be extrapolated from this body of work, I have chosen to describe the bond between art and life which, for over forty years, Pistoletto has brought to the tiny village community of Corniglia, in the heart of Cinque Terre, in the Liguria region of Italy. This is probably one of the most 'resistant' experiences of involvement in a community in the history of contemporary art.

In 1967, after several seasons of creativity pursued with striking dynamics and speed, Pistoletto decided to open his 'studio' to the variegated humanity of his *Mirror Paintings* and to his three-dimensional *Minus Objects*.

This story begins in 1968, at the end of the avant-garde attempt to reconcile the division between art and life, which led to a renewal of the visual arts that has continued unremittingly through the years of the socio-political disengagement of art to the present day. Pistoletto turned his studio into a place of dialogue and experiential exchange, which led to encounters with various figures, including poets, actors and film-makers, which, in turn, gave rise to the Zoo experience. This heterogeneous group, active from 1968 to 1970, was born — in the words of Pistoletto — 'from the idea of creative collaboration, and was perhaps one of the first experiences of transition from an object-based aesthetic to a relational one'.

Theatrical language is an outcome of the merging of artistic disciplines. In this connection, Pistoletto says: 'I certainly didn't intend to go into theatre; I had no desire to switch from the profession of visual artist to that of theatre artist. I wanted to explore other art forms, other instruments, other languages. What I was looking for was an activity of creative collaboration. Sure, when you put together different languages and physically perform, in the end you can also say you're doing theatre. Theatre combines a number of elements — the person, the word, sound, colour, movement, light — in live space.'

The Zoo experience came about during a frenetic moment within the international art scene; in the 1960s and 1970s, the advent of many new forms of drama — some of which were transgressive with respect to the established types — brought to theatre an activity based on collective experience. As in the past, the group became the focal point of a type of drama that denied the primacy of the written word, launching artistic processes alternative to the historic mechanism of the staging of a text. By recovering the centrality of the relationship between group members, this new theatre aimed at communal expressive practices and shared experience, which counteracted the fragmentation brought about through professionalism and delegation.

In this manner, the theatre group was cast as the stem cell of a new sociality and a new anthropological concern; the aesthetic perspective set in motion an ethical reckoning which, by avoiding the risk of self-referentiality, encouraged collective experience. Thus, theatre made an exemplary response to the crisis of the spirit of the era. The expressive language of The Zoo was charged with the same force that gave rise, in Italy, to the Arte Povera movement, of which Pistoletto was a leading figure. On this line of enquiry, the artist says: '…there is the idea of energy, tension and stripping of all that is superfluous. Germano Celant had adopted the "poor theatre" concept pioneered by Polish director Jerzy Grotowski, who believed that the memory is in the muscle and that movement is the root of all true expression. Germano had realized that we were working on basic phenomenology, not for consumption's sake, but in search of the foundation, the root of being.'

In 1968, Pistoletto, his assistant Maria Pioppi, whom he later married, and The Zoo arrived in Corniglia. At that time, the life of the local community was very simple, almost archaic. The newcomers sensed the potential of this secluded place to support a vibrant collaborative laboratory, and it was not long before The Zoo's experiments became part of the villagers' everyday life. The group was inherently open and variable in nature, and it prioritized a real-life approach to theatre over dramatic pretence. In this way, the tough simplicity of the people of Corniglia became a fertile testing ground for the artistic approaches implemented by The Zoo over the next three years.

Interviews with some of the women who have witnessed the long relationship developing between Pistoletto and the community of Corniglia, reveal the simplicity and thoughtfulness that characterized Pistoletto's and Pioppi's rapport with the community from the outset. Licia Spora describes how 'Michelangelo was smart enough to present himself as one of us. He immediately fell into the rhythms and dynamics of the village, and we developed a beautiful human relationship with him and with Maria. Only much later, we realized he was a well established artist. He and all those extravagant people he brought to Corniglia were the spark of village life.' The interpersonal acumen shown by the artist — what Howard Gardner describes in his publications on multiple intelligences and education as the ability to form an accurate and truthful model of oneself and to use it to operate effectively in life — is what helped people to overcome the estrangement caused by the arrival of the extravagant and colourful bandwagon of The Zoo.

The group met daily on one of the village squares, in a series of experiments aspiring to create 'horizontal' creative dynamics, a level playing field between the different components of the group. Pistoletto recalls: 'Anyone who manages a group is likely to become king and then to be alone, and maybe even have a revolt break out. It is a matter of competition. Instead, we wanted to have democracy, so each day there was someone who became the director of the group. This stimulated the creativity of all and offered new themes to be developed together. We called this set of actions the *Minus Man.*'

At nightfall, men and women returning from work stopped to watch The Zoo's experiments in the square; the *Cornigliesi* describe how there was no television at that time, and the group's theatrical improvisations were a sort of live TV for them.

After completing the experience with The Zoo in 1971, Pistoletto and Pioppi remained intimately connected to the inhabitants of Corniglia. A few years later, they decided to open their creative experience directly to the community. A relationship was formed that was, above all, human and familial, which moved into the realm of art. In addition to involving the participation of individuals from Corniglia, the first collaborative action, *The Trombonauts*, was largely inspired by the life of the community. It represented the seagoing of the male villagers, their journey toward the unknown and the dignity of the staunch women who stayed behind, marking time with the regularity of their housework and defining the space of everyday life. White sheets were hung as a curtain, then folded and taken away by the women; at the end of the show a second set of sheets was hung, coloured this time, in a paraphrase of the houses of Corniglia.

In *The Trombonauts*, many of the elements that characterized the fertile season of The Zoo resurface: the unfolding of the story as if it were a musical score; the mood, at once epic and coupled with the everyday; the centrality of music and sounds as building blocks for action and creative collaboration with artists like the composer, Enrico Rava, and the soprano, Shuko Takahashi.

Corniglia once again became a small artistic laboratory, the experiments of which were subsequently transferred to a much larger scale in Atlanta, US, where Pistoletto staged the *Creative Collaboration* which involved the entire city and its official institutions. Over a period of two months, a broad and extensive participation in collective creativity matured, which took different areas of the artistic and political life of the city as their starting points. Of this experience, Pistoletto says: '[…] Maria and I called in Lionello Gennero (formerly part of The Zoo), the jazz musician, Enrico Rava, and the composer, Morton Feldman (with whom I had collaborated in *Neither*). With their help and that of local artists, we did things all over the city, involving adults and children at different neighbourhood centres, groups of actors in shopping centres, jazz musicians in the main square; we staged children's musical events in a big home for the elderly, as well as interventions in small shops and collaborations with Atlanta's young artists in several art galleries.'

When he returned from Atlanta, Pistoletto brought some of the artists who participated in the US experience back to Italy with him. Together with the people of Corniglia, they executed two more actions, *Pecora Cantata* and *Opera Ah*; both were staged in the squares and streets of the small village and both involved the symbols and rituals of the community.

The choice of the title *Opera Ah* refers to the generative possibilities of situations, of openness. Some of the strongest images of the performance are comprised of small groups of women holding combinations of beams to symbolize the architecture of the house. These powerfully sculptural images refer to the centrality of women in the village's social organization. According to Pistoletto, 'Women carried things on their heads, men carried beams on their shoulders. Thus was born the idea of a building made on the heads of women, on which men built their houses. Women have become the elements of memory, stable, proponents of the structure of the house, hence of the village.'

In 1981, Pistoletto and the people of Corniglia produced *Year One*. It was a real theatre project, conceived at the outset to be staged in theatres and galleries. The work was performed at the Teatro Quirino in Rome. Many of the people involved in the project had never left their homeland before. Although it was performed in 1981, *Year One* referred to an unspecified year in the history and places of the world, a year capable of encompassing both future events and, with the retrospective view of the mirror, past ones. In this piece, the *Cornigliesi*, Maria Pioppi and other Pistoletto family members became the 'pillars' to support architectural structures of the eternal city on their heads. The working process this time was much more complex and required the twenty-odd individuals involved in the project to make a daily commitment over a period of about two months.

In connection with this, Pistoletto writes, 'The play can be considered a talking painting, a living sculpture, and at the same time it can be listened to like a composition in which the literary phrases glide along on a musical score. It is the representation of a city where the people are the architecture. It is a civilization that immobilizes people under its heavy structures'.[1]

Year One portrays the history of humanity, from Cain and Abel, Romulus and Remus, Egyptian civilization to Roman, papal power to the conquest of the moon. In the words of Pistoletto, *Year*

One is 'the eternal city inside of which one hears time beat to the point of petrification.'

The stories I hear from those who experienced this adventure have epic connotations. The *Cornigliesi* faced the challenge of a major theatre of the Italian capital with pride and dignity. They understood that an experience that had been crucial to their human and social development also had a great artistic value.

Ten years later, in 1991, *Year One* was presented again in one of the most important contemporary art institutions in Italy, the museum at Castello di Rivoli, and, in 1994, it was staged at the Marstall Theatre in Munich, Germany. On this occasion, *Year One* restaged another important work by Pistoletto, *White Year* (1989). Late in 1988, Pistoletto had declared that the following year would be a White Year; amazingly the events of 1989 did, in fact, give a whole new turn to history (with the fall of the Berlin Wall, the revolution violently repressed in Tiananmen Square, the end of communist regimes). When *Year One — White Year* was staged in Germany in 1994, Pistoletto's daughter Cristina supplemented the original score with vocal compositions based on newspaper clippings narrating the events of 1989. The cast was joined by new participants, the children of the first generation of actors from Corniglia.

In November 2009, almost thirty years after the first performance of *Year One, Year One — Third Paradise* was staged at the Teatro Regio in Turin. On this occasion, the living sculpture was formed by a number of the original *Cornigliesi*, who had truly come a long way to get here, younger villagers who proudly took the place of their mothers and fathers, together with Maria Pioppi and other members of the Pistoletto family, and some of the people who have shared in the experience of Cittadellarte over the last ten years. Cittadellarte is Pistoletto's most recent 'collaborative exploit'; it has sprung from the seeds of experience sewn in the preceding 'creative communities'.

Third Paradise is the point of arrival of these creative communities, an arrival that can no longer be postponed. It has a philosophical goal applied to contingent reality, which the artist's *New Infinity Sign* represents well. The classical infinity symbol has a double loop and a third, central loop that becomes the womb generating a humankind which, having come to mirror itself and to see its own wonders as well as its own destructive impetus, can look at what is around it and

---

1 Michelangelo Pistoletto, Year One, 1981, http://www.pistoletto.it/eng/testi/year_one.pdf.

then turn its attention to redefining a possible existence.

Today, Corniglia is a global tourist destination, one of the pearls of the now-famous Cinque Terre. The inhabitants who have remained in the village are all involved in tourism in one way or another. However, the continual passage of people from all over the world barely touches the lives of the locals and leaves no trace in terms of relationships. By contrast, the cyclical return to the ritual work with Pistoletto, notwithstanding the historical and social changes that have taken place over the years, has become one of the building blocks of the *communitas*[2] of the place.

I was fortunate enough to contribute to the recent creative collaboration, *Year One — Third Paradise*, and what I was able to see, working with Pistoletto in Corniglia, is that this experience has been deeply rooted; it has left its mark on several generations, creating stories, tales and myths that have been absorbed in the social fabric. As one of the key phrases of *Year One* says, 'We've come a long way to get here'.

2   According to the anthropologist, Victor Turner, the creation of communitas
    is based on immediate relationships among group members. Within the
    communitas, without losing the traits that render them unique, individuals
    are conceived as a we 'tending toward a freely chosen common goal'; the
    members of the communitas thus achieve 'an order or quality of human
    relationship that does not have the character of a transaction, as people
    when undertaking actions directed toward others are not necessarily
    moved by expectations of a relationship that serves their own interests'.

About the Political Potential of Contemporary Art

Jonas Staal

Introduction

The political potential of contemporary art in what is sometimes known as the post-ideological era lies in revealing the constant *ideological battle* that is masked by what we jokingly call parliamentary democracy. I see art as an instrument in making this battle manifest again and in showing that, beyond the pathetic democratic conceptual framework — Participation! Diversity! — a genuine *difference* is conceivable.

For an artist like myself, public space is the democratic arena par excellence, the place in which public conflict and confrontation have to take place, the place in which *political existence* takes shape, the place in which we can say that we are not merely dealing with politics but with *our politics*. Not politics in which we contract out our vote, but politics that consists of the process of *learning how to shape it ourselves*. Art is an instrument with which to make this voice not only heard but also *seen*.

The text below further explains these starting points by using three of my projects as illustrations.

Stalinlaan

I would like to start with the history of the Vrijheidslaan ('Freedom Avenue') in Amsterdam, which was the core of one of my projects in 2009. I'll begin by releasing a document, a letter that was a major part of this:

To: Oud-Zuid City District
P.O. Box 51160
1007 ED Amsterdam

Rotterdam, 21 May 2009

Dear staff member of the district of Amsterdam Zuid,

After the Netherlands had been freed from occupation by the Nazis in 1945, the various countries involved in this liberation were honoured by having streets named after their leaders. The Amstellaan became the Stalinlaan, after the Soviet statesman Joseph Stalin. The Zuider Amstellaan and the Noorder Amstellaan were also rechristened as Rooseveltlaan and Churchillaan. When, on 4 November 1956, the Soviet army was sent to the People's Republic of Hungary in order to suppress the massive rebellion of the populace — which started on 23 October 1956 and is known as the Hungarian Revolution — the residents of the Stalinlaan angrily changed their street's name into Vier Novemberlaan. They also sent a request to the city council to either make this name the official one or to rename the street Amstellaan again. A majority of the city council supported the residents but preferred the name Vrijheidslaan. The Mayor and Aldermen agreed with the council members. Despite virulent protests by the Communist Party Nederland (CPN), the decision to change the name was taken in November 1956. The Stalinlaan officially became the Vrijheidslaan.

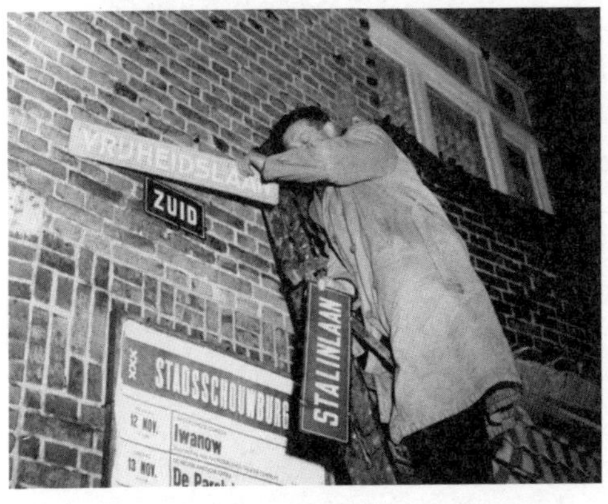

In 1956, the sign of the Stalinlaan in Amsterdam is replaced by one bearing the name, Vrijheidslaan.

On 4 March 2009, the Vrijheidslaan was changed into Stalinlaan through my instructions. With this letter, I send you a street sign for the Stalinlaan, made by the firm, Sign & Traffic. I do this because I am convinced that it was never your intention to repeat Stalin's manipulation of history, for example when he removed his later political opponent, Leon Trotsky, from photos that still showed them together. The street sign meets all necessary requirements for street signs in public space. I hope to have been of service to you by restoring the street sign to its original state.

Kind regards,
Jonas Staal

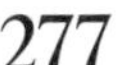

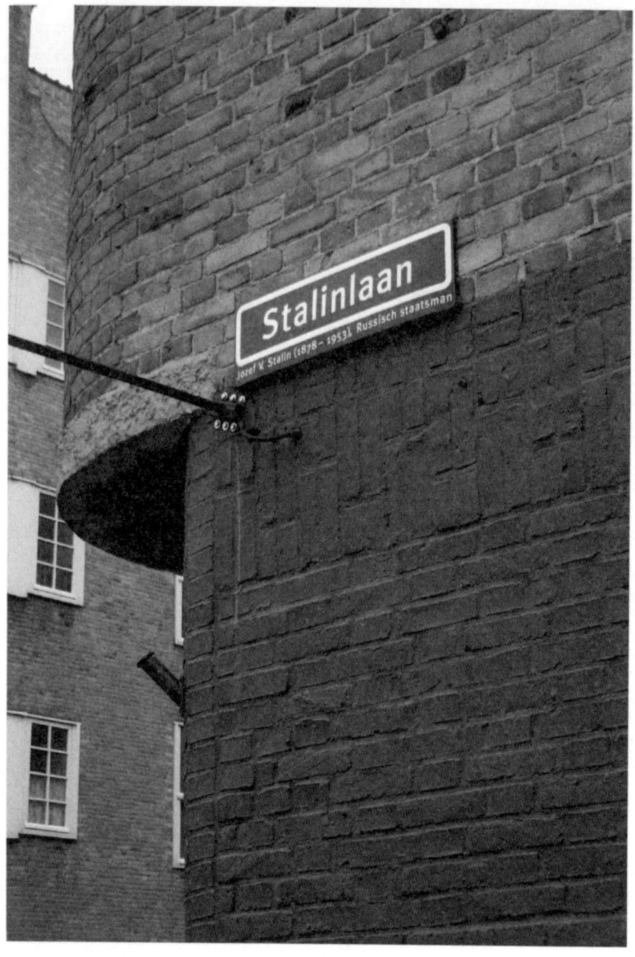

Jonas Staal, Stalinlaan (2009)

Important in this story is that there is no rationally fixed starting point; I could just as easily have changed the Vrijheidslaan into Amstellaan, the name the street bore before the Second World War. Or, using the same line of reasoning, I could have removed the street sign, referring to a time when there was no sign and the street had not yet been turned into an ideological game board for the dominant

278

political order. Getting to my point, there is no clear substantiation of any original name or image that can be the legitimate beginning for a change; there is no old that has to make room for the new, there is merely the *historical urgency* that made the street a place of ideological confrontation and conflict at several points in time.

After World War Two there was an urgency to etch the liberation of the Netherlands into the collective memory, to 'never forget' and to chisel *absolute* gratitude to the liberators into the street scene: there we have Roosevelt, Churchill and Stalin. The Hungarian Revolution *differentiates* the freedom which at first appeared to be unambiguous and was just as unambiguously recorded in a street sign. By 1956, the residents of the Stalinlaan distrusted the freedom brought by the Soviet army under Stalin; this freedom was no longer their freedom. This freedom had been tainted by *ideological interests*, which — beyond the universal democratic peace and human rights — resulted in a political order that had imposed a *lack of freedom* on Hungary.

This experience of historical urgency found its natural conclusion in the proposal to change the name of the street into Vier Novemberlaan, out of solidarity with the Hungarian People and, at the same time, as a *reminder* of the Dutch people's own underground resistance against, and suppression by, the Nazis. The liberators of one country turned out to be the occupiers of another country. The underlying conclusion seems to be that if the Soviets had liberated us for ideologically false motives, *it would have been better if they had not done so at all.*

But then the city council itself intervened. The call from the residents, for a street name that acknowledged the suppression of the Stalinist regime, was erased with which can safely be called the ultimate *hat trick* of parliamentary democracy: the Stalinlaan was rechristened Vrijheidslaan. Because who could possibly take offence to freedom? And wasn't freedom what it was all about in 1945? The answer is No — when the residents came up with a street name out of solidarity, freedom was still a *matter of principle*; the freedom the city council was concerned with had withdrawn from this essential debate and represented a whole new *totalitarian order*.

Because changing the Stalinlaan was *in itself a liberation* — a liberation of the ideological matter that confronted post-war Holland, namely that there is no such thing as neutral, universal freedom; there is only freedom that is established by, and articulated from within, *power politics*. The name Vrijheidslaan created the illusion that liberation by the Soviet army could be liberation *without* signature-

because — so the perverted line of reasoning went — the regained freedom itself was real but the intentions of the soldiers were not. Through the Vrijheidslaan, Amsterdam city council celebrated a *conflict-free freedom* — a freedom without *ideological responsibility*, a freedom with *clean hands*.

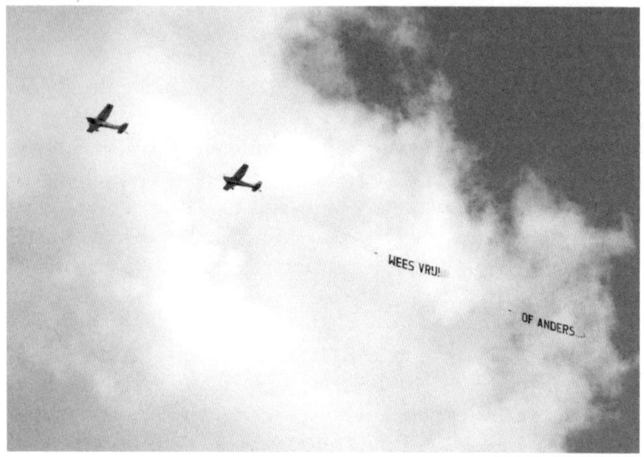

Jonas Staal, Be free! Or else... **(Liberation Day, 2010)**

This freedom is the freedom of *democratic ideology* — a freedom cut loose from the individual interests and barbaric violence of the previous century, a freedom in which everybody can participate and in which everybody must be kept on board, a freedom to exclude fundamentalism, a freedom to just act normal, a freedom to do nothing, a freedom to limit freedom when the terrorist meter hits the red or the street terrorists make the street unsafe as the vanguard of the barbarians who are preparing an assault on the enlightened gates of Europe. This is a freedom that represents her actual counterpart, a freedom that is best understood as *diktat*:

> *Be free!*

This diktat implies a trade-off — something from the past has to be dropped in order to become part of this new *freedom without interests*. At this point, it is important to introduce the historic concept of *iconoclasm* in our time as a concept that can explain the dynamics behind this trade-off: the destruction of the alien — a potentially radically alien culture or position — for the sake of a normative system of values, but *without showing this process or exposing it as such to the world*. This trade-off is only successful when it is not *recognized* as such but presented as a natural process of primitive customs toward Western Enlightenment ideals. Through this process, which aims to establish an absolute, and therefore non-existent, concept of freedom (what do we do once *everybody* has finally been freed?), an interesting ideological battle is taking place.

Replaced Street Signs

The Chinese district in The Hague, for instance, has had its own street signs for some years now, written in both Western and Chinese characters. In itself, the phenomenon of a Chinese district is odd enough; were we to speak about Moroccan or Antillean districts, it would imply disastrous integration and excessive segregation. But, in the case of the Chinese, one of the worst integrated groups in the Netherlands, this is not a problem when it comes to language and distribution. The apparent lack of fundamentalist political or religious character and the — also apparent — *humble attitude* of the Chinese made sure they could taste something of the *freedom without interests* that is so characteristic of the democratic ideology. This implies an acknowledgement of difference — between the Dutch and Chinese culture — that is merely tolerated within the stainless steel framework of the Dutch monument of the street sign. A *difference without a real difference* as an example of Dutch tolerance.

When, propelled by this democratic principle of equality, the writer, Vincent van Gerven Oei, and I extended the principle of this street sign policy, also replacing the street signs in districts with an Arab-speaking majority, we concluded, once again, that the concepts of freedom and equality within the democratic ideology represented a concealed policy of *exclusiveness*. Subsequently, however, the paradoxical promise of democracy — freedom and the right to difference for everybody — requires an unrelentingly consistent action, which, first and foremost exposes the *fear of freedom* when the wafer-thin mask of tolerance and openness falls away.

To return to the concept of iconoclasm — in this day and age, I would not represent this as simply the destruction of one image in favour of another but as a *strategy* in which a view or policy reveals the ideological contradiction. I would represent it as a radical *differentiation* of images that seem normative or absolute to us. The core of my work is the democratic ideology, which I choose not to regard as being elevated above ideological struggles but as their *continuation*.

The Japanese translate our concept of democracy as *democratism* — as one of the great many *isms* in this world — for a reason, and I suggest we follow their example in this.

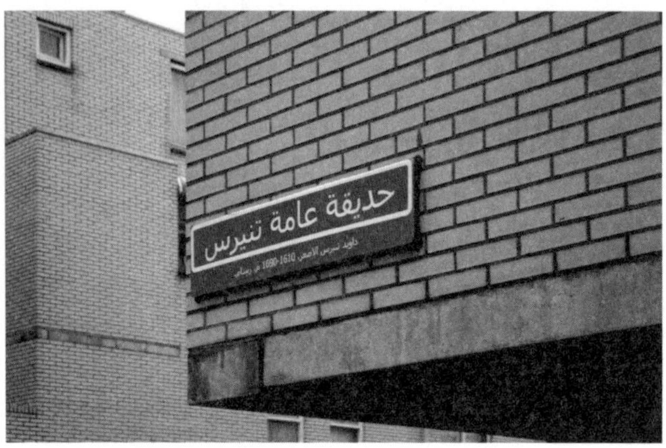

Jonas Staal and Vincent van Gerven Oei, Replaced Street Signs **(2008)**

Monument to the Displaced Rotterdam Citizen

In 2007, the Partij van de Arbeid (PvdA) (Labour Party) politician, Zeki Baran, called for the erection of a *Monument to the migrant worker* in the Afrikaanderwijk in Rotterdam — a sculpture that would be a reminder of the contribution made by first generation migrants to the rebuilding of Rotterdam after the Second World War. It was also intended to show that migration has contributed positively to Dutch culture, becoming part of our culture as well. The sculpture would further serve as a plaster over the still-open wound that the neighbour-hood suffered during the first and only race riots which occurred there in 1972, as a result of the complete lack of support for migrants in society. In that year, the autochthonous population had quite literally dragged migrants and their possessions out of their houses for three days.

Ronald Sørensen, leader of the right-populist party, Leefbaar Nederland ('Liveable Netherlands'), reacted with anger to Baran's pro-posal and stated that 'on balance migrants from Turkey and Morocco have cost Dutch society more than they contributed'. He went on to say that it would be more appropriate if a sculpture was erected for the Rotterdam citizens who rolled up their sleeves after the war, with a 'natural work ethic'. He evoked 'A bronze sculpture of a dock worker and his family, looking around, lost in the surroundings they were expelled from', referring to the exodus of autochthons from the problematic Rotterdam neighbourhoods to the suburbs, the new white bastions of the city — a monument to the 'displaced Rotterdam citizen'.

I called Sørensen about his suggestion and, after consultation with this politician, I decided to accept this assignment and had a three-dimensional scale model made based on his specifications. During an interview with him and Anton Molenaar, the Leefbaar Rotterdam ('Liveable Rotterdam') spokesperson for Youth, Education and Culture, I presented them the rough design. 'You catch me completely off guard with this, but I like it,' was Sørensen's reaction. 'Objectively speaking this design could serve all sorts of purposes,' Molenaar added.

It is obvious that Sørensen's proposal for the monument was primarily meant as a polemical move. His monument to the displaced Rotterdam citizen was intended to direct attention to Baran's — as yet unrealized — monument for the migrant worker, which is why he feels 'caught completely off guard' when he is confronted with a scale model that can be used to produce the actual monument. This doesn't mean that he doesn't want to actually erect the monument; it is merely the first time he actually thinks about it in concrete terms because he didn't take his own proposal *seriously at first*. And we, the audience, can also only see the actual implications of this policy when the image described manifests itself visually, with all its historical connotations, ranging from *social-realism* to the ideals for edifying the people that ex-Labour Party member, Sørensen, put into his creation.

To Recapitulate

In the case of the *Stalinlaan*, the concept of freedom is used to conceal an essentially ideological struggle for the sake of the successful implementation of post-war democratism.

In the case of *Replaced Street Signs*, the exclusive nature of the freedom of democratism is visualized — namely, the totalitarian removal of all the differences that are not system-confirming in nature.

In the case of the *Monument to the Displaced Rotterdam Citizen*, this *exclusive right* to democratic liberties for the autochthonous Dutch is elaborated — the monuments to the migrant worker and to the displaced Rotterdam citizen engage in an ideological battle in the representation of history and *with it*, the meaning of 'our' acquired,

democratic liberties.

Instead of one image of reality nullifying the other one — destroying it — I would like to *realize both monuments* at the same time and have them cancel each other out: the monument to the migrant worker on the Afrikaanderplein with, next to it, the monument to the displaced Rotterdam citizen, running away from it.

Only *in combination* do they form the real monument — monument to the current condition of democratism, a monument that reflects the state of our political debate and the positions in it.

In the *public* confrontation of these images, from the space that is created by their *mutual nullification* lies the potential to find the terms of a new political and artistic freedom. It is this area that I would like to name the *political potential* of contemporary art.

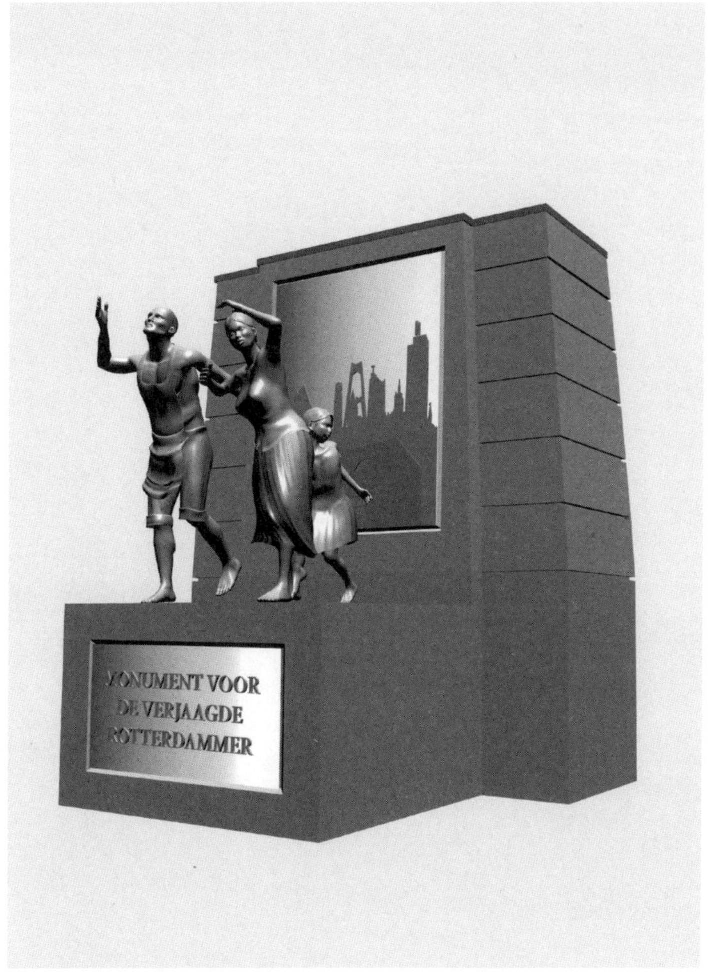

Jonas Staal, Monument to the Displaced Rotterdam Citizen **(2008)**

Ruangrupa
Experimental Video Workshops and Activism in Indonesia

Miguel Escobar Varela

Two men carry boxes from one side of the room to the other, as if they were working for a relocation company. We only know they are there because of their reflections on the screen of an old TV that is lying in the centre of our field of vision. The room in which they are working has huge windows masked with bars. The men continue for a few minutes in their seemingly unending quest to transport the boxes. Suddenly, they start dancing. Their dance takes place just in front of the TV screen, and the dance seems to be for our benefit. The initial impression anyone watching this scene might have is that the men are unaware of being observed. However, as soon as they start dancing, this impression changes. And the observers realize that they have not been able to understand the actions taking place in that room. Whatever is going on in that room is not 'captured' by the reflections on the TV screen.

The previous paragraph refers to a piece of video art called *Dalam Kotak di dalam teralis* (The Box Behind Bars, 2007), which was made during one of the OK Video Militia workshops organized by the Ruangrupa collective in Depok, an area of Jakarta. The video, directed by Brian Genie, Robert M. Syarif, Dimas Djunaedi and Maulani, makes a reference to the distorted way in which television claims to mirror reality. The full power of this metaphor can only be unravelled if we are aware of the complex media history of Indonesia in the past century. In this essay, I will offer a summary of this history, in an attempt to shed light on the relevance of not only the afore-mentioned video, but also the range of workshops and activities organized by Ruangrupa.

In October 2009, when Ade Darmawan and Reza Afisina from Ruangrupa came to the Netherlands, they agreed to meet me for an interview. They had come to Utrecht to develop a project for CASCO (Office for Art, Design and Theory) and to present a selection of video works at the Impakt festival. Ruangrupa (literally meaning Visual Room) was established in 2000. Since then, it has become a prolific platform that is responsible for numerous screenings, workshops and exhibitions in different parts of Indonesia as well as hosting in Jakarta a biennial festival of video art that is the oldest in the country and one of the few operating in South East Asia. According to Ade Darmawan, the artistic director, and Reza Afisina, the coordinator of the Art Lab, the goal of their activities is to foster development of the aesthetic and political possibilities of video, an art form that is not very widespread in their country. Their efforts constitute an attempt to balance the development of the form as an artistic product and its possible meaning for social development and transformation.

For this reason, they organize the international festival and travel extensively to different countries to show works developed by Indonesian artists to a specialist international audience. They are also involved in activities which aim to make the critical and expressive tools of video art available to the widest range of people through workshops, such as the one that produced the video described above, and screenings in different cities in Indonesia. The political significance of these activities will be outlined here.

Before embarking on this endeavour, however, it is important to clarify that not all of the group's activities are directed towards pursuing a political agenda. Only sometimes does the work they develop and showcase have a very clear political message; on other occasions, works are playful, funny or intimate. They are, after all, primarily an artistic organization and not a political group. However, at both a formal and an ideological level, the freedom of expression that is catalysed by their workshops has political resonance, with theorists of video art praising its inherent power as a means for political opposition and a tool for the development of alternative constructions of the self and the political imagination. Although enthusiasm for this approach has waned in the eyes of some contemporary art writers, it is still a recurring theme in media art discussions in Europe and North America. I will only offer a brief overview of these ideas in order to show how the oppositional power of video art is always delimited by a certain *mediascape* and the specific social framework in which video art is developed and shown. In this light, video art as an oppositional tool can only be understood when considered in an historical way, by explaining how its hypothetical power to oppose the mass media functions within time-bound and concrete social environments that generate specific patterns of media relationships. After presenting a bird's eye view of theoretical discussions around media art, I will, thereafter, discuss Indonesia's recent political and media past in order to explore ways in which the claims of video art's oppositional power can hold true in that country.

The Oppositional Power of Video Art

The origins of video art in the 1960s are often idealized as the moment at which 'artists decisively reclaimed video as a creative medium capable of challenging the military, political and commercial interests from which it sprang'.[1] Since then, video art has generally enjoyed a positive reputation within academic and artistic circles, as an effective means of contesting domination.[2] It has been understood as a way of constructing images — or rather, as a plurality of means of constructing images — that are in radical opposition to the way this is done within mainstream media in TV, film and advertising, realms which have been tainted by political and commercial agendas of domination.[3] The way in which media art explores alternatives is by moving away from conventional narrative structures and cinematic conventions, and by generating images in unprecedented ways. For at least five decades, champions of video art have claimed that the very exercise of exploring different ways of dealing with images offers an alternative viewpoint that may be read as an act of political defiance. Festival organizers, art writers and historians who elaborate such appraisals of video art do so by invoking the assumption that political and commercial powers exercise control over society by determining which images are normal, real and desirable. Therefore, the radical visual experimentation undertaken by video artists has the power to expose the constructed character of such images and to bring about awareness of their latent manipulative nature. As a direct consequence of this, video art is said to foster a critical attitude towards the way people relate to images and, by extension, to political power.

An early and well known example of video artwork that aroused this kind of enthusiastic appraisal is Nam June Paik's video account of an official papal visit to New York in the 1960s. As is well known, Paik was one of the first artists to use a portable video camera as an artistic medium rather than just a means of documentation. With this new piece of equipment in hand, the Korean artist set out to record the Pope's visit along the crowded streets until he ran out of tape, presenting this recording to an audience at the Café a Go-Go.[4] The element that made this action especially significant was that Paik screened his version of the event next to a televised account of the same visit, with the uncut version standing out as radically different to the televised one, which was full of commercial cuts and multiple editing. People who comment on the significance of this event — such as Noah Wardrip-Fruin, who praises the work for calling into question the 'sacrosanct status of montage'[5] — defend this practice on the basis of its ability to disrupt hegemony.

However, by the late 1990s, certain writers argued that this radical capacity of video art had been completely eroded; Michael Nash observes that 'the least that can be said is that we have witnessed the death of video art'.[6] Television and film, he argues, have become so self aware that they have turned into their own best critics. As a contemporaneous example, one could mention *The Larry Sanders*

Show,[7] a television satire in which the inner workings of a talk show are exposed, or, in the case of film, *Wag the Dog*,[8] in which a Hollywood producer is hired to stage a fake war against Albania for television. In the light of these examples, the words of Nash ring true: "alternative' video has lost its moral imperative'.[9] One could argue, however, that television's self-reflexive criticism is based on marketing decisions rather than on an ideological discontentment. These types of programmes and films were, quite possibly, designed by producers in order to win the attention of media-savvy consumers in an over-saturated market. Despite this plausible criticism of the ideas proposed by Nash, his point is still noteworthy and relevant. If video art is to regain its critical force in places such as the United States and Europe, it needs to change because the media environment in which it evolved has changed. Thus, the efficacy of video art as a medium depends of the historical and social context in which it operates; in different societies — with different media histories and distinctive *mediascapes* — video art has different opportunities to exercise its oppositional power. Let us turn now to an examination of the ways in which the Indonesian scenario might differ from the current status of the *mediascape* in other places; this will consist of a brief overview of the changes undergone by political and mainstream media influences over the past few decades.

Recent Media History of Indonesia

After Indonesia achieved its independence from the Netherlands in 1949, Sukarno became its first president. He enjoyed a short period in government before being ousted by General Suharto, whose Orde Baru (New Order) is usually depicted as an authoritarian regime. In

1 Catherine Elwes, Video Art: A Guided Tour (New York: I.B. Tauris, 2005), pp. 3-4.
2 Michael Rush, Video Art (London: Thames & Hudson, 2003).
3 See, for example, Elwes, op cit, Rush, op. cit. and Margaret Lovejoy, Digital Currents: Art in the Electronic Age (London and New York: Routledge, 2004).
4 Elwes, op cit., p. 4.
5 Noah Wardrip-Fruin, Introduction to 'Will There Be Condominiums in Cyberspace?,' The New Media Reader, ed. Noah Wardrip-Fruin and Nick Montfort (Cambridge, MA: MIT Press, 2003), p. 463.
6 Michael Nash, 'Vision after Television: Technocultural Convergence, Hypermedia, and the New Media Arts Field,' Resolutions: Contemporary Video Practices, eds. Michael Renov and Erika Suderburg (Minneapolis: University of Minnesota Press, 1996), p. 382.
7 HBO, 1992-8.
8 Dir. Barry Levinson, 1998.
9 Nash, op cit.

order to ensure control of an unstable nation against dissident voices, his administration used techniques of intimidation and institutionalized brutality over a thirty-year period.[10] For the mass media, this meant that a particularly repressive political culture was established;[11] here, I will concentrate on the particular sectors of the mass media which will become relevant to experimental video activists: the realm of the moving image.

As an extension of the authoritarian control that characterized Orde Baru policies, television and film were controlled through censorship. In the case of motion pictures, an institute for film censorship was established, known as Lembaga Sensor Film (LSF), which had to check the content of films requiring permission for public screening. As Sen and Hill note, this was only a symbolic form of control, as the LSF consisted of two viewing rooms which operated for six hours each, five days per week, rendering impossible the actual task of viewing all incoming material.[12] However, as Adrian Vickers explains, many things in the Suharto era worked within the 'helmet culture', a metaphor he borrows from M. Dwi Marianto, who noted the curious helmets people wore in Indonesia when riding motorcycles.[13] In principle, helmets were compulsory as a means of protection from injuries; however, people used all sorts of helmets (including hard hats from the construction industry, for example) which did not really fulfil a safety role but which were successful in allowing motorcyclists to escape paying fines to police officers. Vickers extends this image into every controlled realm, to explain how appearances were maintained; he goes as far as to say that 'the appearance of accurate measurement, of modern surveillance, was important as a *raison d'etre* of the bureaucracy'.[14] With this idea in mind, the limited capacity of the LSF should not strike us as inefficient; rather, it was quite effective in its function as a symbolical reminder of the government's control that induced people not to do what might get them into trouble. Indeed, as Philip Kitley notes, when it came to television and film, some bans never happened because editors, journalists and broadcasters censored themselves.[15]

In television, censorship was a relatively easy task, since, for the most part, only one national station, TVRI, was allowed to exist.[16] This channel had enormous power over the content of the news to be broadcast, which was reproduced by every local station at peak time (7pm). Television — which, according to Sen and Hill, was more a creature of the Orde Baru than any other medium — was a 'key propaganda tool for government policies, and the site for the regime's definition of Indonesian national culture'.[17] This definition included, for instance, the prohibition to broadcast material in any language other than Indonesian or, occasionally, Javanese, a regulation that could be interpreted as a means of reducing the linguistic diversity of the archipelago, where an estimated 719 local languages are spoken.[18] This combination of censorship and programming guidelines acted not only as a tool for controlling the spread of information but also as a form of aesthetic control that encouraged a particular idea of Indonesian culture. Situations comparable to this could be found all throughout South East Asia, where 'television evolved during the heyday of nationalism as a political force, when many states were emerging from diverse racial and language groups. The assertion of the ideal of 'the nation' coincided with the development of a powerful tool for nation-building'.[19] Thus, television was officially presented as a means of dominating public opinion. This situation contrasts with the broadcast policies of Western countries, which enjoy a rhetorical power to offer views that differ from those of government. It is beyond the scope of this essay to measure the extent to which this actually happens; what is noteworthy, however, is the difference in the rhetorical practices of media politics between Indonesia and other places. The overt status of television as a tool of domination was regarded by Indonesian people, especially those living at the peripheries of the country, as a rather oppressive form of representation that offered no space for alternative constructions of Indonesian identity.[20]

10 See Adrian Vickers, 'The New Order: Keeping Up Appearances,' Indonesia Today: Challenges of History, ed. Grayson Lloyd and Shannon L. Smith (Singapore: Institute of Southeast Asian Studies, 2001), pp. 72-84; David T. Hill, The Press in New Order Indonesia (Jakarta: Equinox, 2001); and Jörgen Hellman, Performing the Nation: Cultural Politics in New Order Indonesia (Copenhagen: Nordic Institute of Asian Studies, 2003).
11 An extremely well documented account of these practices can be found in Krishna Sen and David T. Hill, Media, Culture and Politics in Indonesia (Jakarta: Equinox, 2007), in which the situation of media is explained in detail.
12 Ibid.
13 Vickers, op cit., p. 74.
14 Idem, p. 77.
15 Philip Kitley, 'After the bans: Modelling Indonesian Communications for the Future,' Lloyd and Smith, op cit., p. 258.
16 See Sen and Hill, op cit. and Philip Kitley, Television, Nation, and Culture in Indonesia (Athens: Ohio University Center for International Studies, 2000).
17 Sen and Hill, op cit., p. 131.
18 Ethnologue: Languages of Indonesia (2007), www.ethnologue.com/show_country.asp?name=id (accessed 1 December 2009).
19 William Atkins, The Politics of Southeast Asia's New Media (London: Routledge/Curzon, 2002), p. 20.
20 Hellman, op cit.

The Fall of the Orde Baru and Ruangrupa's Activist Practices

The fall of the Orde Baru in 1999, together with its machinery of censorship and control, was seen as a possibility for greater freedom of expression. This historical event overlapped with an increase in the availability of cheap recording devices in Indonesia. From 1995, digital video cameras were released onto the market for relatively low prices and they were immediately accessible to a large sector of Indonesian society.[21] This allowed for a growing number of people to start experimenting with images in unprecedented ways and led Ade Darmawan to explain in interview that 'video art in Indonesia has been developing in a very organic form'. This experimental usage of video is, in his view, almost a natural consequence of the combined significance of the fall of the Orde Baru regime and of the commercial availability of cheap recording devices to a greater proportion of the Indonesian population. However, an important catalyst in this transformation has been the presence of organizations that have encouraged people to experiment with images in creative ways, such as Ruangrupa and Video Babes.[22] Ruangrupa, the oldest of these organizations, operates as an international platform with an extensive network. However, from the point of view of their role as art activists, the workshops that the group coordinates in different cities are the most significant activity. The objective of the OK Video Militia workshop coordinated in 2007 was 'to empower the people, by using the video as a medium for expression, for research, and for reflection on the social phenomena'.[23] In order to achieve this: '[…] the workshop also develops the "quintessence" of each city and town where the workshop is held. We conducted simple researches about the places, regarding the physical aspects or, especially, the socio-cultural aspects, to gain some descriptions about them. We then present the many problems we found to the participants, we re-present them — is it true what the mass media and many people have been thinking about their place of residence? We then asked the participants to explore questions that had never been posed about their environment, and we then developed these questions together and discussed how to present those questions and problems using the medium of video.'[24]

Alexandra Crosby, who witnessed one of these workshops in Padang (Sumatra), explains how Asung, the workshop coordinator, encourages 'participants to use video as a tool to analyze their own local contexts, to ask new questions about familiar surroundings and situations'.[25] After these questions are set out, Asung and his team help the participants to develop strategies to explore them using the medium of video. From March to May 2007, Ruangrupa offered fifteen workshops free of charge in twelve Indonesian cities; they collaborated with high schools, radio stations and other institutions to gather interested people; the equipment used for shooting the films ranged from camcorders to mobile phone cameras, depending on the requirements of the ideas.[26] As may be apparent from the historical overview presented above, an emphasis on the local qualities of the places where workshops are coordinated is important. In the times of the TVRI and the Orde Baru, news coverage was manufactured in Jakarta and there was hardly any possibility for local communities to engage in the representation of their local reality. The OK Video Militia workshop of Ruangrupa aimed to allow this to happen; furthermore, it encouraged free experimentation, breaking away from the aesthetic — as much as ideological — constraints of mainstream film and television. Viewed in this light, some of the enthusiasm that arose in the minds of the early theorists of video art is entirely justified within the *mediascape* of contemporary Indonesia.

One relevant example of a video which both emphasizes the local and breaks away from aesthetic convention is *Rob*,[27] which gives a personal account of the city of Semarang by combining different images of the city, distorted through the use of video editing software to give it a sense of unreality. Other works retain these qualities while simultaneously being more direct in their intentions and messages. This is the case, for example, in *GEMAH SAMPAH: LHO KOK MALAH NUMPUK?* — *Thrashes*[28] which tries to create awareness about a dump in the city of Cirebon as the source of many of its problems.

21 Jayasrana, 2008, quoted in KUNCI Cultural Studies Centre and EngageMedia, Video Activism and Video Distribution in Indonesia (Collingwood: Engage Media, 2009), p. 17.
22 Ibid.
23 Ruangrupa, 'OK Video Workshops,' 2007, www.ruangrupa.org/home/archives/okvideo/okvideo2007.html#workshop (accessed 1 December 2009).
24 Ibid.
25 Alexandra Crosby, 'Ruangrupa: Mapping a Collective Biography,' Gang re:Publik Indonesia-Australia creative adventures, eds. Alexandra Crosby et al. (Sydney, Gang Inc., 2009), p. 131. PDF version available at www.alimander.com/ruangrupa.pdf
26 Sascha Pries, 'Revolutionizing the audio-visual environment,' The Jakarta Post, 15 July 2007, www.thejakartapost.com/news/2007/07/15/revolutionizing-audiovisual-environment.html (accessed 1 December 2009).
27 Dir. Rofikin, 2007.
28 Dir. Sukarya, Sugiana and Gatot Afrianda, 2007.

The workshops conducted by Ruangrupa, therefore, become effective sites at which normative ideas about national and local identity are questioned. The resulting artworks often challenge the power of the mass media to represent social reality; the standard model is contested and alternatives are creatively developed by the participants. In this way, Ruangrupa demonstrates that reality and its mediation are not given; they can be completely altered and numerous alternatives exist. Making palpable the contingency of media reality is a meaningful and important task, when the theoretical power of media art is thoroughly explored in a society with such a complex media history.

Out of Order: Cirkus Cirkör An Interview with Tilde Björfors

Tessa Overbeek

When I first read the sentence, 'Cirkus Cirkör, contemporary circus from Sweden', I was a little surprised by this combination of words. Although I would have no trouble naming novels or films from this country, I had never associated it with circus before. The exuberance, boldness and eccentricity of circus seemed incompatible with the Swedish national character, which is often thought of as restrained, down to earth and preoccupied with safety. However, halfway through their show 'Inside Out', the artists of Cirkus Cirkör had convinced me that Sweden and circus could be a fantastic and fruitful combination. Judging by the thundering applause they received, the other members of the audience felt the same way. This represented another battle won in the fight to prove that Swedish circus could be a success, a fight that was started fifteen years ago by Cirkus Cirkör's founder and artistic director, Tilde Björfors.

'When I first came into contact with contemporary circus, I thought: "If this is needed anywhere in the world, it is in stiff and cold and clean Sweden!"' Björfors said in the conversation I had with her in Alby, a suburb south of Stockholm, where the circus's offices and training hall have been situated since 2000. By the time she first had this thought, in the early 1990s, the afore-mentioned stereotypes about Sweden and the Swedish were rapidly becoming less and less true to reality, a development that will be discussed later.

Since she founded Cirkus Cirkör with a small group of like-minded spirits in 1995, Björfors has devoted large portions of time and energy to her mission, which is to 'establish contemporary circus as an art form in Sweden, artistically and pedagogically, [to] develop and increase the possibilities of contemporary circus culture, [to] put Sweden on the world map of contemporary circus, and to inspire and be inspired by young people and street culture'.[1] Björfors, who was only in her mid twenties at the time, started a quest for support, which meant contacting all the institutions, officials and politicians who could possibly help her realize the young organization's goals. In the end, nobody was willing to invest in contemporary circus.

Undeterred, the *Cirkörers* started their project themselves, using their own resources. This decision turned out to be well worth the risk as, in 1996, their show, 'Ur kaos föds allt' (Out of chaos everything is born), toured the country and performances sold out quickly. That same year, requests started coming in from companies who wanted the circus artists to perform on special occasions, and the summer training programme that Cirkus Cirkör had set up drew 40,000 visitors.[2] Apparently, Björfors' intuition was right, and contemporary circus was indeed needed in Sweden. Cirkus Cirkör has been growing and expanding ever since. The fact that the company has engaged in different types of activities almost from the start makes the people behind it, and Tilde Björfors in particular, true 'trespassers'. They have staked their claim not only in the artistic and educational domains, but also in the business world and the public sector. There is almost nothing the *Cirkörers* have *not* done with contemporary circus, since even scientific research has been added to their practices in the past decade.

In the artistic domain, Cirkus Cirkör has had great successes, both in Sweden and internationally, with shows like '99% Unknown', 'Inside Out' and 'Wear it Like a Crown'. In the educational domain, the company has organized numerous training programmes for almost anyone who wants to practice circus, from the very young to the very old (the book *Inside a Circus Heart* mentions a tightrope walking 99-year-old)[3] and from professionals to amateurs. The circus training for people with disabilities also deserves to be mentioned. Notably, Björfors and her colleagues have also succeeded in offering opportunities to young people who aspire to be professional circus artists. After much lobbying and struggle, they have managed to realize a three-year contemporary circus programme at St. Botvid's Upper Secondary School, and a tertiary programme at the University College of Dance in Stockholm (which, after some strife, is now called the University College of Dance and Circus). In 2005, Tilde Björfors became the first professor in contemporary circus at this institution and the first person to hold this position in Sweden.

In 2007, she received a research grant from the Swedish Research Council for her project 'Contemporary Circus — Transcending boundaries in arts and society'. One of the questions she is trying to answer is what circus can teach us about dealing with risk and chaos. As the first part of this interview shows, this is a skill that both circus artists and directors have to master in order to be able to do what they do. The 'embodied knowledge' that Björfors and her artists have gained through experience is part of the material that is studied in her research project, as will become clear from the last part of this interview.

One of the reasons Björfors thought contemporary circus was needed in Sweden was because, in her opinion, dealing with risk and

---

1   Tilde Björfors and Kajsa Lind, Inuti ett Cirkus Hjärta/Inside a Circus Heart (Norsborg: Cirkus Cirkör, 2009), p. 105.
2   Ibid.
3   Idem, p. 117.

chaos is not something the Swedish are particularly good at. When Sweden was still the prosperous, secure, clean and orderly welfare state that the stereotypes reflect, this was not as problematic as it has become in the past few decades. The nation has since been shaken by the murder of Prime Minister, Olof Palme, in 1986, economic crises, a rise in unemployment, a considerable increase in immigration and other external factors like the EU membership, which have brought about change and uncertainty.

As a result, the values and concepts with which the nation identified have been challenged. When Björfors was discovering contemporary circus in France in the early 1990s, the question as to what kind of nation Sweden was going to be was becoming increasingly urgent. After a long reign by the Social Democrats, the election was won by the centre-right party of the Moderates, empathy with refugees coming into the country had turned into concern and there was rising racism and increased activity by extreme right groups. As has been known to occur in countries where people feel threatened by external factors, many Swedes started to cling to the values that define the idealized version of their nation. These values are represented in common words like 'lagom', 'Jantelagen' and 'trygghet', which any reader interested in Swedish culture almost inevitably comes across.[4]

The first two words are related to the Swedish word for law, which does not seem to be a coincidence. The word *lagom* has no exact equivalent in English, but it means something like 'enough', 'fitting' or 'appropriate'. It is connected to the idea that it is best to strive for moderation, which, in turn, is related to the egalitarian principles that were the basis of the Swedish state.[5] As Björfors states in interview, it is also important to *be lagom*, or normal, for the Swedish. This is where the concept of *Jantelagen* comes in, which is about modesty, not putting yourself above others or standing out from the crowd. One can imagine that these values could help a society to run more smoothly, but they can also have a down side, which is illustrated by Don Belt in an article about Swedish society: '[…]Swedes fear that the lagom ethic, combined with an educational system that stresses uniformity, discourages the best and the brightest — the smartest kid in class, the entrepreneur, the risk-taker, the artist, the inventor — in short, the very kinds of people Sweden needs now, more than ever, to succeed'.[6] This is a fear that Björfors addresses in everything she does, both in the way she expresses herself and in the way she leads her life, as a person who is obviously not afraid to stand out, occupying at least three of the roles that are mentioned in the quotation above.

Trygghet, which means something like 'safety' or 'security', is also an important Swedish value that Björfors tries to challenge. In the booklet that came with the show, 'Inside Out', she included several quotations from psychiatrist David Eberhard. In his book, *In the Land of Security Junkies*,[7] he tries to show how Swedish society is cushioned by the state, which tries to control danger, while many people in the country act 'as if the slightest setback was lethal'. It is ideas like these that Björfors addresses in her research, but also in her shows, though often in a less concrete fashion.

Since meeting brain scientists from the Karolinska Institute during the Nobel banquet of 2002, at which Cirkus Cirkör was invited to perform, Björfors has been fascinated with the workings of the human brain and the way circus can be related to this. She and a few of Cirkus Cirkör's artists have collaborated with these scientists, and the subject also plays a major role in her own thinking, research and performances. One topic she is currently working on is the dynamic between the left and right cerebral hemispheres and the types of information processing that characterize each of them. In most people, the left hemisphere is concerned with processes like speech, language, reasoning and analysis, while the right hemisphere is associated with sensory inputs, auditory and visual awareness, spatio-temporal awareness, creative abilities and humour. While there is much interaction between the two hemispheres, they each have their own way of processing information from the outside world. The right side is supposedly more open to its environment, more oriented towards the general context, while the left side experiences the world around it in a more indirect, ordered, categorized, abstract and 'distant' fashion. One could also say that the left side is more orderly and logical, while the right is more chaotic, but also more creative.

4   **Whether it be** Fishing in Utopia (London: Granta Publications, 2008), a memoir by the English journalist Andrew Brown, who spent many years in Sweden; Dennis Sven Nordin's A Swedish Dilemma: A Liberal European Nation's Struggle with Racism and Xenophobia, 1990–2000 (Lanham: University Press of America, 2005); Modern-Day Vikings: A Practical Guide to Interacting with the Swedes (Yarmouth: Intercultural Press Inc., 2001) by Christina Johansson Robinowitz and Lisa Werner Carr; The Seven Cultures of Capitalism (London: Judy Piatkus Ltd., 1993) by Charles Hampden-Turner and Fons Trompenaars about the Swedish economy; or the article, 'Sweden' by Don Belt in National Geographic, Vol. 184, No. 2, 1993, pp. 8-36.
5   Christina Johansson Robinowitz and Lisa Werner Carr, op cit., p. 71.
6   Belt, op cit., p. 22.
7   Original title: I trygghetsnarkomanernas land: om Sverige och det nationella paniksyndromet (Stockholm: Prisma, 2006). More than the English title, the Swedish title reflects Eberhard's belief that Sweden is in a state of national panic.

In the leaflet that came with the show, 'Wear it Like a Crown', Björfors is quoted as saying: 'Our society, in everything from child rearing to professional life, is structured in the more logical order and systems of the left side of the brain. I see this as a social problem. It is vital that the right side of the brain is given more room.' In this interview, Björfors explains how Cirkus Cirkör has tried to contribute to creating this room, for instance in the projects it has done in communities.

When Cirkus Cirkör moved to the municipality of Botkyrka in 2000, its community work quickly expanded. In the suburb of Alby, with its multicultural shopping centre near the subway station, the changes that Swedish society has gone through are immediately visible. Botkyrka is one of the most international municipalities of Sweden, with residents originating from over one hundred different countries. Because many of these residents are young, the area provides Cirkus Cirkör with many opportunities to interact with the community.

Upon arriving there, the circus artists almost immediately started invading (in the most constructive way possible) local schools and meeting people at youth centres, schools, clubs and in the streets and squares, which also resulted in many collaborations with others who did community work. This approach was repeated all over Sweden, under the name 'Cirkör on tour'. In seven municipalities, training programmes and workshops were organized, not only involving youth, but also local politicians, civil servants and teachers. Afterwards, common goals for cooperation could often be set. In 2006, a few *Cirkörers* even used this approach in Durban, South Africa.[8]

That same year, the show 'Momo or the Battle for Time' was performed with a large number of amateurs from the municipalities of Botkyrka and Skärholmen, who contributed to different parts of the performance. The following year, a deeper collaboration was formed with the municipalities of Järfälla and Landskrona, in which circus artists were sent to interact artistically and pedagogically with people from the local area, taking inspiration from their surroundings. Their performances are created through an open process, address themes such as trust, loneliness and friendship, and are also included in general cultural and school activities in these municipalities.[9] As we shall see, these co-operations often had a positive impact on the people taking part in them. Although Cirkus Cirkör's efforts have led to impressive results, this interview also shows that breaking boundaries is not always easy: trying to make structural and durable changes in municipalities provided many challenges, for instance when it came to working with those making the policies on a local level. At the same time, the co-operations were often a learning experience for all those involved.

In a text she wrote as an introduction to the show 'Inside Out', Tilde Björfors states that her own circus training has mostly been of the mind. That must be true, because somehow she manages to leap between seemingly disparate subjects like circus, society, leadership, the human brain and politics, while at the same time juggling themes like order and chaos, fear and love, having control and letting go of it. But when she finally catches them, opens her hand and lets them unfold, it is revealed that she has been talking about the topic that fascinates her most all along: the relationship between risk and possibility.

8 Björfors and Lind, op cit., 113.
9 Ibid.

Tessa Overbeek

I saw your most recent show, 'Wear it Like a Crown', in May, quite soon after the premiere. Now that it has been performed over a longer period of time, can you tell whether or not it is a success?

Tilde Björfors

It is doing very well. Whether or not it can be called a success depends on how you look at it. The artists really love performing the show. I don't think I have ever been involved in a performance in which the artists felt so proud of it from the beginning and owned every detail. It is a feeling I have been longing for, because one of my goals when I create is that *we* create, that we are all growing through the process; that is more important than the result. I think this show is, in that sense, the best process I have had. This is not true all the time, but I think it is my job as a leader to look at my artists and students as if I were in love. People say that love is blind, but I think it is the other way around. When you are in love, you see someone's highest capacity and you may be blind to everything that is destroying that potential. None of us live to our full capacity; we are all destroying it in different ways. When seeing my artists' highest capacity, I am also challenging them to be more than what they are today. If you talk to the artists of 'Wear it Like a Crown', they will say that they have been challenged to take quite a big step from who they used to be.

Audience-wise, we have also had really positive results, with sold out houses and standing ovations. We are booked one year ahead, but there was also a moment of risk. When we had our premiere at the Södra Teatern [Södra Theatre, a well-known cultural venue in Stockholm], where we are performing now, the pole artist broke her wrist. Finding someone to replace her was difficult, especially in this show, because it is built around who the artists are as people. It is like a composition of their different problems and what they wear in their crowns[10] [their worries and fears]. When you work so deeply with the artists, and use so much of who they are in the performance, it is very hard to replace anyone. It may be stupid to do this, but it is how I want to work. It is very different from working in theatre, which is my background. There you can so easily replace a person, because they are acting in their role. Here, it is much more connected to who the artists are in real life, not only because they are not schooled actors, but also because choosing to work in circus is choosing a lifestyle.

T.O.

In an interview with you in Sideshow Circus Magazine, *I read that something similar happened with one of the artists in your previous show, 'Inside Out'.*

T.B.

Yes, that was on the actual premiere! In the final part, the artist who was playing the lead role was jumping on the teeter board [a type of see-saw, via which acrobats can launch each other high up into the air] and she landed on her neck. It was very dramatic; we were all crying while we waited for answers from the hospital but, in the end, it turned out not to be that bad. I have always thought that risk is an important part of life — that it is important to dare, to challenge your space. To be alive is to grow as much as possible, and when you grow, you take risks. I think it is strange that the word 'risk' has such negative connotations when so much good can come from it. However, after that premiere, I thought: 'shit, who am I? I am trying to present risk as a good thing, while I am actually playing with life and death!' I started to question my outlook on life.

When I first came into contact with contemporary circus, I thought: 'here they show me how much we can do as human beings; they are constantly challenging the laws of gravity and the world.' For me, it was the physical image of what I thought was the meaning of life. That is why I started working with circus. It was like I had found my voice in the world, which said: 'Everything is possible, don't be afraid of being afraid', and so on. When this accident happened, I started to see the fragility of life; I started to doubt whether it was worth taking the risk. Of course, we have to take into consideration how fragile life is. To live is to balance life and death. If we don't dare to stretch [our limits], then we are not living. But we have to be aware that we are human beings and not superheroes or gods. I think that is what 'Wear it Like a Crown' is about for me. It is about dealing with fragility and doubt, with personal problems that you have. If you let them stay in your heart, you allow them to hold a grip over you. But if you put them up in your 'crown', then you are free in your heart and you can do anything. This question about the relationship between

10 This metaphor refers to the idea of not trying to ignore or suppress fear completely but allowing it to have its place and not being blocked by it. The title of 'Wear it Like a Crown' is the same as a song by the Swedish singer, Rebekka Karijord. Music from her album, The Noble Art of Letting Go, also accompanies the show.

risk and possibility has followed me for fifteen years now. I have been working on it, researching it, talking to brain scientists about it, and I still continue to deal with that question. For every performance and everything else I do, I have other questions as well, but when you break them down, you find this question about possibilities and risks.

T.O.

In the booklet that came with 'Inside Out', you have included this part by the psychiatrist David Eberhard, who says that the welfare state in Sweden tries to cushion society and to reduce risk. It does seem like a place where everything is quite orderly and clean and people are seen as somewhat contained. Maybe a country like this could use an outlet of some kind. Do you see that kind of role for the circus?

T.B.

Absolutely. When we started, we were really crazy. We thought we were doing circus for young people, but the age of the audience ranged from five to ninety-nine. It felt as though the Swedish audience had been longing for this kind of madness, where boundaries were broken, including the boundary between the audience and the stage. A circus performance is like direct communication, there is no 'fourth wall', and for me that is im-portant. It is not only the physical way it challenges boundaries. If you look at traditional circus, it is a society outside of society, and as a contemporary circus, we still have that outsider perspective. We are always challenging the world around us; we are walking where we are not allowed to walk. When society says: 'This is how it is and this is how it is going to be', we are always questioning it, saying: 'But you can also walk here, or you can jump, you don't have to stay there.' Circus has a very anarch-istic way of questioning things. You can think about an acrobat. If there is a big wall that cannot be climbed, he will immediately think: 'Can I jump over it? Or can I take three people and they jump onto something and then they propel me, or can I…' When I visited other contemporary cir-cuses, I started to see similarities in their ways of working. When I learnt more about circus history, I found out that, before what we call 'traditional' circus, with a tent, came about, there was a time of a wild, strange, anarchistic way of working. If there was no stage, they just found a new way to do what they wanted. This older type of cir-cus is more similar to what we are doing than the 'traditional' circus is.

T.O.

So, would you say that your circus is about creating chaos in the order of society?

T.B.

For me, the chaos is so important. Without it, you cannot learn or understand something new. Everyone I have talked to, including brain scientists, says learning involves a moment that feels like chaos. Our first show was called 'Out of Chaos Everything is Born'. At the time, I was very intuitive, and I hadn't thought about the role of chaos that much, but I experienced clashes between artists with very different opinions, backgrounds and cultures. In an intuitive way, I felt our work was about making a platform where chaos was actually happening. And that is how I continue to create. I think most people in Sweden are trying to avoid chaos. You can see it in the schools; it is like we are going back to the 1950s, to blackboards and strict rules and punishments, which is very strange. Like David Eberhard said: We are in a new world. The world that we are in now is so much more unsafe. Children do not go to school to get an education for a job for life. No one can count on lifelong employment anymore; some people, of course, but not many. We have to find out how to feel *trygg*, safe, even when the world around us is constantly changing and nothing is certain. This requires learning how to work with your right brain at school and not having more rules. That is what I am fighting for. I think I am quite political in that way.

In our society, people have to deal with risks all the time, and the best way to do this is to work with your right brain. The best example is in art, or fantasy, when you are imagining what can happen. When children are playing they are also getting an important education about the order of the right brain. The more we learn about that, the better we can deal with risk and chaos, because that is where we have the capacity. When we focus too much on teaching them to use the left brain, when they start to read and write so early, and when we teach them about the order of the system and right and wrong, children forget how to deal with chaos. Of course, it is important to also learn about those things, but we should not work only with that part of the brain. What David Eberhard was trying to say, is that when something happens that is not in the logical order, we get shocked and paralysed.

T.O.

Would you say that the circus is one of the places in which people learn to think with the right side of their brain?

T.B.

In circus, both sides need to work at a high level. The traditional circus, for instance in

309

Russia or China, was a lot about teaching artists how it had to be done; it was only about the discipline part, about learning things exactly as they had always been. But that is not the kind of circus that interests me. What interests me is what happens when people have knowledge of the traditional, but they also try to change small things, to carry out a constant research in gravity for example. But a circus artist always needs to have discipline. If you want to be a wire walker, you cannot want it one day and want something else the next day. You have to be on that wire every day for five years to reach a certain level, and you have to do a lot of other things as well, like stretching and working with safety, so a large part of it is about having control. But to be in balance is to always move in and out of balance, and you can never control whether you will stay on the wire. Of course, you can train harder and harder and become better and better, but you could always fall, even if you are the best wire walker in the world. You have to deal with that moment as well, and that is why I think circus artists have such specialized knowledge about life. In some circus disciplines, it really is about life and death. You can train and prepare and try to avoid every risk, but if you are on the teeter board, for instance, at some point you have to let go and when you do, you have to deal with the consequences.

We are taught about control very early in life, and it takes adults a lot of time to learn what it is like not to have control, which is what life is actually about. We don't have control; with death, that is more the case than with anything else. We cannot control it, however hard we try. To live is to not have control. And I think it is wrong to put all our efforts into trying to have control without learning to deal with the fact that we do not. I think that is why so many people in Sweden are on anti-depressants, and I think we could avoid that. Look at society now: companies with strong leaders are crashing, and even the media are starting to lose control. At the same time, in the social media, groups create themselves. People are taking control in completely different ways, and leaders lose control if they try to prevent that. I try to be a strong leader here, but I do that by trying to find the tools to use what is coming from the students in the circus hall, from the artists, from the people in the office. When you have trust in a student, or a person working under you, they can do so much more than when you try to control them. I have seen so much evidence of that, but sometimes I still get into the position where I want to control everything. It is hard not to, especially when people have failed around you. But it is so important, also in an artistic process. If I try to control it, I lose the possibility of getting something more out of it and it ends with where I am. It is interesting to make it go further. That is also taking the risk that it will be a big failure, because I won't know if I can handle the chaos that arises, but to dare to do that is my biggest goal as a leader. So the role of control is different now, and I want to push that a little, with the shows that we do, and also in our community and political work.

T.O.
I read about your community projects in which people from the circus go into schools, and how the circus artists put the teachers on a bed of nails. Could you explain that sentence?

T.B.
We don't want to make it uncomfortable for the teachers, it is done with love. The project is called *Cirkusliv* [circus life], and we have been doing it since 2000. When we go into a school, usually only one person there knows we are coming. In the morning, we move into the school yard with our circus wagons, put up our tents and let students help to find electricity and put up posters. During the day, the artists come into the lessons and put the teach-

ers somewhere, sometimes on a nail mat, and create chaos. At the end of the day, we have a show to which all the students and teachers come. We want to make chaos to show that not everything has to be scheduled and that the teacher can be in a different role. We are literally putting everything upside down. And what we also do is demonstrate something about being normal. I don't know what it is like in other countries, but in Sweden, we are all trying to be normal. It is important from very early on in life. None of us feel that way, but it is important to seem normal. These artists are so not normal, but they are really good at something, so the children are all impressed with these very extraordinary people. What it means to be normal is one of the questions we leave behind at the schools.

T.O.
Speaking of your community work, I read about the prizes Botkyrka has won since you moved here, like the 'Child and Youth Municipality of the Year award', the 'Highest Quality Municipality award' and the 'Cultural Municipality of the Year award', but also about the friction that arose in your cooperation with the municipality…

T.B.
When we came here, we worked very closely with polit-

icians; they were very open to our chaotic and creative energy. They said, 'We have stability and you have creativity and madness and we want to support that.' It was like an explosion, everything went so quickly. This suburb was known as one of the worst in Sweden, but after about two or three years, it started to get all these prizes and the media image of this community changed. The north of Botkyrka used to be the bad part compared to the south, the richer part. The people who live there did not want to call their area part of Botkyrka because they were ashamed of it; they wanted to say that they were from Tullinge [a smaller area within the municipality]. That has changed in the past few years. The people in the south of the municipality are now also proud to be part of it. It is a small thing, but it is about identity. All the municipalities have a line below their name, and before it used to be something like: 'Botkyrka, close to Stockholm'. Now it is 'Botkyrka, långt ifrån lagom', which means something like 'Botkyrka, far from normal'. The word *lagom* is typically Swedish; it means something like 'in between'. It is quite powerful. In Sweden, we all try to be 'in between' — we are not black, we are not white, we are not happy, we are not sad, but we are controlled. For the most part, the municipality has been a dream to work with; it was almost like a love affair. But now, the politicians and other officials want to take back control in the traditional way, instead of using what they are offered and supporting that. Some of the key people we worked with from the start in Botkyrka are no longer here, and with them some of the trust and magical collaboration has disappeared. Now, the political climate is more traditional, with decisions being made at the top. They don't like the feeling of not having control; neither did the people we worked with before, but at least they were not afraid of new thoughts and ideas. The relationship between Cirkus Cirkör and the municipality had such a strong foundation that we could be critical, and so could they. The new politicians and officials have big ideas and plans, but the problem is that they are no longer involving us and other circus and film groups which are supposed to fill these ideas with content and meaning. By doing things without telling us, they think they can control what will happen. If they make the decisions in a small room, without involving the people working or living here, the process does not take as much time. Like with the *Hangaren*,[11] they want to make it a stage for circus and film and everything, but they did it totally over our heads. If they were working with the type of leadership that I was proposing earlier, they would have started with a dialogue; they would see whether or not the people here needed that stage. If they had invited people to take part in a democratic decision-making process, they would probably have the circus and film communities enthusiastically working toward the project, but that kind of process is much slower. Perhaps, in three years, I will have to say that their faster process was a success…

T.O.

So, if you are critical and you want to do something against the people who do things over your head or over the heads of the people who live here, would you include the people who live here in your protest, so to speak?

T.B.

It depends on what we are doing. Some parts of our work need that, but we have been through a long process. In the beginning, our goal was to establish the art form in Sweden and for kids to have the possibility to train, so they could have that physical experience. Be-

cause there were hardly any fans of contemporary circus in Sweden, we had to start everything from scratch. And you could say that we worked fifty percent for the art form and fifty percent for Cirkus Cirkör. Now there are many more companies and an organization that we contributed to, together with other circus companies and schools, called Manegen [Centre for circus, variety and street performance — a trade organization that was founded in 2008 by eighty people who represent different aspects of the art form and industry in Sweden], people are booking performances, there is the university-level circus programme, and a lot of students who have been through our education programme are starting up circus schools all over the country. So it is leading its own life.

There was a slightly problematic phase, when people knew about Cirkus Cirkör as the first to introduce contemporary circus here, but they didn't know that [contemporary circus] is an art form with many different modes of expression. So we worked hard to help other contemporary circus groups grow. When that started to happen, we realized that we also had

---

11 'The hangar' is a large, multifunctional arena that is to be used for circus, film productions and other cultural events. It is intended to house thousands of spectators. In late August of 2010, it was being prepared for its inauguration during Subtopiafestivalen in early September 2010.

to define our unique artistic mode of expression within the contemporary circus community, because Cirkus Cirkör was now one among many groups. Then we decided that what we could do for the art form was to make really good performances and to go international and show the government that the art form has the possibility to fly. So we are now in a phase where we have been developing our art and also our pedagogy. You can go to circus schools almost everywhere, but we want to give something more than just the training. We have the goal of making everyone grow, so we no longer only bring circus to gym classes, because we want to give more space to the artistic and creative aspects of it and not only to the physical part. We also apply it to mathematics and other subjects and do more experimental work. We are not taking the perspective of the people in the community into account as much, because it feels like that is not what we need to be doing at this moment. We feel like we need to develop our tools and our artistic heart and who we are. That way, we go out into the world stronger, knowing more about what we are giving. We have been teaching and doing so much, but we have not been thinking about what was happening and why. Why did so many processes grow out of what

we did, through working with politicians and people in different municipalities? So much has been put in motion, but we wonder, 'What did we actually do?' So, of course, we are working with a lot of people around us, but we are not working with the kids from the municipality in our performances right now. Also because we think it is the municipality's job. It is written in their vision that they want to do that and they have funding for it, but they are not doing it. So that is one of the things about which we disagree.

T.O.

In the beginning of your book, Inside a Circus Heart, *you thank the Municipality of Botkyrka, but also the Swedish Arts Council, the Stockholm County Council and the City of Stockholm, because they provide your financial basis. Don't you feel limited in how critical and autonomous you can be, since you are, in a way, dependent on these institutions?*

T.B.

We are not so dependent. We have support, but it is quite a small amount from each one, compared to what we have in total. I feel that we have had phases during which we were totally working to please all the supporters, and that was a hard time. The first seven years were like being on a highway; we were totally following our hearts and our vision. We had so much to do and to create, and we were unstoppable; if there was no way to go, we created one. It all happened very quickly, and we didn't really think about it. After a while, we got different kinds of support and moved here, but we didn't have enough money to make our own creations; we always had to work together with different institutions, like the Royal Dramatic Theatre.[12]

I kind of liked it, because it was also a way of getting out into the world, influencing it with circus. But somewhere we got lost and I felt like we were living to please all these others. We were given some money to tour all over Sweden, some money to do a lot of work here in the municipality, some money to do work in Stockholm and, at that moment, I wondered, 'why am I doing this?' It was quite hard. After a while, that started the process that led to 'Inside Out'. When we made that show, we used all of the money, even though we didn't know whether it would be a success or not, because we needed to have a performance without any collaborations. We wanted to create circus, not theatre circus or anything. So we said, 'OK, we will risk that they take back their funding.' We did that because we needed to show what we wanted to do, and that was to create a circus performance, which has a different rhythm. We got funding from the state, but we had to create a performance every year, and perform in certain places in Sweden. But we knew that if we put everything into 'Inside Out', we would have to perform it for many years. We also wanted to go international. Luckily, nobody took back their funding. Now 'Inside Out' is touring the world and Sweden is proud, but we took a big risk.

T.O.
And now that you are also successful as a company, do you feel you can be more critical and autonomous?

T.B.
Yes, since then, we have done what we want. Why I sometimes say bad things about the politicians is because I think they are doing things the wrong way, although some of them think we are right. Introducing a new art form in Sweden wouldn't have been possible without some friction and conflicts with politicians and officials. For example, there is an education minister who wants to go back to the 1950s, taking away all the aesthetic learning processes in school, and I have

---

12 The result was the very successful production Romeo and Juliet (2002).

been explicitly critical, writing an opinion piece that got a lot of support from aesthetics teachers. I am not afraid of authority. It is more like the opposite. I have worked with state television and I was being very positive, but the only person I was fighting was my boss. That is typical me. I am not good at being strategic. If I have a goal and I think something is necessary, I can fight as much as is needed. The people who hated me while I was doing that, sort of respected me after a while. It is not about me being rich, but about more kids having the possibility to train in the circus or for more audiences to see it.

T.O.

In your book, there is a quotation from someone who compared your circus to a jester in medieval times, who was invited to amuse the ruler, but who was also the person who could criticize him, who had permission to do so in a light way. I think that is an interesting comparison. Do you also study this role in your research about circus as a way to transcend boundaries in art and society; is that an aspect of it?

T.B.

Yes, it is one aspect of it, but I wish we could study it more. I really think [being a circus company] is a good camouflage. We have really made advanced changes in the municipalities because we don't seem dangerous: for example in the north of Sweden, which ended up with two gymnasium programmes, but also in the south, and here in Botkyrka. Kajsa [Lind, vice president of Cirkus Cirkör,] used to be a consultant for big companies before she came here, but most people don't know that. So we can come in and make quite big changes with the leaders and the ruling politicians and make them see things in a new light, make them realize that investments in young people's creativity are investments in growth, for example.

T.O.

So people thinking you were harmless and funny helped when you were trying to make changes. Has it happened in more places than just Botkyrka that, once they found out that you are not so harmless, they 'stepped on the brakes'?

T.B.

I don't know if it's as simple as that. When you undertake processes like this, you need to find people to play with. In all the places where we have been, there has been at least one person who was really interested and doing a lot of good work in their surroundings. One thing that we give as a criterion for coming into a municipality at all was that they find out what kinds of activities young people in their municipalities do and want to do. So the people who want to bring us into their municipality start an investigation, because often they don't even know this. We don't want them to bring us in to force their young people to do circus when they actually want to do something else. We also want the people to see what they already have in their community. Is there someone who is interested in co-operation, or someone we can support? That is because we want the project to continue, even when we move away. This approach is why we have succeeded in some places — because the local people have created something themselves. Young skiers and snowboarders in the north of the country, for instance, were inspired by our Young Cirkör ensemble and started their own ensemble, called Winter Street. They perform all over the region and are still growing. But sometimes we might have been somewhere for three years, giving energy, knowledge and support and things that were in flow suddenly stop because people say, 'This project is over.'

We have also been in the midst of internal fights between political departments. Sometimes, departments were not talking to each other, and we were trying to make them see that they were both doing the same thing and that maybe they should collaborate, when they had been working side by side for ten years without seeing it. Sometimes, these processes are a lot about power play and you can be in the middle. One of the things we have learned is that it is heavy stuff to be involved in. I am so happy that we have done it and I believe we will continue doing it, but there could be an easier way to make changes than having us driving these big processes, because they are very heavy. There is a never-ending row of obstacles; there are always things that need a push. It's never just about starting up a new education programme, for instance. We dive into national economics, school politics, the way accountants measure buildings (as investments) and teachers (as costs) in schools, and so on. If we are making performances that can make things happen, then that is where we have to put our energy. So we haven't stopped doing it, but we are trying to do it in other ways.

T.O.

So now you are reflecting on what you have been doing and why things have or have not been working. Do you now believe that you can possibly have more effect through the art itself, did I understand that correctly?

T.B.

Yes, and also through the pedagogical processes. I am at the end of three years of research, and finishing and presenting that will be the next thing for me to focus on. We will know more about methods and tools. For dance and theatre, there are many theories and concepts, but we have nothing to describe circus. That was also the reason why I started my research project, and started visiting circus colleagues around the world. I have been one of several researchers from different scientific fields who are working on the same research project, so it's hard for me to say what the final result of the project will be. In part, it will be about what circus can teach us about risk and control and letting go of control, and how you can transfer this knowledge to other fields. For instance, circus artists and teachers have been working with Masters students in economics and management. The students and artists created workshops for each other, and the result was surprising for the economists, but not for me. The management students had a lot more to learn from the artists about risks, markets and communication than the other way around.

T.O.

And when it comes to the performances, do you think you would ever make a performance that is more explicit when it comes to how you see the world? I think your per- *formances can definitely transfer a certain attitude that everything is possible, and they give audiences a very positive feeling, but would you ever make your message more concrete or rational?*

T.B.

I don't know! That is the difficult part when you try to let yourself be guided by your intuition — then I am not deciding myself. Well, of course I am deciding myself, but it's not like I think, 'Oh, this would be clever to do…' When I do something for Cirkör, I am honest and true and everything I do comes out of my question about the relationship between risk and possibilities. It is never just for entertainment; everything comes back to answering that question. I think I have something that is very 'Cirkörish' that I want to communicate with a big audience, or with a normal audience. And then it cannot be too narrow. So, even when I create it and I think I am being clear and serious, it comes out abstract and funny. And the artists I work with also like to have a laugh. You can see that clearly in 'Wear it Like a Crown', for example. My father saw it at the premiere and when he saw it again a couple of months later, he said, 'It is so much lighter now!' And that is not me, but the artists. I think I could find ways to transfer what I am thinking to the stage, but I am not sure. Sometimes I get long letters from people who have seen 'Inside Out' or 'Wear it Like a Crown'. The show they have seen did not always change their lives, but it changed their way of thinking, or it helped them to do something they had to do. So I don't know if I need to be more precise…

T.O.

Do you mean that you are happy when people take their own meaning out of the shows and apply them to their own lives, and that, if you were more precise, you would rob them of that possibility?

T.B.

Yes, it was obvious with 'Inside Out'. When we got the first reviews, every critic had seen different things and different parts, but they were all things I had worked on. They had seen different layers and that was very interesting, but none of them had seen them all. There are few people who actually follow my thoughts. I want to make art, and it is important for me that the audience is able to enjoy a performance without needing an explanation. It should talk to people in one way or another, talking through itself, so that it is the viewer who finds out what it says. It is how I have been taught about art, and how I think about it. However, with 'Wear it Like

a Crown', I had a talk with the audience after the performance, and people said: 'it was so good to hear about your thoughts, I saw so many more layers and I have to go and see it again!' So I am no longer sure that it is wrong to describe what you have been doing, but you have to find a way for everyone to see and understand it. I don't know how to do that yet.

T.O.

So, for now, you leave it a little bit open, and, by getting all those letters, you know that it is working somehow, that everybody takes something out of it?

T.B.

Yes, but also with artistic research — not research about art in a university context, but research in art. In Sweden, this is still quite new and developing. I think that this kind of research may be the platform for thinking about questions like this. I miss that a little. While creating 'Inside Out', I thought I could discuss the process and everything behind it, and I was longing to have people to talk to. But, as soon as a show was being performed, I found out that nobody was interested in talking about the struggle to get there; they just wanted to know whether it worked or not. I think that art investigates real stuff, the same way scientific research investigates things, but there is no way to find out what is actually happening. There are more people doing research on us than with us. This becomes clear from my interviews with artists about their art. A researcher I work with who specializes in theatre was a little embarrassed because she was trying to describe the art, but the artists were describing it with much more flesh and blood, from eight years of daily experience. Of course, what they say is deeper in some way, but it is still 'funny'. I think it is also something about the right and the left side of the brain. Fifty years from now, artistic research may be on the same level as scientific research. Right now, we think of scientific knowledge as the truth, and artistic knowledge as cute and enjoyable and good for people who are rich enough to have it, but I think it's important.

Björfors remains convinced that circus can offer a specific kind of knowledge, and she might very well be right. To conclude this article, it seems important to think about what a society can learn from circus as an art form.

Apart from the mind-, mood- and maybe even life-altering artistic experience and amazement at human potential that shows can offer, contemporary circus can possibly offer a critical, yet light, perspective on society and everything that is thought to be 'normal' within it. It can be thought of as a 'dismeasure', against the 'measure' of society,[13] a place in which chaos can arise, and it can function as a counterbalance to all the order that is enforced by society. The *Cirkusliv* example illustrates how circus can be used to bring about 'symbolic inversion' in the Bakhtinian sense, in which existing hierarchies of power are temporarily turned upside down. Although the order is usually restored afterwards, it can make people more aware of a status quo that is not normally called into question.

But, more importantly, thanks to the opportunities to 'try it yourself' that have resulted from Cirkus Cirkör's initiatives, any member of Swedish society can benefit from the 'embodied knowledge' that is gained through the stretching of one's own limits, or the breaking down of one's own boundaries, not only through the ideas of professionals that are currently being gathered in Tilde Björfors' research, but also at first hand. Could it be that experiencing the effort, the risks, the fear and the failures, or the elation that comes with finally mastering something that used to be beyond your reach, actually makes more of an impact than when you are being told or shown what it is like? This question remains unanswered for now, but maybe Björfors and her co-researchers can change that.

Björfors makes a convincing case for the ability of circus to offer lessons on how to deal with chaos, risk, fear and letting go of control; lessons that seem very valuable, not only in Sweden, but also in other nations that are coping with a rapidly changing society (including the Netherlands). The necessity to adapt to changing conditions is relevant for both the autochthonous inhabitants of a country and those who are moving into it. A place where standing out from the crowd and being far from normal is encouraged, rather than being frowned upon, could be beneficial for both these groups of people.

Whether circus can actually achieve these results remains to be

13 See the interview with the Italian philosopher, Paolo Virno, in Pascal Gielen and Paul De Bruyne, Being an Artist in Post-Fordist Times (Rotterdam: NAi Publishers, 2009).

seen. What seems already proven, judging by the way in which Cirkus Cirkör has succeeded in establishing the art form in Sweden, is that determination, enthusiasm and boldness can be infectious. Although the road to success has not been without bumps, this circus company has been welcomed with open arms by audiences almost from the start. Again, one can question whether it was the circus performances themselves or the attitude of the performers that caused this reaction, but it reminded me of this quote, which also appears in a shorter version elsewhere in this book:

> We still don't know, Spinoza says, what a body can do and a mind can think. And we will never know the limits of their powers. The path of joy is constantly to open new possibilities, to expand our field of imagination, our abilities to feel and be affected, our capacities for action and passion. In Spinoza's thought, in fact, there is a correspondence between our power to affect [...] and our power to be affected. The greater our mind's ability to think, the greater its capacity to be affected by the ideas of others; the greater our body's ability to act, the greater its capacity to be affected by other bodies. And we have greater power to think and to act, Spinoza explains, the more we interact and create common relations with others.[14]

To me, that is exactly what Cirkus Cirkör is about: using their amazing abilities to act to reach out to the world around them, and trying to affect it to such an extent that everybody grows in the process. Björfors clearly believes that the body's ability to act and the mind's ability to think are also connected. So the question is: could it be possible that experiencing the type of circus for which Cirkus Cirkör is famous is beneficial not only for physical, but also for mental flexibility? Could it also affect the way people see the world? So far, Björfors's performances have not been explicitly subversive, but they do convey a very contagious belief in what human beings are capable of, and they have resulted in some strong reactions from audience members.

It may not be possible to express a stronger or more explicit message through the performances themselves, since it could conflict with the way Björfors wants to work with her artists — using their own personalities and input — which could dilute any message she tries to convey. Doing so may not even be necessary, since people already transfer the belief in human potential to their own lives, as evinced in the letters and other reactions Björfors has mentioned, or they may feel compelled to try circus themselves, in order to explore their own possibilities.

The idea that one's ability to act also increases one's ability to be affected is very compelling. In order for the answer to the question I posed earlier to be affirmative, 'bodily' knowledge might have to be translated into mental knowledge somehow, to become useful in everyday life, or the knowledge might need to be transferred from the stage or circus hall to society. Or could the mere *feeling* of being capable, in a more general sense, be enough to deal with the challenges life poses? To consciously try to improve one's ability to be affected may seem counter-intuitive in a day and age filled with threats and uncertainties. It would seem logical to close oneself off, to put up walls and try to avoid any change.

Although this strategy may appeal to some, it seems quite difficult to maintain. Apart from that, as Björfors tries to make clear, it also limits all possibility for growth. The alternative is not to be reckless, nor to try to suppress the fear that comes from being exposed, but to be open, to be affected, to be afraid and to accept it. What seems necessary for this kind of attitude, both in individuals and in communities, is faith in human potential, in the qualities that one has to offer and those that others can offer in return. Only then can the fear of being overwhelmed, uprooted or flushed away be overcome, and only then can something be achieved that surpasses the capacities of one entity. This is maybe easier said than done. It might require a lot of practice and it may even be risky but, as Cirkus Cirkör has proven many times, sometimes you have to take risks to prove that something is possible.

14 Michael Hardt and Antonio Negri, Commonwealth (Cambridge, MA: Harvard University Press, 2009), p. 379.

Epilogue
Jan Fabre
The Revolution in My Own Flesh

Luk Van den Dries

Jan Fabre (b. 1958) is an accomplished artist. From an early age, he had been making installations in his parents' garden, he observed insects, applying his unique imagination to them in his drawings, and wrote plays about real or made-up family members, often as characters in cruel tragedies. In those works of art, Fabre created his own universe according to his own laws, the most important being the power of imagination, which is why he continuously transforms the objects he observes; scarabs are given a strange tail or the head of a fountain pen, women's tongues spurt from the plughole of the bathtub. Even back then, Fabre was fascinated by bodily fluids.

The various branches of art that Fabre continues to practise (sculpture, drawing, film, opera, dance, theatre, drama) continually cross-pollinate; fascinations leap from one piece of art to another. For example, in *Hour of the Blue* — the magical transition from night to day in which everything in nature grows still and energy builds up before it bursts out — Fabre examined the blue hour in every possible way until he knew its deepest core and penetrated its secret. That scientific nature, the continuous conduct of new experiments, characterizes all his working processes. His artistic engine is a kind of laboratory in which he tests everything and explores the frontiers of the universe he has created.

From 1978 onwards, Fabre has kept a diary, during which time he has created an impressive number of solo performances, not only in his native town of Antwerp but also in Amsterdam, New York, Milwaukee and other places. Consistent with the performance tradition of the 1970s, he uses these performances to seek the frontiers between fiction and reality, by introducing 'real' moments into an artistic context (such as making drawings with his own blood) or by confronting reality with artistic actions (by using himself as a living installation in a display case). In *Money Performance*, Fabre challenges the relationship between artist and audience/consumer, by making a collage from the admission fees charged to the audience or by burning it and forming words like 'money' and 'culture' from the ashes. Even back in the late 1970s, Fabre made all his drawings with a blue ballpoint. For a long time, it was his artistic hallmark. He drew on everything: shoeboxes, bodies, himself, walls, playing cards, reproductions of classical masterpieces. Once again, he explicitly entered into a dialogue with existing tradition; it was as if he wanted to draw himself into the lineage of his many predecessors. His blue scratches consumed the previous artwork, re-drew it, made it empty and filled it with his own visual language.

In diary entries from this crucial period in his oeuvre, several excerpts of which are published here, we are confronted with a hybrid of the artist and private person (it is difficult to distinguish between the two). Fabre has not yet 'broken through' in the art world, he is still finding his own style; tirelessly he creates action after action, meets other artists, discovers soul mates, develops a language. This exploration could be called political in the post–1968 (feminist) meaning of the term in which the personal is political. Fabre follows the same line consistently and radically. His body, his fascinations and obsessions are part of a hyper-personal universe, a field of activity of his own artistic self-creation. He invents himself a bit like a demiurge; he creates his own organic life form with an unremitting belief in the power of metamorphosis and transformation. It is evident that he often clashes with society; he explores the boundaries of what Marcuse calls repressive tolerance, challenging the moral crusaders or falling prey to the violence of the extreme right. Fabre thrives on conflict, he goes looking for it, he needs it. He can only fully define himself within the friction of resistance.

Here, we track Fabre from 11 March 1978, in the midst of his self-revolution, to 19 July 1982, the evening of the premiere of his theatre production *Het is theater zoals te verwachten en te voorzien was* (It is Theatre as to be Expected and Foreseen), the show that was to be his international breakthrough.

Antwerp, 11 March 1978
The new revolution
will occur
not in the outside world
but in our own flesh.

Bruges, 11 May 1978
I don't understand it all very well but I feel it physically.
With open mouth and greedy eyes I saw the old unknown
masters glorify the suffering of Christ.
Stigmata, those opened wounds
They are red lips,
bleeding mouths,
menstruating cunts.

Bruges, 15 May 1978
I bought Gillette razors

And in my small hotel room
I cut myself
in my forehead.
Let the blood of my thoughts drip.
It became a series of beautiful drawings.
(I had the thrilling feeling I was doing something forbidden).

Antwerp, 20 May 1978
Last night was the premiere of *Zeven Manieren om aan de Kant
te Blijven* (Seven Ways of Staying Aloof) by René Verheezen.
The actors and actresses had apparently played well because
the applause was loud and long.
I couldn't figure it out.
That response, that success.
To me the actors were supposed to be satyrs, tormentors and
gods.
And I felt they were so goody-goody and tame, in other
words, too 'Flemish'.
To me theatre should be a party of untameable energy!
But who am I?
A young Apollo (so the theatre manager calls me),
a young Greek god who doesn't yet realize he has no part in
a Flemish drama.
I represent the eighth way of staying aloof.

Antwerp, 24 June 1978
Today I worked for dough.
With an advertisements painter Blommaert in Borgerhout.
Painted letters all day long.
The 'O' is damn hard by hand.

Amsterdam, 7 August 1978
I stayed at the Stedelijk Museum from 11 o'clock till 5
o'clock.
And then I wanted to stay in that timeless bar of the
American Pop Artist Edward Kienholz.
A heaven for artists
where you can speak with the dead.
But the attendants discovered me and gently threw me out.

Amsterdam, 10 August 1978
I like watching porn.
I fantasize lustily.
Those bodies in mock ecstasy
have a Christian theatrality
I am delighted by those women who suck dicks full of lust
and conviction.
They resemble singing angels.

Amsterdam, 15 August 1978
Today!
Completed an action.
In the middle of the red–light district I stood motionless in
the middle
of a small bridge that connects two canals.
I had memorized a single French sentence:
'Mon l'art grotte au coeur de la vie'.
And I cried out that sentence for three full hours in every
possible way.
The reactions were very surprising,
from comical to extremely aggressive.
Maybe because they didn't understand the French.

Amsterdam, 16 August 1978
The Dutch, open curtains
and an exact imagination?
The Flemish, closed curtains
and an imagination that has no bounds?

Antwerp, 5 September 1978
I am content.
I heard today I can design the décor
for Paul Koeck's new theatre play.
A socially committed writer with a vision.
Paul Koeck is a man after my own heart.
Two years ago, we didn't know each other,
we saved each other from the claws of a gang of dangerous
Flemish Lions.
We were in the wrong café,
for the right reasons.
The sympathetic boys from the Vlaamse Militanten Orde

lustily started singing German marching songs.
And since we didn't sing along
we became dangerous enemies of the Flemish Republic
(a revolting utopia)
who had to be lynched.
With Paul's physical bravado
and my big mouth
we made it out alive
with trembling legs.
Since that night we have been comrades
that sprinkle each other with red wine.
I will happily design a fantastic décor for Paul Koeck.

Antwerp, 12 September 1978
Woke up again this morning
dressed in my bath tub.
The water was freezing cold.
The last I remember, I was drawing
and I had taken sleeping pills that had no effect at all.
So I kept drawing.

Antwerp, 29 September 1978
The most important tool of the actor
is his imagination.
And if that imagination is lacking,
then what do you do?
Then you have to replace the actors with animals!
The animals will save the theatre!

Antwerp, 25 March 1979
I have isolated myself for a few days and nights now.
It is 6 o'clock in the morning.
Before me on a dish lies a beautiful collection of cigarette
butts
I picked up from the ground.
My ration for the hours to come.
Every butt will taste particularly good
in the knowledge that I ran out of cigarettes
and the shops won't open for hours.

Antwerp, 15 April 1979
Dressed in a fancy starched captain's uniform with cap

I crawled onto the roof at 17.00 hours
of the Central Station (direction Keyserlei)
and tied myself up.
For almost four hours I called, ranted and raved
through a copper ship's horn
'I want to sell the North Sea.
I want to save the North Sea
Who wants to buy the North Sea
to save the North Sea?'
Nobody heard or saw me.

Antwerp, 7 May 1979
Saw a magical performance
With two loudspeakers, a pair of high heels, an electronic
violin and the aura of the American performance artist
Laurie Anderson.
Was it her aura that made the energy and sound visible and
tangible?
Even the simplest acts she performed completely entranced
me.
Every detail of her performance reverberated.
I felt as if my body became a sound box.

Firenze, 9 October 1979
Today I disappeared again.
I existed so little
that I no longer even had a personality.
I was a prisoner in my own body.
My body was a grave of which people occasionally
lift the tombstone to see
if the living corpse still lies there.

Antwerp, 11 January 1980
It is night.
It feels right.
Performed *The Rea(dy) Make of the Money Performance* last
night.
I had my nerves in check and my energy was focused.
The concept was right.
What the audience came for
what they had read in the papers

scandal and success,
they didn't get.
I gave them confusion
and a new performance.

Antwerp, 13 January 1980
The eighties, we are the new wave.
THE 1980s WILL BE IMPORTANT.

Antwerp, 12 February 1980
Making things fail and misunderstood, I am a crack at that.
Maybe it is my way of waging war against the codes used in
the art and theatre circuit.

Antwerp, 20 February 1980
I am fed up with conceptual art.
Art has nothing to do with the democratization of
knowledge.
An audience that understands everything makes everything
mediocre.
I hope my 'self-portraits' remain inexplicable.
Art that only touches the brain does not go far.

Antwerp, 1 March 1980
6.45 in the morning.
Back from the corner of Gasstraat and Van Schoonbekestraat.
Drew on the sixth Bic advertising pillar.
A self-portrait as a mouse and underneath it the text 'I AM A
KILLER'.
I sat in the police station for an hour and a half.
They treated me as if I was mentally disturbed.
This time I was good and smart and kept my body under
control.
The perfect patient is the tamed patient who adjusts
subserviently to the authority of the police or doctor. The
patient who accepts the deformation of life in the institution
or prison and views every protest as a symptom of his illness.

Antwerp, 8 March 1980
Stuck around in café 'Het half soeke' in the Hoogstraat with
Wil Beckers and Leo Geerts until dawn. Leo Geerts is unlike

most Flemish writers. I enjoyed getting to know this man
better. He at least is not frustrated like those other Flemish
writers I have met. And apparently they are all forced to
become school teachers. Because despite a lot of government
subsidies they cannot sell their books full of Flemish boorish
curses and incest stories, not even in Romania.

Antwerp, 11 March 1980
Went to the premiere of Leo Geerts' new text theatre
Vrij België. For a change the Nieuw Vlaams Theatre (Wil
Beckers) has an exciting author with a strong text and still
they manage to kill the play before a single word is spoken.
We live in 1980 but the décor radiates the naturalism of
1880.
Wrong décor, wrong text direction.
'Language forms man more than man forms the language'
Goethe wrote. Sadly enough this hasn't seeped through yet
in Flemish theatre.

Antwerp, 20 March 1980
Discovered Sir Francis Bacon.
I haven't been outside in a week.
I barely sleep and eat way too little.
But I feel strong enough to change the world.
The essence of Bacon's oeuvre and *Nova Atlantis* in particular
discusses the renewal of man. And right now there is nothing
more exciting than thinking and fantasizing about that.
Particularly if you have only drawn yourself for months.

Amsterdam, 3 April 1980
I am taking my time installing *Money Art*
Everything has to hang exactly right.
I do everything myself.
Measure everything and hammer every nail into the wall.
I enjoy using the level
to check how good my eye is.
(The poetry of the detail.)

Amsterdam, 7 April 1980
Visited the hall with the Malevich paintings
in the Stedelijk Museum.

Warm and brilliant.
I only knew the Malevich oeuvre from images.
In reality they are pretty rough paintings, you can see the
paint layers.
Nothing polished, the surface is like sandpaper.
I stood eye to eye with the genesis of abstract art.

Amsterdam, 8 April 1980
Went back to the Stedelijk Museum.
A discovery for me: The Dutch artist
Ger van Elk.
Playful, funny and daring
Almost un–Dutch.

Amsterdam, 9 April 1980
Life in self-imposed exile
over Galerij Exile.
Too much of a good thing.
I want action tonight.
My body grunts, it is extremely hungry.

Amsterdam, 11 April 1980
Today I undertook an action
on the Damplein.
I called out for an hour
'Never trust a hippie!'
Until they beat me up.
I was lucky
half stumbling, I walked away,
ran away.
I couldn't do anything back
because ten Dutchmen
can beat a cow to death.
My nose bled and my jaw still hurts.
and I can feel my kidneys nagging.

Amsterdam, 23 April 1980
I am sick of Dutch tolerance.
Tom, Dick and Harry can all drivel their free opinion
and they have to listen to each other politely.
(that is why these Dutch are so bored and why they come

to us in Antwerp to make so much noise and such a racket
when they are allowed away from their tolerance for a short
while.)

Antwerp, 23 June 1980
Met Joseph Beuys.
Fascinating personality.
A death's head with skin
and with diamond eyes
that look right through you.
At the end of the evening
he made a drawing
(on the paper table-cloth)
and dedicated it to me.
To me this drawing means
a transferral of energy
from a young artist (Joseph Beuys)
to an old artist.

Antwerp, 20 July 1980
First gathering with the actors of my theatre project *Theater
geschreven met een 'K' is een Kater* [Theatre written with a K is
a Tomcat] on the first floor of the Jules de Geyterstraat (Kiel).
I think it went well.
I explained my concept with about forty small drawings I
hung on the wall. And I read out loud the text that I wrote
together with Alex van Haecke.
I am a director with an idea, an analysis and a solution.
I hope this isn't really true and that I can give more.
Violent contradictions, that is what the theatre needs.

Antwerp, 5 August 1980
Theatre needs the mentality of the performance arts.
This mentality will scour away the frontier between illusion
and reality.
A graze will appear, in which I will happily sprinkle salt.

Antwerp, 12 August 1980
I wish I could multiply myself.
Then I would crawl inside the actors' bodies.
Wear their bodies like a costume.

And play all the scenes myself.
Their intestines I would use as props (food, musical
instruments, bags, rope…)
But I am afraid this is impossible.
And I am afraid my actors will live happily ever after.

Antwerp, 25 August 1980
I wish the air would bleed when the actors are performing
their most extreme deeds.
I wish the objects in the scene would become fluid when the
actors aren't using them.
I wish the performance would work like a drug and the
audience would leave the theatre hallucinating.
And stayed stoned for weeks.

Antwerp, 16 September 1980
My creativity is always intractable.
Tonight was the premiere of *Theater geschreven met een 'K' is
een Kater.*
The actors were too nervous.
The performance was too fierce, too aggressive and too
dangerous.
I am glad nobody got hurt.
But I am content with the abandonment and the generosity
of my actors.
I am proud of them, that they went this far for themselves
and for me.
The viewing habits of the audience were clearly shook up.
Some left the hall early with a lot of noise, comments and
yelling.
They didn't exactly wish me and my actors well.

New York, 10 March 1981
I go to all the nightclubs
that will let me in.
I don't have a lot of money
but dance many nights
from champagne glass to champagne glass.
I drink from the glasses of the disco stars and arty-farty
comets
when they exhibit their 'moves' and their 'poses' on the

dance floor.
I am a vagabond-de-luxe that can jive (copied it from my
father).
With style I survive Manhattan and experience 'the big
apple'.

New York, 17 March 1981
My performance *Art as a gamble, gamble as an art* was sterile.
It was too intellectual and too conceptual.
The critics that had to gamble against me
behaved like shy bad actors.
And when I directed them
when they read their scribblings out loud
they refused to follow me musically.
They were too concerned about their ego
that was in the 'spotlight'.
There was no action, no reaction.
While I was working
I kept having the feeling
that I was creating an installation with dead extras.
The applause was solid.
The reactions afterwards, good.
Someone said
'Intellectually it was very dense and rich.'
Yeah, bollocks.
I wanted the exact opposite.
I wanted to bring about a physical sensation in the audience.
I wanted their body to think
not make their brains feel.

Milwaukee, 10 May 1981
Arrived, didn't even open my suitcase.
And worked the rest of the day in the hall of Theatre X
Company
Construction — technics — lights.
And at 11 o'clock at night I started the dress rehearsal of the
American premiere of *Theater geschreven met een 'K' is een
Kater.*
I played too.
The other actors didn't spare me.
I ache all over, tomorrow I will be black and blue I guess.

Wil Beckers, general manager of the Nieuw Vlaams Theatre, played his part as writer with the right stoicism.

New York, 4 February 1982
Performance art has great economic value (priceless) but virtually no economic power.
It refuses to play by the rules of the art market.
No gallery and/or collector can buy it or sell it.
Is there anything better than knowing that no one can own you?
That is why performance art is an important medium.
It enquires after the essence of art.
And confronts the artist with his own physical and mental frontiers.
Making him ask the most essential questions about himself, his work and the general transience of life.

New York, 15 February 1982
I have danced in front of the Empire State Building.
Thinking I will dance here until the building disappears.
I stopped after 43 minutes and 40 seconds.
And walked to Soho to look at a few exhibitions.
It was a gorgeous day, a beautiful imprisonment chosen of my own free will.
(I talked to no one today.)

New York, 23 May 1982
Met Hugo De Greef from the Kaaitheaterfestival in Brussels today.
We made a fantastic bargain.
I gave him my script-concept
of *Het is theater zoals te verwachten en te voorzien was*
and he gave me a carton of red Belga cigarettes.
I was glad to light up a real cigarette again.
He smokes too.
We clicked.
We will see what the future brings.
Does he have the 'guts' to present my work
in that tiny conservative monkey land?

Herentals, 3 July 1982
Auditions for my second theatre project *Het is theater zoals te verwachten en te voorzien was.*
Marc Vanrunxt for kinetics, and me for the play.
Have seen an astounding number of actors and dancers strikingly resembling animals.

The most interesting assignment,
where the actors couldn't hide behind the mask of acting,
were the repeat assignments.
When I saw a move, a sentence, an emotion,
that gave the impression of being genuine,
I made the actors and dancers repeat it 50 times.

Herentals, 19 July 1982
There is an abundance of inspiration and material.
It will be a 24-hour performance.
All day and night.
Even the eating, crapping, drinking, pissing and bleeding of
the actors and dancers
I will use and stage.
The performance will have all the themes of the classic
Greek drama.

Afterword

Rien van der Vleuten

& Arts in Society Series

Afterword

The lectorate Arts *in* Society is one of the tools with which Fontys University for the Arts (Tilburg, the Netherlands) participates in the debates on the place of the arts in the contemporary world. The work of the lectorate resounds both inside the institute and in (inter-)national debates. The importance of being present in the debates increases day after day since the arts and art education have been caught up in a whirlwind of rapidly changing attitudes towards the content, financing and social relevance of art and art education.

This book is yet more evidence that Fontys University for the Arts is well aware of how important reflection is in a contemporary art institute. For the students, the staff and the art world in the broadest sense of the word.

Rien van der Vleuten
General Director

Arts in Society Series

Community Art: The Politics of Trespassing is the ninth publication in a series of publications of research studies and books that map the interaction between social changes (social, economical, political and ecological transformations) and artistic practices. Inspired by the critical social sciences the lecturer studies the possibilities of an ideological (re)positioning of the arts in society. The series is open for publishing proposals in the form of essays, theoretical explanations, practically-oriented research in the arts and research studies.

Earlier publications in these series:

— Gielen, P. (2007). *De Kunstinstitutie: De identiteit en maatschappelijke positie van de artistieke instellingen van de Vlaamse Gemeenschap.* Antwerpen: OIV.
— Gielen, P. (2008). *Het gemurmel van de artistieke menigte: Over kunst en post-fordisme.* Tilburg: Fontys.
— Gielen, P. (2008, 2nd ed.). *Kunst in netwerken: Artistieke selecties in de hedendaagse dans en de beeldende kunst.* Leuven: LannooCampus.
— De Bruyne, P. (2009). *Een stoet van kleur en klanken: De muziek van Luc Mishalle & Co.* Ghent: Academia Press.
— Gielen, P. and J. Seijdel (eds.) (2009). *The Art-biennial as a Global Phenomenon. Strategies in Neo-Political Times* (Open: Cahier on Art and the Public Domain 16). Rotterdam: NAi Publishers/Amsterdam: SKOR.
— Gielen, P. and P. De Bruyne (eds.) (2009). *Arts in Society: Being an Artist in Post-Fordist Times.* Rotterdam: NAi Publishers.
— Gielen, P. (2009, 2011, 2nd edition). *The Murmuring of the Artistic Multitude: Global Art, Memory and Post-Fordism.* Amsterdam: Valiz.
— Gielen, P. (2010). *Hasselt: Op weg naar een artistieke biotoop?: Hasselt als kunstenstad.* Tilburg: Fontys.

Biographies

Bertus Borgers is a musician and co-founder of the Rockacademy of which he became the managing director in 1999. Before that, he helped to set up pop teacher training at the Rotterdam Conservatory. Borgers came into the public eye through his appearances as a guest saxophonist with national celebrities like Herman Brood, Golden Earring and Raymond van het Groenwoud as well as through his accomplishments as the singer/songwriter in his own bands. Borgers has released eleven albums from his own repertoire, recently including songs in the Dutch language.
Contact hoi@bertusborgers.nl

Luigi Coppola is an Italian artist who works primarily in performance art. His artistic research focuses on relational dynamics, stressing the conceptual aspects of order in the social mechanism. Traces of his performance process have been displayed through different media, such as live performance, photography, installation and video. He trained both as a scientist (in environmental engineering, undertaking a doctorate specializing in risk analysis) and in the art field (visual and performance art). He is a close collaborator of the artist, Michelangelo Pistoletto, in Cittadellarte.
Contact coppolalu@gmail.com

An De bisschop obtained a PhD in Educational Sciences at Ghent University, Belgium (2009). For her thesis, entitled *Community Arts as a Discursive Construction,* she was also associated with the Western Cape University in Cape Town, South Africa. She is currently the director of Demos vzw, a Flemish organization that aims to offer equal opportunities for underprivileged people to participate in the arts, sport and youth work.
Contact An.debisschop@demos.be

Paul De Bruyne is Associated Lector *Arts in Society* at Fontys College for the Arts, and a lecturer at Maastricht University, the Netherlands. His 2009 monograph on multicultural music was called *Een stoet van kleur en klanken. De muziek van Luc Mishalle & Co.* In 2009, he and Pascal Gielen co-edited *Being an Artist in Post-Fordist Times.* He is a playwright, director and dramaturge of theatre. His plays have been produced in the Netherlands, Belgium and China, and he has directed plays in Belgium, the Netherlands, Kenya and China.
Contact p.debruyne@fontys.nl

Miguel Escobar Varela is interested in the interaction between traditional and new media in Indonesia. He is currently a doctoral candidate in the Theatre Studies Programme of the National University of Singapore. He has worked in different countries as a performer and a cultural manager and holds an MA in Arts and Heritage, Policy, Management and Education from Maastricht University. Contact m.escobar@nus.edu.sg

Alison M. Friedman is founding director of Ping Pong Productions (www.pingpongarts.org), which facilitates cultural exchange projects and collaborations between Chinese and international performing artists. Since 2002 she has worked in China, where she has served as International Director for Beijing Modern Dance Company, managed Oscar and Grammy-award winning composer/conductor Tan Dun, and produced international dance festivals in Beijing. Friedman lectures widely about contemporary performing arts in China. She was awarded a Fulbright Fellowship (2002–2003) to research the development of modern dance in China, and a 2009–2010 Arts Management Fellowship at the John F. Kennedy Center for the Performing Arts in Washington, DC. Contact alison@pingpongarts.org

Pascal Gielen lives in Antwerp, Belgium, but is professionally based at the University of Groningen in the Netherlands as a sociologist of the arts. Together with Paul De Bruyne, he is also director of the research group and book series *Arts in Society* (Fontys College for the Arts). Gielen has written several books on contemporary art, cultural heritage and cultural politics. In 2009, he co-edited the book *Being an Artist in Post-Fordist Times* with Paul De Bruyne and, in 2010, he published his new monograph, *The Murmuring of the Artistic Multitude: Global Art, Memory and Post-Fordism.* Contact p.j.d.gielen@rug.nl

Sonja Lavaert is a philosopher and Italianist, lecturer at the Department of Applied Linguistics of the Erasmus University College Brussels and at the Free University of Brussels. She has written about Machiavelli, Spinoza and radical Italian philosophy. In 2010, she published her doctoral thesis, *Het perspectief van de multitude. Agamben, Machiavelli, Negri, Spinoza, Virno.* She is also a painter. Contact Sonja.lavaert@vub.ac.be

Hans van Maanen, former Head of Department of Arts, Culture and Media Studies at the University of Groningen, is now a dramaturge and emeritus professor. His main area of research is the functioning of the arts in society, particularly theatre. He is a member of the editorial boards of the *International Journal of Cultural Policy* and the series *Themes in Theatre,* and a consulting editor for the *South African Theatre Journal.* He served as vice-chair and general executive for the Fund for the Stage Arts of the Netherlands and is now chair of the Arts Council of Groningen. His most recent book publications are Van Maanen, Kotte and Saro (eds.), *Global Changes: Local Stages* (2009) and *How to Study Art Worlds: On the Societal Functioning of Aesthetic Values* (2009). Together with Andreas Kotte (University of Bern), he co-chairs the international Project on European Theatre Systems (STEP).
Contact j.j.van.maanen@rug.nl

Alida Neslo was the managing director of DasArts, an international Masters training programme, centred on research into theatre and dance studies, at the Amsterdam School of Arts. She was also managing director at New Amsterdam (DNA), the oldest intercultural theatre company of the Netherlands, and simultaneously managed its pre-theatre training facility, ITS DNA, as well as her own company, the DNA (lab). She was discovered while on stage by the legendary Flemish director, Tone Brulin, and worked for his avant-garde international travelling company, TIE – 3, for several years. She grew up in Surinam, studied in Flanders and Senegal and has lived and worked on four continents. She was a member of the Commissie Cultureel Verdrag Vlaanderen-Nederland [Flanders-Netherlands Cultural Treaty Commission] and vice chairman of the Amsterdam Kunstraad. She currently lives in Surinam.
Contact Olsen296@hotmail.com

Lionel Popkin is a choreographer and performer whose current work deals with issues of cultural transmission and hybrid identities. Recent works include And Then We Eat (2004), Miniature Fantasies (2006), and There is an Elephant in this Dance (2009). Popkin was a dancer in the companies of Trisha Brown (2000–2003), Terry Creach (1996–2000), and Stephanie Skura (1993–1996). He is currently Associate Professor of Choreography and Performance at the University of California, Los Angeles (UCLA).
Contact lionelapop@aol.com

T e s s a   O v e r b e e k studied Arts, Culture and Media (BA) and Literary and Cultural Studies (MA) at the University of Groningen, with a focus on cognitive approaches to art and culture. She has been teaching courses in Art Sociology and Academic Writing at the department of Arts, Culture and Media of the University of Groningen and has been working as a freelance writer, editor and researcher.
Contact tsoverbeek@gmail.com

H e i n   S c h o e r works as researcher and lecturer at Fontys College for the Arts and teaches on soundscapes and acoustic ecology at the University of Applied Sciences, Darmstadt. He has a history in audio engineering and cultural science and writes and composes conventional music as well as acousmatic pieces. His PhD thesis, entitled *The Sounding Museum*, covers the theoretical and practical aspects of the mediation of North American indigenous cultures by means of soundscape composition, namely representation issues and best practices when in the field, in the studio and in the museum.
Contact hein@schoer.net

R i c k y   S e a b r a was born in Washington, DC, but currently lives alternately in Rio de Janeiro and Brasilia. He has a BFA in Communication Design from Parsons School of Design and a Masters in Design Research from the Design Academy Eindhoven. He works as a theatre artist, curator and cultural advisor all over the world.
Contact yo@rickyseabra.com

J o n a s   S t a a l is a Dutch visual artist whose work reflects the relationship between art, politics, ideology and publicity in varied, often controversial ways.
Contact info@jonasstaal.nl

K l a a s   T i n d e m a n s has a PhD in Law and works as a teacher/researcher at the Department of Audiovisual and Performing Arts of Erasmus University College Brussels and the Free University of Brussels. As a guest professor, he teaches at the Antwerp theatre school and at the University of Antwerp. He is active as a dramaturge with the Antwerp players' collective, De Roovers. He also writes plays. For *Bulger* (2006), a play about children killing another child, which he directed at the Brussels youth theatre, BRONKS, he received the 2008 New Playwriting Prize at the Theatertreffen in Berlin. In 2009, he wrote and directed *Sleutelveld,* a play about war, memory and

fairytales. Tindemans publishes writing on legal-philosophical issues, politics and theatricality, ancient tragedy and contemporary (documentary) theatre.
ContactKlaas.tindemans@skynet.be

Luk Van den Dries studied German philology at the Free University of Brussels and has worked in the field of theatre studies since 1980, first at the Free University and, later, as professor at the University of Antwerp. His research focuses on post-war Flemish theatre, about which he has published extensively in (inter)national trade journals. His book on Jan Fabre, *Corpus Jan Fabre* (2004), has been translated into seven languages. Since 2004, he has worked as a dramaturge on some of Fabre's productions, such as *Tannhäuser* in De Munt, *Histoire des larmes* (Avignon) and *Requiem for a Metamorphosis* (Salzburg). In 2008, he and Louise Chardon founded AndWhatBeside(s)Death, a production platform they used to create, e.g., *Ayïn- La baignoire du diable* (2008) and *Sensorama* (2009).
Contact Luc.vandendries@ua.ac.be

Quirijn Lennert van den Hoogen, PhD, studied Business Administration and Arts and Arts Policy at the University of Groningen. For several years, he worked as an official for cultural policy in the Netherlands at provincial and municipal level, and for the Association of Dutch Municipalities. Since 2008, he has taught Art Sociology and Arts Policy at the University of Groningen. He is editor-in-chief of the Dutch *Handbook for Cultural Policy* and a member of the Project on European Theatre Systems.
Contact Q.L.van.den.Hoogen@rug.nl

Bart Van Nuffelen was born in the surreal land of Belgium. Between 1973 and the present day, he has overcome many obstacles to become director of the phenomenal MartHa!tentatief, a high-profile Antwerp-based theatre company. In that capacity, he writes and produces ever-improving plays about untameable life in the city at the beginning of the twenty-first century. 2011 saw the première of *Polen op zondag*, a monumental play about a small park in the heart of the city.
Contact kolonelboemboem@hotmail.com

Karel Vanhaesebrouck is an assistant professor at the Faculty of Arts and Social Sciences of Maastricht University and is a theory lecturer at the Department of Audiovisual and Performing

Arts of Erasmus University College Brussels, where he coordinates the performing arts section and teaches courses in theatre history and cultural history. He is also a guest professor in theatre history at the actor's department of the Conservatory in Liège. He has published a book-length study *Le mythe de l'authenticité* (2009) and co-edited volumes on David Mamet, on tragedy and on art and activism. His scholarly work has been published in journals such as *Poetics Today*, *Textyles*, *Phrasis*, *Theatre Topics*, *Image & Narrative*, *Contemporary Theatre*, *Critique* and *Etudes Théâtrales*.
Contact k.vanhaesebrouck@maastrichtuniversity.nl

Index of Names

A   Abramović, Marina 217-219, 230
Acogny, Germaine 115
Afisina, Reza 288
Agamben, Giorgio 184
Ai Weiwei 205
Alfred, Bruce 252-256, 258-260, 262
Alfred, Darren 254, 259
Alfred, Marcus 260
Alfred, Pewi 260
Anderson, Laurie 331
Ariosto, Ludovico 191
B   Bach, J.S. 119
Bacon, Francis 191, 333
Bakhtin, Mikhail 26, 173, 188, 191
Baran, Zeki 282, 283
Basquiat, Jean-Michel 186
Beckers, Wil 332, 333, 338
Beckett, Samuel 249
Belt, Don 302
Bettine, Sergio 172
Beuys, Joseph 167, 335
Bial, Henry 213
Bifo (Franco Berardi) 186
Björfors, Tilde 10, 299-323
Blommaert 328
Boccaccio, Giovanni 191
Boltanski, Luc 174, 180, 214
Boontjes, Gerard 155
Borgers, Ruud 151, 154, 156, 158-160
Borja-Villel, Manuel 168
Bourdieu, Pierre 173
Bourriaud, Nicolas 17, 18, 26
Brecht, Bertolt 184, 212
Breton, André 227
Breytenbach, Breyten 112
Brown, Andrew 303
Brulin, Tone 111
Bruno, Giordano 191
Buckley, Mary 125
Bush, George W. 220, 234

C   Cameron, James 227, 228
Canetti, Elias 248
Caravaggio 173
Careri, Francesco 246
Celant, Germano 268
Chaput, Martin 246
Chaucer, Geoffrey 191
Chazallon, Martial 246
Chiapello, Eve 174, 180, 214
Chomsky, Noam 170
Churchill, Winston 279
Clement, Tom 99, 100
Clinton, Hillary 138
Cobham, Billy 157
Cohen–Cruz, Jan 20
Cole, Nat King 140, 141
Collor de Mello, Fernando 143
Confucius 9
Cranmer, Doug 254, 256
Crosby, Alexandra 294
D   Darmawan, Ade 288, 294
De Greef, Hugo 338
De Palma, Brian 219
Deleuze, Gilles 171, 178, 215
Deng Xiaoping 196
Derrida, Jacques 52, 215, 230
Derschmidt, Friedemann 244
Dick, Beau 258, 259, 262
Djunaedi , Dimas 288
Duncan, Isadora 139
Duncan, Robert 258, 261
Dvořák, Max 172, 174
Eberhard, David 303, 308, 309
El Ouazghari, Mohammed 44
Ellington, Duke 156
F   Fabre, Jan 10, 325–327
Fang, Adrianne 125
Farris, Julie 144
Feenstra, Wapke 243
Feldman, Morton 269
Finley, Karen 127, 230

Flaubert, Gustave 173
Fleck, John 127, 230
Florida, Richard 27, 242
Fo, Dario 79
Foucault, Michel 30, 52, 53, 56, 170, 171, 215
Fox, Josh 225
Frey, James 95
Francis of Assisi 179, 187
Friedman, Milton 216

G Gadzina, Cezariusz 43
Gandhi, Mahatma 234
Gardner, Howard 268
Geerts, Leo 332, 333
Genet, Jean 212
Genie, Brian 288
Gennero, Lionello 269
Giddens, Anthony 244
Gielen, Pascal 80–82, 87
Giotto 187
Gitelman, Claudia 197
Goethe, J.W. 333
Goffman, Erving 55
Gomez, Antonio 104
Goya, Francisco 168
Graham, Dr. 137
Gramsci, Antonio 175
Granula, Dr. 137
Gray, Spalding 213, 229
Grazhoppa 42
Groot, George 85, 86
Grotowski, Jerzy 268
Guattari, Félix 178, 215

H Habermas, Jürgen 110, 112, 118, 120, 244
Haim, Mark 125
Hall, Carolyn 125
Hall, Stuart 52
Halprin, Anna 219
Hamilton, Ann 136
Hancock, Herbie 157
Hardt, Michael 3, 4, 19-21, 166, 176, 181, 184, 188, 189
Hassler, Laura 150, 151, 158, 159

Hassler, Wendy 151-154, 159
Hegel, G.W.F. 179
Helms, Jesse 25
Hill, David T. 292
Hillaert, Wouter 93
Hillman, Grady 25
Hitler, Adolf 20, 169
Houston-Jones, Ishmael 125
Hoving, Lucas 197
Hughes, Holly 127, 230
I   Isaac, Waylon 261
J   Jabor, Andrea 141
K   Kant, Emanuel 176
Kaprow, Allan 219, 221
Karijord, Rebekka 307
Katz, Jonathan 233
Kellogg, Dr. 137
Kennedy, John F. 215, 216
Kennedy, Robert 215, 219
Kienholz, Edward 328
King, Martin Luther 215, 234, 235
Kitley, Philip 292
Kleinhout, Simone 23
Koeck, Paul 329, 330
L   Lacan, Jacques 215
Laermans, Rudi 79
Lawrence, Stephen 233
Lazzarato, Maurizio 31
LeComte, Elizabeth 213
Leno, Jay 138
Leopardi, Giacomo 191, 192
Lepecki, Andre 219
Letterman, David 138
Lewinsky, Monica 138
Lind, Kajsa 316
Löb, Heidrun 253
Lugg, George 125
Luhmann, Niklas 76, 77, 170-172
M   Machiavelli, Niccolò 185, 190
MacPherson, Crawford Brough 183
Mafaalani, Ola 85

M Malevich, Kasimir 333, 334
Mandela, Nelson 119
Mann, Emily 229
Mao Zedong 9, 196
Mapplethorpe, Robert 25, 26, 82
Marakchi, Abdallah 40
Marazzi, Christian 186
Marcuse, Herbert 29, 80, 241, 327
Marianto, M. Dwi 292
Marinetti, Filippo 227
Martin, Carol 3, 9, 212-214, 223-229, 232-235
Marx, Karl 70-72, 189
Masschelein, Jan 249
Maulani 288
McLuhan, Marshall 222
Meade, Margaret 54
Michelangelo 179
Miller, Tim 127, 230
Mishalle, Luc 37, 40, 41, 44-47
Molenaar, Anton 283
Moore, Michael 79
Mroué, Rabih 223, 232
Musil, Robert 170

N Nam June Paik 290
Nash, Michael 290, 291
Negri, Antonio 3, 4, 9, 19, 20, 165-192
Newman, Fred 230
Newman, Vera 259, 260, 262
Nichol, Lina 259
Nicolas-le Strat, Pascal 188
Nielsen, Douglas 197
Niemeyer, Oscar 142, 143
Nussbaum, Martha 77

O Obama, Barack 207, 234
Obrist, Hans Ulrich 169
Oral, Nazmye 85

P Palme, Olof 302
Parks, Rosa 235
Pearson, Mike 246
Philippe, Gérard 190
Piacenza, Peggy 125

Picasso, Pablo 179
Pinault, François 180, 184
Pioppi, Maria 268-271
Pistoletto, Cristina 271
Pistoletto, Michelangelo 10, 265-272
Politi, Giancarlo 184
Pollock, Jackson 167
Postman, Neil 112
Potter, Jonathan 56

R Ramdas, Anil 92
Rauschenberg, Robert 167
Rava, Enrico 269
Reagan, Ronald 220, 221
Reinhart, Charles 196, 197
Riegl, Alois 172, 174
Roosen, Adelheid 83, 85, 86
Roosevelt, Franklin D. 279
Ruzante 191

S Saneh, Linah 232
Schechner, Richard 3, 9, 211-225, 226-235
Scheffer, Paul 94
Sen, Krishna 292
Senghor, Léopold Sédar 115
Sennett, Richard 32
Shakespeare, William 55, 189, 191
Shang, Ruby 197
Shapiro, Michael 53
Shuko Takahashi 269
Simons, Maarten 249
Skura, Stephanie 131
Sloterdijk, Peter 186
Smith, Jack 225
Sørensen, Ronald 282, 283
Spinoza, Baruch 19, 171, 176, 177, 185, 189-191, 322
Spora, Licia 268
Sprinkle, Annie 138
Stackhouse, Sarah 197
Stalin, Joseph 276, 279
Stanescu, Saviana 213
Stienen, François 79
Stitou, Rida 45, 46

Suharto 291, 292
Sukarno 291
Svanvick, Don 260
Syarif, Robert M. 288

T Tardaguilla, Eduardo 99, 100
Teirlinck, Herman 111
Thatcher, Margaret 220
Thompson, E.P. 70, 71
Thoreau, Henry David 234
Thorson, Morgan 125
Threadgold, Terry 52
Tito 185
Tönnies, Ferdinand 33
Trotsky, Leon 277
Turner, Victor 273

U Ulay 218
V Van den Dries, Luc 79
Van Elk, Ger 334
Van Erven, Eugène 79
Van Gerven Oei, Vincent 281, 282
Van Gogh, Vincent 179, 203
Van Haecke, Alex 335
Van Kerkhoven, Marianne 79
Van Looveren, Marie 78
Vanrunxt, Marc 339
Vawter, Ron 225
Verbrugge, Ad 110
Verdonck, Benjamin 16-18, 20, 21, 23, 29
Verheezen, René 328
Verstockt, Dirk 138
Vickers, Adrian 292
Virno, Paolo 3, 19, 169-172, 174, 180, 181, 184, 214, 321
Visser, Gerdien 152, 154, 158, 159

W Wadhams, Mariah 260
Wang YuanYuan 204
Wardrip-Fruin, Noah 290
Warhol, Andy 186, 223, 224
Wasden Jr. (Wa), William 257, 259, 261, 262
Washington, Dinah 138, 139
Wayland-Smith, Sarah 144
White, Cynthia A. 4-6

White, Harrison C. 4–6
Whonnock, Sean 258
Winehouse, Amy 156
Williams, Raymond 70
Willie, Sandi 259
Wittgenstein, Ludwig 52, 53
Wölfflin, Heinrich 174
Wong, Shirley May 104, 106

Y
Yang Meiqi 196

Z
Zapruder, Abraham 229
Zaugg, Rémy 24
Zhang Changcheng 3, 9, 195–208

Geographical Index

A   Afghanistan 234
Africa 40, 45, 115–117
Alabama 235
Albania 291
Albanians 150, 152, 153, 154, 157, 158
Albuquerque 140
Alert Bay 252–257, 259, 261
Alkmaar 151
America 118
Amsterdam 80, 81, 83, 116, 138, 140, 142, 157, 243, 276, 277, 280, 326, 328, 329, 333, 334
Antarctica 181
Antwerp 29, 41, 42, 92, 93, 102, 111, 326–333, 335, 336
Asia 225
Atlanta 269, 270
Austin 219
Australia 29
B   Balkans 150, 153, 185
Beijing 208
Belgium 8, 23, 37, 47, 92, 115, 141
Belgrade 185
Berlin 29, 140, 143, 145, 271
Blessey 24
Botkyrka 304, 311, 312, 314, 316
Bourgogne 24
Brasilia 139, 142, 143
Brazil 117
British Columbia 253
Brussels 8, 35, 37, 45, 155, 241, 338
C   California 24, 25, 131
Caribbean 110, 114
Chicago 143, 215
China 9, 133, 196–199, 202, 205–208, 310
Cinque Terre 272
Cirebon 295
Copacabana 136, 144
Cormorant Island 253
Corniglia 265, 266, 268–272
D   Dresden 145
Durban 304
Dutch 279

E   East Germany 145
Eindhoven 139, 140, 151, 153, 157
Europe 3, 8, 36, 37, 41, 43, 70, 82, 110-112, 114, 118, 138, 145, 154, 166, 185, 225, 241, 280, 289, 291

F   Flanders 8, 53, 54, 57, 59, 66, 67, 70, 71, 78, 92, 97, 111
Flemish 93
France 23, 30, 79, 92, 180, 184, 215, 302

G   Germany 92, 115, 271
Ghent 70, 225
Great Britain 29
Greensboro 234
Groningen 8, 83, 84
Guangdong 196
Guangzhou 133
Guinea-Bissau 104

H   Hanover 145
Havana 145
Herentals 339
Holland 83, 186, 279
Hollywood 291
Hungary 276, 279

I   Iceland 191
India 113, 231
Indians 95
Indonesia 10, 287-289, 291-295
Iran 231, 235
Iraq 227, 235
Israel 231
Istanbul 145
Italy 79, 180, 184, 186-188, 190, 266, 268, 270, 271

J   Jakarta 288, 293, 295
Japanese 199, 282
Järfälla 304
Java 113

K   Kinshasa 104
Kosovo 150-155, 160
Kosovars 152, 153, 158

L   Landskrona 304
Latin America 40
Lebanon 232
Leuven 97

Liguria 266
London 140, 184, 185, 240, 241
Los Angeles 95, 124, 125, 130, 140, 143, 219
Louisiana 212
M Macedonia 151 160
Madrid 168, 177
Maputo 247
Marseille 247
Mexico City 215
Milwakee 326
Minneapolis 125
Mississippi 24
Mitrovica 9, 149–158, 160
Montpellier 188
Montréal 241
Moroccans 37, 44, 85, 45, 95
Morocco 45, 282
Munich 169, 271
N the Netherlands 2, 23, 28–30, 84, 92, 150, 152, 153, 157, 243, 276, 279, 281, 288, 291, 321
New Mexico 140
New York 125, 127, 128, 130, 136, 137, 186, 196, 217, 219, 225, 226, 230, 235, 290, 326, 336–338
North America 252, 254, 289
North Carolina 234
Nuremberg 20
P Padang 294
Padova 191
Pakistanis 95, 104
Paramaribo 8
Paris 5, 140, 142, 166, 183, 185, 187, 215, 219
Petra 145
Philadelphia 130
Poles 95, 96
Pristine 156
Reims 190
Rio de Janeiro 136, 142
Romania 333
Rome 145, 270
Rotterdam 243, 276, 282–285
Russia 186, 310

S   San Francisco 137
San Marcos 125
Seattle 125, 130
Semarang 295
Senegal 115, 117
Serbia 9, 150, 160
Serbs 150, 152–154, 158
Shanghai 145, 199
Skopje 151, 152, 154, 155, 159, 160
South Africa 8, 53, 54, 64, 67, 68, 71, 304
South America 144
South East Asia 288, 293
Soviet Union 182
Spain 168
Stockholm 219, 300, 301, 306, 312, 314, 315
Sumatra 294
Surinam 8, 92, 110, 114, 117, 118
Sweden 300–304, 308–313, 315, 316, 319, 321, 322
Swedish 300, 302, 303
Switzerland 252

T   Tennessee 160
Texas 219
The Hague 281
Tilburg 152–154, 157, 159, 243
Toubab Dialaw 115
Toulouse 140
Turin 271
Turkey 282
Turks 37
Tuscany 94, 95

U   United States 9, 24, 25, 29–31, 124, 125, 130, 137, 138, 166, 187, 197, 207, 213, 215, 226, 228–233, 269, 291
Utrecht 288

V   Vancouver Island 253
Veldhoven 157
Veneto 191
Venice 166, 167, 172, 180, 187
Vienna 172–174, 244
Vietnam 234, 235

W   Waalwijk 153
Walloon 92

Washington DC 125, 127, 128, 130, 142
Wat Po 145
West Africa 113, 115
Western Cape 8, 54, 61, 62, 64, 66–69
Western Europe 110, 112
Y   Yugoslavia 117, 150, 185
Z   Zurich 252

Colophon

Community Art: The Politics of Trespassing
Editors Paul De Bruyne, Pascal Gielen
Antennae Series n°5 by Valiz, Amsterdam
Part of the Fontys-series 'Arts *in* Society'

Authors Bertus Borgers, Paul De Bruyne,
Luigi Coppola, An De bisschop, Miguel Escobar
Varela, Alison M. Friedman, Pascal Gielen,
Sonja Lavaert, Alida Neslo, Tessa Overbeek,
Lionel Popkin, Hein Schoer, Ricky Seabra,
Jonas Staal, Klaas Tindemans, Luk Van den
Dries, Quirijn Lennert van den Hoogen,
Hans van Maanen, Bart Van Nuffelen,
Karel Vanhaesebrouck
Translation Dutch-English Annemieke van Baal
Copy editing 100% Proof, Els Brinkman
Design Metahaven
Paper inside Munken Print White 100gr, 1.5
hv satinated mc 115gr
Paper cover Bioset 240 gr
Printing and binding Ten Brink/Euradius, Meppel
Published by Valiz, Amsterdam, 2011; second edition 2013

Colophon

The authors and the publisher have made every effort to secure permission to reproduce the listed material, illustrations and photographs. We apologize for any inadvert errors or omissions. Parties who nevertheless believe they can claim specific legal rights are invited to contact the publisher.

Distribution:
USA: D.A.P., www.artbook.com
GB/IE: Art Data, www.artdata.co.uk
NL/BE/LU: Coen Sligting, www.coensligtingbookimport.nl
Europe/Asia: Idea Books, www.ideabooks.nl

ISBN 978-90-78088-50-9
NUR 646
Printed and bound in the Netherlands
Reprint, 2nd edition 2013
www.valiz.nl

This publication was made possible through the generous support of
Fontys College for the Arts, Tilburg

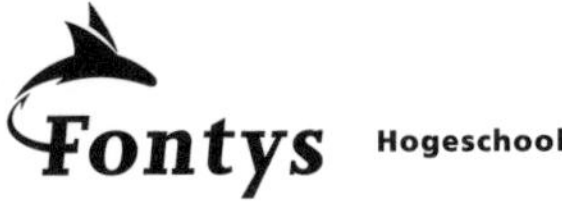

Antennae Series:

The Fall of the Studio: Artists at Work
edited by Wouter Davidts & Kim Paice
Amsterdam: Valiz, 2009 (2nd ed.: 2010),
ISBN 978-90-78088-29-5

Take Place: Photography and Place from Multiple Perspectives
edited by Helen Westgeest
Amsterdam: Valiz, 2009, ISBN 978-90-78088-35-6

The Murmuring of the Artistic Multitude:
Global Art, Memory and Post-Fordism
Pascal Gielen (author)
Arts *in* Society
Amsterdam: Valiz, 2009 (2nd ed.: 2011), ISBN 978-90-78088-34-9

Locating the Producers: Durational Approaches to Public Art
edited by Paul O'Neill & Claire Doherty
Amsterdam: Valiz, 2011, ISBN 978-90-78088-51-6

Community Art: The Politics of Trespassing
edited by Paul De Bruyne, Pascal Gielen
Arts *in* Society
Amsterdam: Valiz, 2011 (2nd ed.: 2013), ISBN 978-90-78088-50-9

See it Again, Say it Again: The Artist as Researcher
edited by Janneke Wesseling
Amsterdam: Valiz, 2011, ISBN 978-90-78088-49-3

Teaching Art in the Neoliberal Realm: Realism versus Cynicism
edited by Pascal Gielen, Paul De Bruyne
Arts *in* Society
Amsterdam: Valiz, 2012 (2nd ed.: 2013), ISBN 978-90-78088-57-8